D1384287

GEORGE PERLES

The Ride of a Lifetime

George Perles

with

Vahé Gregorian

SAGAMORE PUBLISHING
Champaign, IL 61820

Production Manager: Susan M. McKinney
Dustjacket and photo insert: Michelle R. Dressen
Editor: Susan M. McKinney
Proofreaders: Phyllis L. Bannon, Mary Jane Harshbarger

ISBN: 1-57167-022-x

Printed in the United States.

This book is dedicated to my family.
To my wife, Sally; my mother, Nellie; and my late father, Julius.
To my children, Kathleen; Terrance and his wife, Tracy; John and his
wife, Amy; my grandchildren, Nicholas, Michael and Kendall; and
my third son, Patrick.

Contents

Acknowledgments

There are so many people I wish to thank. To our relatives: Joe Romain; Aggie Conti; Ann Marie Eastman; Dennis Simmons; and Bill, Shannon, and Shaunna Bradford. Special thanks to Ken Hoffman for his assistance on this project. From our many great years at Michigan State, I wish to thank all my assistant coaches: Henry Bullough, Charlie Baggett, Larry Bielat, Steve Beckholt, Dino Folino, Steve Furness, Ted Guthard, Pat Morris, Buck Nystrom, Willie Peete, Norm Parker, Bill Rademacher, Nick Saban, Pat Shurmur, Kip Waddell, Morris Watts, Bobby Williams and Ed Zaunbrecher. The excellent support staff: Mary Kay Smith, Pam Henning, Renee Gagnier, Jeff Monroe, Sally Nogle, Bob Knickerbocker, Troy Hickman,Dave Henry, Gary Raff, Gary Van Dam, Charlie Wilson, Greg Croxton, Ed Rutherford, Tom Shepard, Dean Olson, Cecil Mackey, and of course, Doug Weaver.

From the outstanding Pittsburgh Steeler years: the late Art Rooney; his son, Dan Rooney; and Head Coach Chuck Noll and the fantastic assistant coaches: Dick Hoak, Woody Widenhofer, Charlie Sumner, Bob Fry, Tom Moore, Lionel Taylor, Paul Yram, Dick Walker, Bud Carson, Tony Dungy, Dan Radakovich and Ned Mervos.

Thanks to my good friends with the Detroit Red Wings and Tigers organization: Mike and Marion Ilitch, Gary Vitto, Mike Dietz, and Gino D'ambrosio. To Frank Pappas, Dan Henry, Dr. James Murray, and to all of my players throughout the years. To Peter Secchia, Frank Kelley, Monty Story and Chris Bergstrom.

Finally, I must remember and thank those who influenced this "Ride of a Lifetime" who are no longer with us: my mother-in-law and father-in-law, Gladys and Donald Bradford; Don Barrrett; Jack Farrell; President Hannah; Jack Breslin; Father Mac; Biggie Munn; Duffy Daugherty; and good friend Rollie Dotsch.

—George Perles

This project was conceived and engineered by Mike "Burn The Boats/Get It Done" Ward of the aptly named Visions Sports Management Group. I'm grateful to Mike for his energy, commitment and assistance in every facet of the book. Special thanks, also, to Ken Hoffman, the Michigan State University sports information director. Ken was generous with his time and resources.

Peter Bannon of Sagamore Publishing stoked our own excitement about the book with his immediate enthusiasm, and Sagamore's Susan McKinney and Michelle Dressen provided their expertise.

Visions' St. Louis-based attorney, Mark Dunn, St. Louis writer/attorney Michael Kahn and University of Missouri football coach Larry Smith helped me learn what I was getting into, and I also appreciate the counsel and assistance of my colleagues, including: Dick Weiss, Skip Myslenski, Andy Bagnato, John Garrity, Jeff Gordon and John Duxbury. The stellar work of the *Detroit News*, *Detroit Free Press* and *Lansing State Journal* provided excellent background, as did Lynn Henning's *Spartan Seasons* and Jack Ebling's *Spartan Champions*.

One of the banes of such an extensive interviewing process is transcribing the hours of tape recordings. Andrea DeBaun-Markward and Marna Clark got over their impulses to kill—I think— and did excellent, essential work. I also thank Jeryldine Tully for her advice, not to mention her Macintosh computer and crash-course computer lessons.

Mike Smith, my deputy sport editor at the *St. Louis-Dispatch*, believed in me before I did a few years back. I'll always be thankful to Mike and Bob Pastin for getting me started in sportswriting. Thanks, also, to Dan Kelly, my sports editor at the *Columbia Missourian*.

One of the reasons this book idea intrigued me was I not only played football, sparingly, at the University of Pennsylvania, but I also was brought up in an academic environment— and have seen its virtues, eccentricities and treacheries. My parents, Clare and Vartan, somehow thrived in that atmosphere, despite being burdened with warmth, character, wit and principle. Sometimes, the good guys do win. My efforts in this book are devoted to them.

—Vahé Gregorian

Foreword

I've closely followed the career of George Perles since he was assembling those brilliant Pittsburgh Steelers defenses during the 1970s. He formed those defenses with the same ingredients he would use to rebuild the Michigan State program—tenacious, hard-nosed, fundamental football. I also appreciated that he did it at Michigan State with an emphasis on academics and citizenship and building character. His teams were known for being physical but clean, which is an excellent reflection of their teacher.

We had some great competition with the Spartans, and I'm sorry George won't be there to continue our season-ending battles for the annual Land-Grant Trophy. It will be hard to replace George as a coach and almost impossible to replace him as a person. It's a shame that he got trapped in all the political conflict at Michigan State, because with the service and commitment he gave for 12 years as head coach—and many more as a student and an assistant—he should have been honored instead of fired. I'd like to have seen what would have happened if some department head fired an English professor who had served the school with such distinction for 12 years.

When Penn State was admitted to the Big Ten Conference, George was one of the first to give me a congratulatory phone call—and it came from a cellular phone on his practice field at the Aloha Bowl. He also invited me to come to his golf outing in East Lansing that year to help raise money for the Special Olympics. In honor of George I even wore a green tie for a speaking engagement there.

George's warmth, good humor and sincerity made him one of the most respected and well-liked men in our profession. I'm sure George would never say this, but in a way that made him much like his idol: Duffy Daugherty.

If his coaching career is over, I'll always be proud to know that I coached against George in his last game. As excited as we were to know we were going to the Rose Bowl as undefeated Big Ten champions after our victory, I approached George with some sadness after the game. As we shook hands, he smiled and told me to smell the roses for him. I laughed and promised we would. I hope that as George stops and smells the roses now, he knows what an outstanding contribution he made to college football and how much of a difference he has made in the lives of hundreds of young men.

—Joe Paterno

Introduction

This is how it ended for Michigan State University football coach George Julius Perles last fall: In a preposterous flurry of skullduggery and intrigue, perpetrated by a former White House operative, perpetuated by a trustee who boasted that he had stabbed a corpse, and administered in the spectacle of a virtual public execution broadcast live on statewide television in Michigan.

"An outstanding season" was what Michigan State president and erstwhile deputy director of presidential personnel Peter McPherson had said Perles needed to keep his job, and McPherson remained spectacularly vague about that imperative even as he fired Perles on November 8, 1994.

"As I said all along, I would know [outstanding] when I saw it — and I did, indeed," said McPherson, sounding much like former U.S. Supreme Court Justice Potter Stewart on the topic of pornography.

As if this weren't hullabaloo enough, it all was framed by a lurid backdrop: A disillusioned, disgruntled and apparently disoriented former Michigan State football player named Roosevelt Wagner in October told *The Detroit News* he once had stalked Perles for two days with two loaded guns and the intention of murdering him.

"I followed him everywhere he went; he didn't even know I was following him," Walker said in a tape-recorded interview that he would later deny having given. He added, "I had this whole scenario made up in my mind. I was gonna kidnap him and take him and shoot him somewhere in all them woods in Mason. Wouldn't nobody ever found the body."

Absurd as this all may sound, it was in many ways a mere microcosm of Perles' 12 fascinating years as MSU's head coach.

For all his sterling accomplishments — the 1988 Rose Bowl victory and six other bowl appearances, the 56 Academic All-Big Ten Conference citations, the nine first-round National Football League draft picks — Perles also continually meandered into maelstroms. Many involved the most fundamental issues in modern collegiate sports:

Athletics vs. administration. Gender equity. Accountability of student-athletes. Allegations of improprieties in the program.

"I would never have stayed at Michigan State if I knew there could be so much conflict about it, or that my staying could somehow hurt the school," Perles says now. "I would have taken the job with Green Bay [in 1988] or with the Jets [in 1990] if I had known what was coming."

But indeed, from the moment he accepted the head coaching job at his beloved alma mater, Perles' regime seemed condemned to controversy — and conundrums that could have confounded Solomon.

"The tragedy of it all is that none of it had to be this way," said John DiBiaggio, the former Michigan State president — and one-time Perles booster — whose grappling with Perles became a focal point of Perles' era. "George and I could both still be there."

Unnecessary or not, the theme was previewed and perhaps sown from the outset. To hire Perles in late 1982, Michigan State and Perles had to finagle their way out of his glistening contract with the Philadelphia Stars of the fledgling U.S. Football League. The opportunity to embrace the Michigan State job was startling to Perles, who in 1980 had been crestfallen when he was bypassed for this, his most coveted of positions, in favor of the inauspiciously appended Frank "Muddy" Waters. Perles doubted he would be considered again, particularly so soon.

But when Waters, a sweet, sincere man who had been cruelly miscast, was ousted after going 10-23 in three seasons, Perles was the immediate object of athletic director Doug Weaver's fancy.

As for that pesky three-year, $400,000 contract with the Stars? Hopscotching around such annoyances isn't unusual in coaching, but the breaking of this covenant carried a particular stigma: Perles had been hired just five months before and had yet to coach the Stars.

Still, Myles Tanenbaum, the Philadelphia businessman who owned the Stars, appreciated Perles' position.

"George was really in a bind," said Tanenbaum, who later would send Perles a congratulatory telegram for winning his first game at MSU. "At some point before then, we had talked about that we wouldn't stand in his way if a better opportunity came along.

"But give us a break here. It was totally beyond our anticipation or comprehension that it would occur before the first season."

During a well-stoked lunch meeting to settle the matter, a skittish but resolute Perles was overcome with emotion as he told Tanenbaum and Stars general manager Carl Peterson there was no material incentive that could keep him in Philadelphia. On the whole, and for less money, he'd rather be in Michigan.

"I'm going to East Lansing," he said, "if I have to walk."

With that, Tanenbaum hugged Perles — and informed him that the Stars soon would be compelled to sue Michigan State. The suit asked for $1 million and was settled out of court for $175,000.

That sum was easily eclipsed by revenue from revived attendance at Spartan Stadium the next season. But that sum also swiftly became a point of divisiveness at Michigan State. "Perlesgate," then-Michigan State trustee Peter Fletcher called the transaction.

"I do not believe there is any such person as a Pigskin Messiah," Fletcher said then. He referred to the $175,000 as "hush money" and added, "Ladies and gentlemen, there are more important things in this life than passing New Year's Day in Pasadena."

Not all agreed with Fletcher. Many, in fact, exulted.

"When George got hired, they had a reception at Longs and the lines were just like The Godfather coming back. They were coming out to greet George as a savior," said Joel Ferguson, the aggressive Lansing businessman who was among the board of trustees' most influential voices.

It was Ferguson, once a fiendish backer of Perles', who last fall took issue with commentary that he had betrayed Perles and behaved like Brutus stabbing Caesar. His curious defense: "I didn't stab Caesar, I stabbed 'Bernie.' You know, the corpse from

'Weekend At Bernie's' "? Ferguson later apologized to Perles for the remark.

No one was more pleased about Perles' appointment than Perles. He was giddy, if not delirious. He had been steeped in the tradition of legendary MSU coach Biggie Munn, given up a knee for and idolized Munn's successor, Duffy Daugherty, and met his future wife on a blind date at Michigan State.

Many Saturdays during his decade as a Pittsburgh Steelers assistant coach were spent concocting ways to tune in MSU broadcasts in his car, which he pretended to wash or wax for the benefit of neighbors. "A son of Michigan State," Perles calls himself, and his rabid allegiance is undisputed among those who know him best.

"No one could be any happier than I am today," Perles said at his introductory news conference. "The only thing about this is you can't feel like this every day. I wish I could bottle this up and keep it for the rest of my life. . . . In some ways, this is a storybook. It's like a movie."

Hokum? Maybe. But it was authentic, vintage Perles hokum.

"He's totally genuine; there's not a false bone in his body," said John McVay, the San Francisco 49ers vice president who gave Perles his first collegiate coaching job as an assistant at Dayton. "I'm certain that he has green blood in his veins."

Ultimately, though, the storybook would disintegrate into a soap opera, if not a Shakespearean farce. And that green blood, some suggested, was more indicative of a man transfused with — and transfixed by — money than anything to do with Michigan State color or ceremony.

There are many who blame Perles for the ruckus that distinguished much of the last half of his dozen years at Michigan State. He was a bully consumed by ambition, they say. A master of leveraging. He was alternately accused of being fickle and stubborn, and his filibusters about loyalty were scoffed at. His demise could have been called, "The Taming Of The Shrewd."

"Somewhere along the line, we all lose our way; hopefully, we find it again," said former Michigan State athletic director Merrily Dean Baker, who qualified her comments by noting she had known Perles only during the final three years of his tenure.

"But when you profess loyalty to a place or to a dream or to an ideal, that's quite different than professing self-loyalty.

"And self-loyalty is what I continue to see being portrayed here by George. If you were loyal to George, George was terrific to you. But that's not loyalty to an institution."

"He should have shown loyalty to his players," Ferguson said, "and gotten rid of some of those deadbeat assistant coaches he had . . .

"Here's George, who used to brag that he never fired anybody. Hell, I hired a guy and made him my sales manager on a Monday. I fired him on Saturday. I could see he wasn't going to get me to the level I needed to get to, so I gave him a couple months' pay and sent him on his way."

Yet there is profound evidence that Perles oozes many enviable qualities: honesty, gratefulness, benevolence and well-directed loyalty. Ask, of all people, Tanenbaum.

"George was very straightforward and sympathetic," he said. "He was torn, and it was legitimate. That's what made it so tough all-around."

Ask former players, from Mean Joe Greene, whom Perles coached through four Pittsburgh Steelers Super Bowl championships, to Lorenzo White, the Heisman Trophy contender and one of the heroes of the enchanted Rose Bowl season. Ask officials with the Special Olympics, for whom Perles has raised nearly $300,000 by spearheading golf outings in the last eight years.

"I'm very compassionate toward the Special Olympics because of my good friend Paul Teets' son, Michael, [former assistant coach] Norm Parker's son, Jeff, and my good friend Ron Palmer's daughter, Laura," said Perles, who slowly tilts his head and sighs at the thought of the children running to the golfers at the end of the fundraiser. "It's one of the few charities where you can really touch someone. Feel them! All charities are good, but some of them you can't get your hands on and get the great feeling you get from hugging these kids and seeing these kids. And one thing we know for sure. All those kids are going straight to heaven."

Especially, ask the men who grew up with Perles near Detroit's hardscrabble Vernor Highway during the depression. The boys with whom he hopped cars and crashed weddings and gorged down "loose ones" at Duly's. The 14 boys he volunteered to join the service with, so they could all be assured of going through basic training together. The men he still considers among his intimates, even if he was the only one to graduate from college — and even if he now hobnobs with the likes of Michigan Attorney General Frank Kelley and former Ambassador to Italy Peter Secchia.

"He never forgot us guys," said Jimmie Teets, who runs Veterans Fence Company, which Perles helped found when they got out of the Army. "That's one of the things I admire so much about him. He can't do enough for you if he's your friend. But don't cross him."

"George is an intensely loyal guy, to a fault," Secchia said. "To where the past is as important as the future. . . . He's a big, lovable Teddy bear, but he's a blocking back, not a tailback."

"He's a passionate guy; whether you agree with him or not, he believes things deeply. George just keeps coming at you. There's nothing that can slow him down. Maybe temporarily, but nothing really slows him down," says long-time friend Joe Farrell, now the assistant to the dean of the MSU College of Human Medicine.

Farrell says he will remember forever the way Perles consoled him when Farrell's son died unexpectedly in 1985.

"All of my life, my friends have tended to be people who stood out and marched to a different drummer," said Kelley, in his 34th year as attorney general. "My friends would probably be characterized by others as different, and to the degree they are different, they are more attractive to me because I'm kind of an iconoclast. I look upon life in somewhat of a satirical way, and I tend to gravitate toward people who understand the ironies of life. George, with his background, was one of those. Most of my friends are bigger than life, and he certainly is.

"He never forgets his roots, never for a minute forgets that he's done a lot of hard work but also had a lot of good fortune. And he's never done what most men do and rationalize good fortune into a feeling of self-accomplishment, and develop the attitude that since they're self-made they can be selfish and forget their past. I can't stand phony bastards, and there are too many of them in the world. George is not that way, and neither am I."

Skeptics notwithstanding, it's also hard to ignore this part of the composite picture: Perles' fervor and utter absence of affect when he speaks of loyalty. He pounds his dining room table. He bellows. His left eye moistens, a function, he says, of a "dry eye" condition. Only coincidence, of course, that it tends to dampen at times of peak emotion.

"I had a lot of good things happen to me because of the loyalty of other people," Perles said. "You give it, you get it. Everybody in the world talks about loyalty, but we shouldn't even have to talk about it. If you don't give it, you don't get it. You might get something fictitious. You might get something that looks like it but isn't it. It's a two-way street."

This, his critics say, is a facade, masking a manipulative, opportunistic spirit. Their censuring stems largely from three Perles forays and parlays: marching proudly from Philadelphia to Michigan State; converting an offer from the Green Bay Packers into a virtually unprecedented 10-year contract in 1988; and wresting Michigan State's athletic director job, to go along with his football job, after a courtship with the New York Jets in 1990.

That final coup — approved by the board of trustees over DiBiaggio's vehement objections — fatally ruptured Perles' relationship with DiBiaggio and created a shrill national furor. "ANYTHING ELSE, COACH?: Shame on Michigan State for caving in to George Perles," was the headline in *Sports Illustrated.*

Ferguson, a peerless Perles advocate until the final year, tried unsuccessfully to douse the outrage, which included a failed student initiative to recall him and other trustees who had lobbied for Perles.

"This story is history. [The media] is milking this," he told the *Detroit Free Press* at the time. "Why don't you let Noriega escape so you can make it front page again?"

But the questions were valid, even essential: How could the trustees victimize their own appointee, DiBiaggio, a principled man who simply saw the jobs as "separate and distinct?"

"The real issue was not George Perles," DiBiaggio says now. "He was really insignificant in the matter."

How, DiBiaggio and three of eight trustees argued, could Perles be allowed to become his own superior?

"I honestly believe that institutional credibility and integrity in the future could be in jeopardy," DiBiaggio said then.

And how dare Perles negotiate again, just two years after accepting the 10-year contract and proclaiming his life-long allegiance to Michigan State?

"I don't respect [Perles]," then-trustee Dean Pridgeon told The Associated Press at the time. "He's short on integrity. He doesn't honor contracts. . . ."

Call Perles an extortionist, then, but take note of his peculiar modus operandi: In all three cases, Perles was approached and flirted with by enticed prospective employers, not vice versa. He was hardly rattling a tin cup. In all three cases, he chose Michigan State for substantially less financial gratification than he was being offered to leave. He, in fact, performed the athletic director's job gratis—not to mention so adroitly that the department showed a $3.6 million profit in his two years. The department lost about $1 million in the following two years.

And for someone supposedly consumed with money, he has spent a lot of time giving it away, or disdaining it. Seldom does Perles accept the ample money to be made for speaking engagements.

So if he is guilty of anything, Perles says, it is of being willing to listen and of diligently trying to reinforce his family's security. And besides. . . .

"Hello," he says, answering one of his two seemingly surgically connected cellular phones. "Wrong number. Oh, that's OK. Want to talk?"

He disconnects the line and laughs.

"I'll talk to anybody, anytime," he says. "If *The New York Times* called you, wouldn't you listen? And what's wrong with me shooting for the moon, anyway? This is still America, isn't it? And I'm a hell of an American."

Or, as *Detroit Free Press* columnist Charlie Vincent put it during the height of the A.D. frenzy:

"He does not want to rob banks.

"He does not want to mug people.

"He does not want to deal in drugs.

"He wants to coach football and direct an athletic program."

To truly grasp and put in context Perles' legacy at Michigan State, where he leaves second only to Daugherty in victories, one must also gaze through the mucky prism of politics inherent in the framework of the university, which perhaps is just like any other university . . . only more so.

The very foundation of the school, inaugurated as an agricultural college in 1855, was questioned when then-Governor Austin Blair sneered at its location as it was being built in the dense forest that was East Lansing.

". . . In the woods, as if our young men need to be taught the business of chopping and logging," hrrumphed Blair, according to Lynn Henning's book, *Spartan Seasons*.

But the seeds of disruption weren't planted until 1963, when the state's Constitution was written with a provision for electing trustees at Michigan State, Michigan and Wayne State to eight-year terms as part of a statewide partisan ticket.

At the time Perles' fate hinged on the trustees, Michigan was one of just five states to allow voters to elect trustees for major public universities. Among the flaws of that system: Candidates are often placed on the ballot as patronage, and voters around the state would have scant knowledge of or interest in a local candidate's stance or record. In most states, those positions are appointed by the governor and thus held at least remotely accountable to him or her.

The inherent problem is apparent, even to those outside the system. Bowling Green football coach Gary Blackney, for instance, removed his name from consideration at Michigan State after Perles was ousted.

"They have an elected board of trustees there," Blackney, considered one of the hot commodities in college coaching, told Knight-Ridder newspapers. "You could find yourself in disfavor there very quickly."

Even in an ideal world, though, the set-up is fraught with boobytraps. Mark Twain suggested averting eyes from the making of laws and sausages; to that list we would submit the gore of university administrative politics.

The board selects the president of the university and deputizes him or her to run the institution — but to be accountable to the board, on which individuals may have brimming agendas or whims of their own. With little accountability of their own. And when *those* conflict . . .

Former Michigan State President John Hannah, who left MSU in 1969 after 28 prosperous years, helped adopt the 1963 Constitution and later was aghast at his realization of the Pandora's Box of political gamesmanship he had helped pry open.

"John Hannah once told me that the biggest mistake he ever made was having elected trustees," said DiBiaggio, now president of Tufts University.

Secchia, who interviewed for McPherson's job, also is well-acquainted with the excesses and vulnerabilities of the system.

"Michigan State is an archaic political system," said Secchia, the former GOP national chairman. "There is no way in God's scheme of things that trustees at the university should be elected by the public. The public has no idea who they are, and these people get elected and then they think they've got a mandate to make policy, when in essence, the only reason they got elected is that they're on a particular ticket that wins.

"The governor knows that it needs to be changed. Most learned people know that it needs to be changed. It just isn't changed because it's part of the Constitution. It's too hard to do."

And athletics often has a way of illuminating and amplifying conflict on any university's board — or, say, between that board and the university's president.

"The athletic department of a university is kind of a pawn," Kelley said. "If the president is a jock type, or a frustrated athlete type, and likes football or likes the coach personally, then you have no problem. But about half the time, the academic president has pressure on him to de-emphasize sports. And they will tend to do so. And what you had here during George's tenure was a standoff between the board and the president."

So what might have been an old-fashioned, bareknuckled power struggle between coach and president was contaminated by trustee intervention. That, of course, was their prerogative, but such puppeteering renders the presidency flaccid and tempts chaos.

Initially, the board's meddling favored Perles. But not without a price. It boomeranged on Perles in the end, when two pivotal board seats were taken over in 1990 by trustees — Dee Cook and Jack Shingleton — who were sympathetic to DiBiaggio and shared his priorities.

So take a glimpse at the Michigan State Administrative Funhouse, where the children's game of Rock, Paper and Scissors seems to be the guiding force:

—One former trustee once flipped a lit cigarette on DiBiaggio's carpet, ground it out with his foot and said, "See, I can do anything I want."

"That was a nasty issue," Secchia said. "It was a battle, initially, between [the trustee] and DiBiaggio, and DiBiaggio put George into it because George was being defended by [the trustee]."

—One former trustee had a secret accord with McPherson, who was by all accounts oblivious to the intricacies of the athletic department, that left that trustee essentially in charge of athletics.

—Ferguson unabashedly uses expressions such as, "We should have taken DiBiaggio out sooner" to describe his solution to the Perles-DiBiaggio imbroglio. "DiBiaggio said, 'You usurped my authority,'" Ferguson said. "I said, 'There's no such word, no such phrase. You either had the authority, or you didn't. Obviously, you didn't.'"

—The governor's office wouldn't hesitate to make "suggestions" to DiBiaggio about Michigan State athletics.

"You talk about power politics and ego," DiBiaggio said. "That was awful."

He added, "I really believed in the place . . . but it was the worst situation imaginable."

—Baker, who became athletic director in the wake of DiBiaggio purging Perles from the position in 1992, was left flapping in the tempest when DiBiaggio stunningly announced his resignation after her first day of work.

"It was terribly unfair to her," Secchia said. "And it wasn't that she got flung to the Ol' Boys' network. It was the fact that she became [DiBiaggio's] symbol of defiance. She had to wear all the baggage. . . . She was left to babysit a monstrous situation."

Baker, who had wanted to fire Perles in 1993, then was stripped of any real or perceived clout when McPherson was nudged into making the stupefying and undercutting maneuver of putting associate athletic director Clarence Underwood in charge of revenue sports. She was forbidden by McPherson — or perhaps by McPherson's trustee confidante — from even attending Perles' final news conference.

As for her relationship with Perles?

"I don't know if you would even call it a relationship," Baker said. "It was just kind of a macabre dance for three years. A Dance Macabre."

Perles, who was furious when one of Baker's first moves was to try to cashier his longtime friend Larry Bielat, grits his teeth with some regret at the mention of Baker: "I can look back and say that in some situations dealing with her, I was not my normal self."

So Baker, who resigned in January, as much as anybody came to understand and even symbolize the Rubik's circle that has engulfed Michigan State athletics. Although Ferguson says she was her own worst adversary, it's clear she was snarled in the gridlock among DiBiaggio, Perles and the trustees.

"I knew I was going into a mine field, but I didn't even have a lead dog," said Baker, who says swimming from Turkey 20 miles across the Bosporus Sea in her 20s prepared her to survive the infested waters at MSU. "What I see is an institution that has subordinated its values to politics. I think people with petulantly political agendas have been allowed to prevail, and when you have politics being applied at an institutional level, there's the tendency to have one or two individuals surrounded by a group of sycophants who do their bidding in order to receive favors."

"And that's why it becomes a political satire," she added, laughing. "I mean, do you know of anywhere else in the country where the chairman of the board of trustees calls the athletic director demanding to know why she won't approve an order for 30 sweatshirts for the coach? That's the level of micro-management I had visited on me for three years.

xxii

"It's not a typical democracy, when we take our vote and the prevailing consensus is what we go with. It's like, 'I'm on the minority side, I didn't get what I wanted, so now I'm going to try to dirty it up a little and ultimately get what I want.'

"You know, I had a person on the board of trustees who didn't want me to be athletic director, so he voted against me. Well, he lost. I was selected. But he started, even before I arrived, trying to change that around to get what he wanted."

That person was the omnipresent Ferguson, who lost his place on the board last fall. (Election day, incidentally, was the day Perles was fired). Ferguson had objected to Baker because her orientation was in women's athletics.

"I never was thrilled about Merrily coming in here because if your goal is to win in basketball and football, why would you hire someone who has no experience in either?" said Ferguson, who owns Channel 57 in Lansing. "If I want to be the best station . . . I pick up a trade magazine and I see that the top three shows in syndication are 'Wheel,' 'Joker' and 'Jeopardy,' so I make a phone call and find out when the renewals are up. And I go out and I buy up all three shows. Because I know if I want to get to that level, I'm going to have to have the right type of product and talent.

"So I didn't have a problem with Merrily. The only thing with Merrily was that where she wanted to go was not where the institution wanted to go."

He added, "The problem with Michigan State is we've never had shared vision."

Even within this myopic, dizzying and volatile world, Perles originally flourished. That was as much a function of his management style as it was of his recruiting success and cutting-edge training regimens. It was a manner honed by four men whose pictures were perched over Perles' shoulder in a single frame in his office: Daugherty, McVay, Chuck Noll, coach of the Pittsburgh Steelers, and Ed Rutherford, Perles' coach at Western High and later his colleague at Michigan State.

"George had a way about him where he could take a group of people and take each person's strengths and weaknesses and be able to let them be themselves but be able to melt that pot into a successful mold," said Nick Saban, whom Perles befriended when Saban as a novice hung around Steelers camps, whom Perles hired on his first MSU staff — and who now is succeeding Perles as Michigan State head coach. "I always thought that was a unique thing. I had to learn how to do that, because it wasn't one of my strengths.

"He gave you responsibility, and you did it and he never second-guessed you, whether it worked or didn't work. It takes a special kind of person to be able to do that. . . . He was not egotistical at all about giving other people credit and promoting them. Some people in this profession are always afraid that if you promote other people you will eventually hurt yourself."

But the off-field shenanigans inevitably had consequences on the field. After whisking the Spartans to a 54-36-4 record and bowl appearances in six of his first eight seasons, Perles went 19-26 from 1991-94 and twice suffered losses to . . . Central Michigan? His own consumption with all the flap, Perles concedes, may have cost a game a year, which could have transformed the pedestrian 1992 and 1994 seasons into face-saving bowl years.

So, what, then, to make of Perles, who has been revered and reviled and still mystifies. He is a simple, but not simplistic man, a Will Rogers of malaprops such as "ice cubes in the veins" (describing someone who is poised) and "shooting the fat" (having a conversation) and almost always the pulse of the party. "Social director," Noll used to call him.

"I never had more fun with any friend in my life than I have had with George Perles," said Pitt coach Johnny Majors, with whom Perles runs Coach Of The Year clinics.

"George is the kind of person," Weaver said, "that you remember, in a lot of ways like that old *Reader's Digest* column: 'the most unforgettable character I ever met.' George is the type of guy who would have been in that. For a lot of reasons."

He is 61 years old now and spends his days lunching and playing gin at the no-frills Sip'N'Snack in Okemos, swimming at the Michigan Athletic Club and hovering around his home playing host to a bewildering gaggle of friends whose bargings and goings have made his life a "Seinfeld" episode.

"This really is a flophouse, isn't it?" he says, laughing, as his front door swings open again.

He has time now to consider his days at MSU. Perhaps they ended too soon. Perhaps they ended too late. Perhaps he should have been nicer. Perhaps he should have been meaner.

Perhaps he would have done it all the same.

"George is no different than Mulroney or Shamir or Margaret Thatcher or Gorbachev or Mitterand," Secchia said. "When you've been around a long time and the world is changing, your supporters get older and therefore the intensity of your support gets weaker. Your friends come and go, and your enemies accumulate.

"Michigan State got to the point where the old traditions that George was so loyal to, Duffy and Biggie and the John Hannah era, had passed. They didn't mean anything to the DiBiaggios and [trustee] Dee Cooks. That doesn't mean that the DiBiaggios and Dee Cooks were wrong. It just means that the music had changed, and George was doing the same old dance and probably didn't see that."

If so, Perles still has reason to learn the nuances of the new steps.

No, he doesn't have designs on the Michigan State president's job, as he joked when he was asked about his future plans at his firing:

"If the presidency were open," he said, looking at McPherson, "I'd apply. And that's one job I know I could handle.

"I'm just making fun," he added. "Getting a little sticky in here, and I'm just trying to have a good time."

Perles, in fact, has stayed on good terms with McPherson. He answered a recent phone call from him thusly: "President! How you doing?" After an informal chat about Perles' still-pending settlement, Perles guffawed and said, "You shouldn't have fired me. We'd make a good team."

But in what could be the clinching — and, to some, clenching — twist to the whole affair, Perles has become enamored of running for the board of trustees in 1996.

"Bad dream, huh? *I'm still here*," he said, laughing. More seriously, he said, "I would have a pure attitude and would be doing what you should be doing with the position, and that's to watch over the university for the taxpayers of the state of Michigan. . . . I think I can contribute to the well-being of the university, and that's what I want to do."

As for coaching again, Perles thinks it unlikely. And that's fine — at least until he tailgates at Spartan Stadium this fall. For now, being fired for the first time seems to amuse him more than haunt him.

"Here's how you get out of this game without being fired: You win a championship, you get on a plane . . . and you fly into a mountain like Knute Rockne," he said. "Or you win a Super Bowl and come down with a terrible, terrible disease like cancer . . . like Vince Lombardi. And that's too high of a price.

"Besides that, they get everybody."

What a ride it was, though, before they got George Perles.

The Shadow Knows

I keep everything on my calendar. Last November 8, I wrote in it, "Election Day" and "Got Fired — 10:45 a.m."

First time in my life I got fired. So what? I finally joined the club. I'm one of the boys now. And like I told the media that day, to say this was a surprise, you'd have to believe in the Easter Bunny. And I didn't just fall off the Christmas tree truck.

Maybe it really was over in 1988, when the board of trustees gave me a 10-year contract after Green Bay offered me a job. I remember talking to John DiBiaggio, our president then, and he said I should go if it would make me happy. I remember laughing when I got off the phone and saying, it was funny, it almost sounded like he meant it. But we were real close at the time, so I didn't dwell on it too much.

All the real problems probably started in 1990, when the trustees gave me the athletic director job over DiBiaggio's objections. Boy, was he steamed. Suddenly, everybody's drawing up sides. President DiBiaggio finally left, but the battle was just beginning.

Anyway, the jig was basically up for me on March 2, 1994. I had just gotten back from a Red Wings hockey game at the Joe Louis Arena in Detroit, and my son Pat was watching the Channel 10 news. They were in a commercial, but Pat said that the lead-in was that there was a memo about me. When the news came back on, they reported that the memo said I had to have an "outstanding season" in 1994.

Or else.

That was at 11:20. At midnight, Peter McPherson, DiBiaggio's replacement, called me. He said he had pressure from a board member and that there was a memo from Merrily Dean Baker, the athletic director, saying that she wanted me fired. He said he wanted to talk to me the next day. I said, "Fine."

We met in his office, the president, vice-president Roger Wilkinson and our senior associate athletic director, Clarence Underwood. Merrily was out of town, but she was on the speaker phone. She admitted on the phone that she had recommended firing me. But she said she had never written a memo. Something smelled.

The president seemed mixed up, and someone must have made up that memo and leaked it. There's speculation that he, coming from Washington, liked to leak things. And one of our trustees, Joel Ferguson, who was with me a lot of the way but bailed out in the end, says McPherson wanted to get rid of me after we lost to Louisville in the Liberty Bowl at the end of the 1993 season.

You're always looking over your shoulder a little when the people who hired you leave, and I knew Merrily and McPherson already had a problem with me. Plus, they'd been sore at me because of some comments I made at a banquet in Tokyo when we were there to play Wisconsin. Everybody was making all this racket about what a huge big deal this game was for Wisconsin, since they could get to the Rose Bowl with a win, and I got up and made kind of a rude reply to it all. Probably shouldn't have said it. But it's hard for me not to say what's on my mind.

"McPherson thought that speech was totally against any kind of protocol," Joel said. "Then in the Liberty Bowl, it was a miserable night and we punted twice inside Louisville's 35-yard-line. True story. That stuff works when you win ugly, but when you lose ugly, you're in serious trouble. McPherson wanted him out on the spot.

"My position was twofold. You're already almost into January, and you don't want to make a change in the middle of recruiting. And two, if you're a new president setting standards for the guy, you've got to at least give the guy some lead time and notice. An 'outstanding' season was the compromise."

But there were other trustees putting pressure on McPherson. Especially Dee Cook. I think she was carrying the ball here. She was a high school classmate of DiBiaggio's, and I think she thinks that I had something to do with him leaving and always resented me for that. I might be wrong, but that's how I feel.

She didn't want to talk for the book, but she did say she was one of the ones who wanted me out because it was best for Michigan State. If that's the reason why, then I can respect that. I've never even sat down with Dee Cook for five minutes. I'd love to take her out to dinner, have a cocktail or two and interview her. Ask her what she thinks I did:

Did I take the athletic director job knowing that DiBiaggio didn't want me to? Yeah, I did. What choice did I have? I tried to leave, and the board wouldn't let me leave.

Did I put athletics ahead of academics? Hell, no. How many guys do I have to graduate to prove that?

Did I use Green Bay to get a 10-year contract and an annuity? Yeah. Is this America? We call that "supply and demand." I mean, if no one wants you, you're not going anywhere.

And thank God I did get that contract. Because if I hadn't, Sally and I would be out here with a tin cup now since they unloaded me. I mean, I'm living proof. They put a guy on the street.

I don't know what else Dee could say or ask. But I could answer any questions from her or anybody else, because we never did anything sneaky or with the wrong motives.

Anyway, the whole thing in March made me feel lousy. I've seen situations like that, when you give people ultimatums. It's no-win for the individuals involved, for the school and even the administration. Everybody loses, because the press now has a field day going over every game, every decision, with a microscope. You know you're going to have a season with many, many distractions because of that statement. When you go public like that, that's a kiss of death. And, really, they'd have been better off firing me then than putting us through the agony of the season.

Of course, that was what was really beautiful about the "outstanding season" idea. Because the president would never say what it meant. Probably only The Shadow knows what he meant. Oh, and Joel, who always seemed to know what the president was thinking.

"'Outstanding' year was just supposed to be better than the previous year," Joel said. "My position was that if George made one of the Big Ten-designated bowls that would be acceptable. But we didn't say that, because 'outstanding' was even more general."

So if we'd have gone to a bowl game, McPherson could have said we needed to get to the Rose Bowl. Or if we'd have gotten to the Rose Bowl and lost, he might have said, "Uh-uh, that wasn't outstanding."

What is outstanding, anyway? Couldn't it be having the biggest come-from-behind victory we ever had at Michigan State, like we did against Purdue the week after they announced I was done? That could be construed as outstanding. I mean, you could look for outstanding things in the way kids handle adversity. You could go 0-11 and have an outstanding season.

Or you could go 11-0 and not have one. You could have hot dogs acting up, wearing Army fatigues and all the other nonsense that went on at Miami. Or you could have an outstanding season if all the kids were being good citizens and got their grades.

The point is, you can make it anything you want. You could make it good if you're looking for good, or you could make it miserable looking for bad.

The skids were greased.

But I had to find a way to ignore it, somehow. I didn't talk about it with the team, because I never wanted to give them an out. I tried to stick with what I always say: "Work hard, keep your mouth shut and good things will happen." We put that inside our Gator Bowl rings after the 1988 season, which we started ugly: 0-4-1.

Some people thought I could have saved myself in the end by firing some assistants. They criticized me for not doing it. Isn't that silly to take something so good and pure and clean and make a negative out of it? Well, I would never, ever fire an assistant coach. I'm from the school of Duffy Daugherty and Biggie Munn and Woody Hayes, and you never heard of those people firing anybody.

Why not? Because loyalty is hard to find these days. It's like a precious gem.

And I think part of my job is to know the strengths and weaknesses of the people who are working for me. Obviously, we all have strengths, and we all have weakness. There isn't anybody free of that. But I could not ask my coaches to do all the things they do without giving them something.

And what I gave them was the loyalty of knowing that they never would be fired. Their wives and kids would never be put in the street. Looking back on it, I'm more proud of that now than I ever was.

To be able to do that, of course, you have to do an exceptional job in the first place in hiring people. Which I did. You have to research it. You have to really know your people.

The second part to all this is that there are a lot of people who, when you don't win as many games as they would like, always look for a reason. Something you did wrong.

So if you don't fire people and don't win enough games, they'll come back on you. But if you did fire people and didn't win enough games, well, then they'll say you shouldn't have fired them. Or if you don't win enough games and you practice at night, they'll say you should practice in the day. If you don't win enough games and practice in the day, they'll say you should practice at night. The point is that anything you do can be held against you. And is.

I always figured we would win enough games, anyway, and that I'd feel good about treating people right. After all, I still have to shave.

Even with us being doomed, there were times I let myself wonder if we just might make it, anyway. After we beat Wisconsin, the Rose Bowl champs, we were 2-2. But then we lost three in a row, the last one to an Iowa team that was down to its fourth-string quarterback. Not good.

That's when Joel came over to tell me that this wasn't an outstanding season. And he went public with it, too. One of the Detroit papers had a huge headline the next day: "Bye, George?" When people accused Joel of stabbing me in the back, he said he had stabbed a corpse. Kind of a mean, sarcastic statement.

Why Joel was the one saying this stuff about my job I wasn't sure, but the president was in Asia.

Joel said he was sorry later, and it was no big deal to me. I went to see him in his office this summer, and when I walked in I laughed and said, "Here's the corpse." But my mom didn't like reading that line, and had I been him I'd have felt a lot better if I'd have hung in there with me all the way.

We beat Indiana at home the next week, a nice win, and one that gave me my 72nd victory — second only to Duffy at Michigan State. I liked that.

But now came all this cuckoo stuff with Roosevelt Wagner. Whew, how 'bout Rosie?

He made all these wild accusations that there had been grade tampering and payoffs and other National Collegiate Athletic Association violations in our program. But those interviews with him you couldn't make heads or tails of. Even though he made a lot of contradicting statements, Michigan State is still cleaning all that up with investigators. No one's said boo about how the investigation's going.

Doesn't bother me, though, because we always were clean. I have nothing to hide. Nothing.

Rosie also told one paper that he had stalked me and was going to try to murder me and dump me in the woods behind my house. This was kind of a bizarre thing. Strange stuff. Now you've got the bullets coming from everywhere. The president, the board, the media — and a guy saying he's following you around with loaded guns wanting to kill you.

You know, when you look back at it, you say, "Whew, we did a pretty good job getting through this obstacle course without anyone getting seriously hurt." I mean, I got fired. So what?

Rosie last played for us in 1991, and the papers said he believed I had somehow tried to keep him from getting drafted by the National Football League. That's not true. In fact, it's ridiculous. We helped all our kids, but he left a year early. That might have hurt him. And I'll tell you, if you're good enough, the NFL will draft you.

So it wasn't anybody's fault. I guess he just wanted the NFL so bad he was looking for someone to blame, and who would be easier to blame than the head coach?

This all made Sally very uneasy. I suspected it was a lot of talk, so it didn't make me too fearful. I wasn't spending any time looking out my windows or checking my rear-view mirrors. What was I going to do, look around corners for the rest of my life? But it brought it to our attention to the point where we got a restraining order.

Anyway, we went on and beat Northwestern and we were 4-5. We could go to a bowl if we won our last two, and we'd deserve it because those thoroughbreds at Penn State were last on the schedule. Maybe beating them would have been an "outstanding" thing to do.

Joe Paterno, the Penn State coach and my good friend, before the season had tried to speak up for me. He seemed to know the score, judging from the words he used.

"George will be fine because he's an outstanding coach," he said at the Big Ten Kickoff Luncheon. "College presidents are like coaches. Once in a while, we say things we don't mean, too."

This was becoming a beautiful national story. The media had something to write every week, even if there was nothing going on. And it seemed like there was always something going on.

They were selling T-shirts around town: "George's Farewell Tour." The *Lansing State Journal* published a reader poll that said I should be fired. At one game, my son Terry and a former player of mine, Jim Rinella, got in a scrap with a fan who was holding a "Fire George" sign above the tunnel.

People who do those kinds of things don't mean it personally, but sometimes they don't think about that there's more to the person on the sideline than just being a coach. They forget that you're a person, too, with a family that might be sensitive.

I actually was handling it all pretty well, because I had to, and I've always said a little bit of humility wasn't going to hurt me or anybody else. Besides, I knew if they did do anything to me they were going to have to give me a lot of money because of my contract. But it was getting really tough on the kids and my assistants, and that hurt me.

Now, just before I really started kidding myself about having a chance, it was November 8. The president called me that morning and asked me to come over to his place.

I knew what was up, but he surprised me by implying he wanted me to resign. I told him, "No way I'm resigning." I couldn't go back and face my assistant coaches or my players, who for better or worse are like my sons, and let them feel that I had abandoned them.

And I don't like playing games. If you're going to fire me, fire me. There's no use trying to cover it up; you're not fooling anybody. So the president said, "You call your attorneys, I'll call mine and we'll meet this afternoon."

So we met at my attorney's, three of them and three of us, and they said we'll get this all settled in 60 days and they were going to have a press conference that afternoon. I said, "Fine." Then the president said he wanted me to go to the press conference with him, and I said no. I still don't know why he wanted me to do that. Maybe he just wanted to get it all out of the way at once.

I wasn't going to have any part of it, but then he said he'd have compassion for my coaches if I would do it. So I decided I could handle being fired on live TV if it would help them get paid longer. I said I wanted to have the press conference at 5 o'clock, during practice, so there wouldn't be any players or assistants there.

I went and talked to the team for about five minutes before practice. I didn't get into any emotional mumbo-jumbo with them. Just told them that the administration had fired me but that they shouldn't worry about that and should just think about preparing for Purdue on Saturday. Boy, they were getting a heck of an education through all this, maybe even more than what they were getting from their books.

Then I went to the press conference. The president came in and threw out some malarkey about how well we did in our era, while I just sat there watching him take questions for a few minutes. Didn't bother me. I like to listen.

A lot of the papers took pictures of me wiping my left eye while I was sitting there, and they thought I was crying. But it was a dry-docker. I've got a dry eye, which means that it leaks sometimes.

It was funny. The president never used the word "fired." He just said, "George will coach the remainder of the season and will not coach next year." Then he said something about working out a settlement for the remaining three years on my contract and then he said this:

"I ask all Spartans everywhere to join with me . . . by supporting the Spartans against Purdue this weekend and in the final Big Ten game against Penn State. Knowing George as I do, the best way to honor Coach Perles is to support his players and his coaches with the enthusiasm that they deserve."

He also said, "We're an institution that abides by our contracts."

Wasn't that something?

When it was my turn, I tried to make a few debate points. It was one of the few times I ever used notes because I had so much to say. Usually, I don't use notes or even plan my speeches because I speak from the heart right at the moment. Besides, I don't like to wear my glasses in public.

"Let me give you a couple facts," I said. "I had three years remaining, and I wanted to coach the three years. And I couldn't. And so, I've been fired. And that's a breach of contract. Now, those are facts. Clear, clear facts."

Then I bragged a little, about winning 61 percent of our Big Ten games, going to seven bowls and winning the Rose Bowl for Michigan State for the first time since 1956. I got kind of worked up then, thinking about Duffy and how I had wanted to be a bridge back to his tradition.

"There are about 10 men in the country that have been at the same place as long as we have — probably nine now," I said. "And I don't know how many were graduates of that school. But I call myself a son of Michigan State because I went here. I have 22 years here either as a student or a coach. My wife went to school here. Two of my sons played for us here. . . .

"I hope I know the coach who succeeds me. I will help the coach who succeeds me. I will be in this town. I will be in the parking lot. I will be in the press box."

I'm sure that press box statement surprised some of the reporters. Made them a little uncomfortable, probably. But in my contract I negotiated two lifetime press passes. If that makes them a little edgy, that's OK. They'll get over it. I want to see what goes on up there, how the writers come to their opinions and conclusions.

I've actually always enjoyed dealing with the press, even though some of them don't realize it or maybe don't feel the same way about me. It's a big game, really. But I think the media deserves to have answers for their questions. They have tough jobs.

Like during that news conference, Terry Denbow, the university publicist, tried to interrupt the media while I was up there talking and said, "One more question." I said, "No, Terry, we're going to take all the questions they have."

I wasn't going to let him end it. I wanted to make sure that anything they wanted to ask, they got to ask. I resent press conferences that are fixed. I mean, why show up at all if you're just trying to hide? That would be kind of silly.

To me, it's a great challenge. The harder the questions the better. A lot of times after a game, I'll just stand up there and ask myself the really hard questions to take them off the hook and keep them from embarrassing themselves. Plus, that way I get to ask the questions the way I want to ask them.

One of the reporters on November 8 reminded me that I liked to say wins are like weddings and losses were like funerals. So what was being fired like? I laughed and said, "This is purgatory."

But I was joking. In fact, I planned to have a party at my house that night. If I'd have had enough room, I would have invited the media.

I remember hearing that when they fired Muddy Waters, the coach before me, he answered his phone the night before by saying, "City Morgue." But I didn't feel like that. I guess I'm just not that way.

Different people are made up differently chemically, psychologically. When I got fired, I felt bad for maybe a week or two, then it was on to other things. I'm grateful that's the way I react. It's no credit to me. It's just the way I am.

I'm not bitter. I don't hold grudges. If they wanted me out, that's fine by me — as long as their motives were pure and they were trying to do what they thought was best for Michigan State. I mean, I should have been teaching volleyball in some smelly gym. Or working on an assembly line at Ford.

"I've had so many good things happen, no one deserves that much," I said at the press conference. "I would be the lousiest person in the world to say I was shortchanged in the game of football."

On Saturday, we beat Purdue 42-30 after trailing 21-3. The players poured Gatorade over me and lugged me toward the center of the field. They didn't carry me all the way off, though. I must have been too much of a load.

We were 5-5, and it might have been interesting for the administration if we'd have beaten Penn State the next week. I mean, they would already have fired me and we'd have been going to a bowl. You don't think somebody would have thought that would sell a few tickets?

That would have been perfect. But the Nittany Lions beat us 59-31, and it was time for me to move on.

2

Potato Loaf
and Street Fighting

It all started for me in 1934 at 7728 Pitt Street, Apt. 2, where I spent the first 17-and-a-half years of my life. My parents, Julius and Nellie, didn't buy their first house until 1951. That was in Allen Park. They paid $12,550 for it, and they lived there until my dad passed away in 1969. My mom sold it in 1972.

So I was born and raised on the west side of Detroit, near Central and a block off the old Vernor Highway.

I'm very proud of the old neighborhood, and I take people there to show it off every chance I get. I took DiBiaggio there once, and he loved it.

I hear I get a little absent-minded when I go around there, getting sentimental. Last time I took some friends through, they told me I ran about five stop signs pointing out the sights.

One of the best sights for me is Duly's Place. I can't remember the last time I left Detroit without stopping at the counter at Duly's and having "loose ones" — unpacked hamburger shoveled into a hot dog bun and smothered in chili and onions — or an "a la mode" — a bowl of chili covered with a scoop of onions. Add a Duly's dog, and you've eaten what we call a hat trick.

I've always been thankful that I was born and raised there, because that's where I learned one of my finest lessons: Loyalty. I don't think you're born with it. I think you learn it.

And I think the reason we learned it on Vernor Highway was because it was a tough neighborhood, and if you didn't have friends — salt-of-the-earth, true friends, and lots of them — you had a chance to get beaten up every day. You'd get your block knocked off. So you became very loyal to each other for survival.

Every ethnic group you could imagine was in the neighborhood. There's even a banquet hall on Vernor called "The Melting Pot." A lot of different blood was around: Irish, Polish, African-Americans, Mexicans, Armenians, Germans, hillbillies and, of course, Lithuanians, like me. I'm a thoroughbred.

I slept in the Murphy bed that rolled out of the closet in the living room, and we always had a clean, nice apartment. Across the street was where we had our Victory Garden after World War II. I had an urge to stop by to see the apartment a few months ago, to show it to a few friends and my son, Pat. The woman who answered the door was dressed only in a towel, and she said if she knew I was coming she would have dressed up.

Under the circumstances, we didn't ask to go in. I asked her if they still had the Murphy bed in the closet and she said, "Is that what that was? They don't have it there no more."

There were probably 100 tenants in those apartments, and we all shared a clothesline out back. But there were no children allowed after I was born, so I was the only kid around. That's why I was everybody's gopher.

Gopher for bread, gopher for milk, gopher this, gopher that. I used to help the caretaker, Mr. Watts, water the lawn, shovel the coal and shovel the snow. He kept me pretty busy. Maybe that's why they wrote this about me at Western High in the prophecy of the January Class of 1953:

"George Perles will land a position on the Los Angeles Rams but between seasons he will shovel snow and sweep streets to keep in good shape."

My dad was a payroll clerk at the Ford Motor Company, the Rouge Plant, which at one time was the largest plant in the world. When Mr. Henry Ford worked there, the only cars on the lot were Fords. It's not that way anymore.

My father was a coal miner's son from Plymouth, Pennsylvania. His father got killed in the mine when my dad was just in eighth grade. So my father left school and worked in the mines to take care of his mother, two sisters and his brother. He worked there until he turned 21, then he came to Detroit and got a job with Ford as a badge checker at Gate 4. He was never late for work, and he never let me be late for anything, either.

He was a pretty smart guy, so he moved up. Good basics. Good speller, good math and beautiful penmanship. He was formal, too, sometimes wore his old dress clothes to mow the lawn.

And he really liked routine. On Friday nights, he'd play euchre with the boys at the bar at 7777 Dix. On Saturdays he'd always take my mother out to see friends. He took the Baker streetcar to work, the Baker Bullet. We'd eat dinner every day at 5, then he'd read his paper and doze off and go to bed.

Speaking of the paper, I was a newspaper boy for a while. But I lost my paper route the first day of high school. I entered school at mid-year, and the basketball coach saw me and wanted me to go out for the team. So after school I went to the gym, even though that's the sport I wasn't very good in. At the end of the practice, you had to make six foul shots in a row before you could leave.

Well, I couldn't make them. I kept going and going, but I just couldn't do it. It was embarrassing, and I got home so late that day, the paper station was closed and I lost my job. Battled with newspapers all my life!

Since it wasn't common for men to show affection in those days, the way my dad did it was to serve guests in his home. He couldn't say how he felt, so that's how he did it. That was a form of love for him, and it's still a very pure form of love for me. I like nothing better than to have my family around or my friends over and do things for them. Like him, I have a hard time saying the word, "Love." And besides, it's too easy to just say you love somebody.

What my dad and my mom really liked to serve was Lithuanian kugelis, or potato loaf. I still make it all the time. I call my mother — she's 87 now — every time I make it. But I know the recipe by heart:

Five pounds of Idaho potatoes, plus one onion, peeled and grated by hand — it's not the same with a blender. Mix in six eggs, a half-pound of melted butter and a touch of salt mixed into a batter. Bake at 350 degrees for up to two hours until browned. Then you slice it and serve it with butter and sour cream.

Sally's specialty is Oyster Stew, which she likes to serve at Thanksgiving. Anyone can cook, but I think what really makes or breaks a good cook are soups and sauces.

My mother really was a great mother. She took me to church at St. Peter's every Sunday. Religiously. And she was the disciplinarian. One of the greatest punishments I'd get was to be kept in. It was like being caged up. I'd claw at the window.

She'd also use the cat-o'-nine-tails when you had a spanking coming, and it gave her some leverage. Believe me, you were concerned if you got caught acting up. When she unloaded . . . I mean, whew, boy. I guess the strongest thrashing I got was for missing catechism once.

I didn't miss it again. That was a good reminder.

"All he'd have to do was look at it," she said, "and he'd turn white."

She was born on Dearborn Avenue in Del Ray, a little area of Detroit, and lived right behind the railroad tracks. She was the only one in her family born here. Her brother and sister were born in Europe. She used to tell me stories about how she'd climb on the boxcars and throw off coal. Then she and her brother would put it in boxes to take home. They didn't have much.

Her mom died young, from one of the childhood diseases. Her pop, he lived to be a pretty old man, but he got up in the middle of the night to go to the bathroom once and he picked the wrong door. The bathroom door was right next to the staircase. He fell down the stairs and died.

In a lot of ways, I think I might get my toughness from my mother. Once, she brought a bat out to break up a fight at the playground.

"After that," she said, "there was no more trouble with those boys."

During the war, she even went for a few hours a day and worked down at the Rouge Plant.

"My husband didn't want me to work, so I went on the sly," she said.

She was more sports-minded than my dad, too. She would pitch and catch for a local softball team. She used to go to Tigers games with her friends and sit in the upper deck eating the baloney sandwiches she had made. One day, she even caught a foul ball.

"Didn't catch it, exactly," she said. "But I jumped over some seats and scrambled for it."

I'd go to the Tigers games, too. Only we would take rags and dust seats. That's how we got in. Sometimes, you'd get a tip, sometimes you wouldn't.

My goal in life when I was 10 years old, I remember telling my mother, was to play professional baseball and make $50,000 a year and drive a black Cadillac. That was it in those days. The most a major-league player was making then was about $50,000, and a black Cadillac was the epitome of automobiles — in my neighborhood, anyway.

I thought about all that when my friend Mike Ilitch, the owner of the Tigers and Red Wings and of course, Little Caesar's, invited me to lead in singing "Take Me Out To The Ballgame" at Tiger Stadium during the seventh-inning stretch of a game in 1992. I stood on top of the dugout in my coat and tie and belted it out. In the days of the old neighborhood, I could never have envisioned anything like that.

I guess my best friends were the Teets brothers, Paul and Jimmie. They lived a block-and-a-half away at 2412 Springwell. There were seven kids in their family, quite a lot of action, and since I was an only child I tried to hang out over there a lot.

My best friends at Western High — "Western High, we're here for youuuu" — were Joe Carruthers and Joe Selasky. They both were partially Lithuanian, also, and we were the heart of the offensive line. Selasky was the center, Carruthers was the left guard and I was the right guard.

My friends and I didn't have much money, but we found plenty of ways to have a good time. We used to get around the city in the winter by hopping cars. We'd jump on the rear bumper and slide on the ice all the way to wherever we were going. You had to duck so the drivers wouldn't see you. That was a big event.

The dead giveaway at home was when you wore holes into your boots. Or sometimes when you'd let go, your gloves would stick to the bumper and you'd lose a glove. So you had to be careful of that and watch out for those dry spots so you wouldn't ruin your boots, or there'd be trouble at home. And you didn't want to be seen doing it near home, because the neighbors always were pretty quick to squeal on you, too.

Another unconventional way we got around was across garages. Down the alleys, we could go from one block to the next without hitting the ground by jumping from garage to garage. They were close together, but not so close that there wasn't a little risk involved. We could get into jams for that.

Those were part of the growing pains in our neighborhood, where we were always playing games and looking for good times. My friends and I spent most of every day together.

Sometimes it was basically just playing sports. We'd play baseball just down the block, on a cinder lot behind Harms Elementary School. When it was time for dinner, my dad would step out and whistle for me to get home. I'd dash in, eat as fast as I could and be back out without missing an at-bat.

But we were very creative and resourceful, too.

For a long time, we offered pick up and delivery car-washing at Teets' house. We got quite a few customers. We did a good job, but the best part was taking the cars for a little ride on the way back — especially if it was a fancy car.

Once, I got a little carried away with my dad's car, a '48 Ford. I squealed the wheels in the alley behind school and I dropped the transmission. We took it into the shop at school, and I thought it would be fixed in a day. But it took two weeks, and we repaired it with different pieces from all kinds of cars. They never did mesh together. It sounded like a coffee grinder from then on. I don't think my dad ever figured out what happened.

There were quite a few times we would get all dressed up and crash wedding receptions. That was a good, cheap party, a poor boy's entertainment. You had to buy a wedding card first, then you were all set. You had a 50-50 chance of not getting caught. You just had to guess right if someone asked you whether you were there on behalf of the bride or the groom.

It wasn't all living larks, though.

Whether you wanted to take part or not, inevitably there were fights. Not between friends but between gangs. I don't mean gangs like they have now. There were never any knives or guns or weapons of any kind. None at all. But because everybody kind of had their own turf to guard, there were a lot of fistfights in the neighborhood.

Kevin McGuckin and I were the real fighting son-of-a-guns. But we didn't look for trouble, and we weren't bullies or mean.

OK, there was that time as a catcher that I let a high fastball go by and hit the ump, but he had it coming. So I guess we didn't take a whole lot, either. I guess that's where I learned how to fight for what I believed in.

But I later came to understand that mental toughness was much more important than physical toughness. Physical toughness is going to leave you, but something that you can always have and will always need is your mental toughness. You can't belly up and buckle under when times get tough. Anybody can be mentally tough if they work at it, and that's what we always tried to teach the players:

If you play the game within the rules and with mental toughness, when you come in here I'll hug you no matter what the result of the game was.

Anyway, I guess I had managed to develop quite a reputation as some kind of ruffian.

After my sophomore year at Western, the football coach was leaving and the new coach, Eddie Rutherford, asked him about the team he was going to be inheriting. He sent him a telegram with a scouting report that mentioned me prominently. It said I had the potential to be a pretty good player — if they could just keep me from fighting long enough.

"Seems he has a temper," Eddie remembers the telegram saying. "And I also heard he was kind of a ringleader around Vernor."

So Eddie offered me a deal. If I didn't get thrown out of any games for fighting, he was going to give me a jacket. I was excited. So, naturally . . .

"Well, he got kicked out of the first game," Eddie said.

I'm not sure exactly what happened in the game, but I think it had something to do with me and the other team's center. In the old days you didn't have facemasks. So when you played over the center, if you wanted to get him, you would just take the top of your helmet and bash it into him. It was tough on his face. And then of course the guy retaliates, and you've got a skirmish going. That wasn't exactly what Eddie was hoping for out of me.

"We had a long talk, and he really straightened up after that," he said. "So I gave him a jacket anyway."

I was All-State in 1951 and 1952, and we had good teams. Eddie likes to tell the story about me taking out three guys on one play, and also about what happened against Denby in our opening game my senior year.

"They ran the opening kickoff back for a touchdown, and George gathered the whole team together around him and yelled, 'That's all they're getting,'" he said. "And that's all they got."

We went to the Soup Bowl, and went to Tiger Stadium to play the city championship, the Goodfellows benefit game. That was neat for Joe Selasky, because he came from a family of 13 kids and once had gotten shoes and fruit from the Goodfellows.

Around school, I guess I was pretty much known as a jock and a funny guy. Here's what some of my classmates had to say to me on the backs of their senior pictures:

—"It has been nice having you as a friend and laughing at your clever wit." — Henry

—"A really swell guy who really plays his heart out." — Lenny

—"The greatest athlete Western has ever had, excluding nobody." — Lupe

—"A fine athlete who always played for the school." — Bill

—"A guy who's tops with me. . . . Thanks for giving me so much encouragement during the football seasons." — Don

—"A swell guy to know." — Alice

—"The greatest guy I've ever known. I have always thought I was the luckiest guy in the world to play on the same teams as you." — Bob

—"Commercial law would have been dull without your remarks." — Barb

—"To a swell fellow full of fun." — Joan

—"One of the craziest characters I've met." — Dolores

—"Always stay as nice as you are and you'll get far in life." — Alice

—"The guy ... that I'd like to have protecting me." — Sara

—"I'm very glad your game never went to your head." — Margaret

—"You are one of the most comical guys I have ever met." — Shirley

—"My grade-school sweetheart. I'll never forget the time you beat me up. Best of luck to the nicest and friendliest guy I know." — Mary Ann

—"To a very nice guy I never knew." — Fred

—"It's been swell sitting next to you in Comm. Law, even though we have our spats." — Marilyn

—"The only guy I would give my left arm for." — Joe

—"To a real great one I didn't really care for, but after I got to know you — and almost too late — I found out what a terrific guy you really are." — Lillie

Even if it sounds like I was kind of a slacker in school, I actually wasn't a bad student. Michigan State was recruiting me pretty hard, though, and the recruiters were fussy about the academic situation.

"I certainly hope that you enjoyed your visit to the campus Saturday, and I am sorry that the weather was such that you were not able to see the campus when it was really at its best," one of the Michigan State assistant coaches, Don Mason, wrote in a recruiting letter dated November 26, 1952. "Also, it is our hope that you enjoyed the game and suffered no ill effects from sitting in the rain on that particular day. We were glad that it turned out as it did, as it always gives everyone a chance to play, which is the thing we strive to do on every occasion.

"Don't fail to keep up in your studies even [if] your eligibility may be expended, as your final standing in the graduating class is the only means of obtaining scholarship aid in any Big Ten College. I understand that your marks could stand a little boosting, so it might be advantageous for you to make every effort to raise your rank in your graduating class. . . . Just a word to the wise."

Michigan State was having great success in those days. In fact, the Spartans were national champions in 1952. But I was getting looked at everywhere. I could have gone to Notre Dame, Michigan, Ohio State, Tennessee, Michigan State — any school I wanted to.

And I had made a pact with Joe Selasky and Joe Carruthers. We were going to go to the same school. Joe Selasky didn't get the same honors that Joe Carruthers and I had gotten, so he didn't get the same attention from the college scouts that we did, even though he was every bit as good, if not better.

So I made a deal with the University of Tennessee, which had just finished going to about eight bowls in a row at a time when there were only probably four bowl games being played in the country. I told them I would come to Tennessee if they would bring Joe Selasky with me and then a year later, when Joe Carruthers graduated, bring him in, too. Tennessee went for it.

Before I left for Tennessee, I played some semi-pro ball that summer for a team called the Detroit Tars. One of my teammates was Doug Weaver, who later would be my coach, boss and friend. I think the Tars were paying $50 a week, which now that I think about it could have gotten me in trouble.

"It was probably illegal as hell by today's rules that George was being paid right before he went to Tennessee," Doug said. He was about to join the Air Force then. "Anyway, right off the bat, it was hard to believe that George was 17 or 18 years old. He was mature beyond his years, and he'd knock your butt off. He was completely unintimidated by older guys, and I also knew then that he was sort of irreverent and clever.

"George just had grown up differently. All that Vernor Highway stuff was legitimate and real. That would be a great song, a great TV show, a great book."

For various reasons, it didn't really work out at Tennessee. After five days there, Joe Selasky felt like he had to go back home to help his family. Remember, they had 13 kids, so they needed the income he could get going back to work for DeSoto. And I only ended up staying at Tennessee one semester. I earned 11 credits, and I liked Tennessee. But it just wasn't for me.

The next fall, I transferred to Florida State and I was there for about a month of pre-season practice. But I was homesick the whole time, so I came home, back to the neighborhood.

I wasn't working, and I wasn't really sure what to do next with my life. About all I was doing was hanging out at the Sunset Pool Room with my buddies.

3

The Buddy System

Jobs were scarce in those days, right after the Korean War. About the only place you could find work was at one of the car factories, and I thought a lot about doing that. I would have tried to work with my father if I did.

But the Army had a pretty good deal going then. They had a buddy system; if you volunteered to go in with a friend they'd guarantee that you could stay with him all the way through basic training camp. I guess it was a way to encourage you to join.

I don't know how the idea really came to us, but once it did it caught on quick. So 15 of us went to Fort Wayne, Indiana, and upped our draft numbers and joined the Army for a two-year hitch on April 13, 1954.

It was quite a scene. Fifteen of us, wearing our street clothes and raising our hands together to be sworn in. The newspaper came to take a picture. What were we thinking?

Who knows, but we're all still pretty tight: We still get together all the time, and those guys buy more than 60 season tickets to Spartan games. We had a reunion in 1993. It was our 39th, as usual just to be different.

Boy, was the Army sorry it had that deal. Imagine: 15 buddies out of Detroit. Me, Kevin McGuckin, Jimmie Teets, Joe Brennan, Jack Farrell, Jerry Woods, Bob Dillon, John Kilbane, George Ballard, Bob Treece, Larry Kroll, Russ Crawford, Tony Felice, Don Barrett and Dan O'Connell. We had a lot of fun. We definitely made the most out of training camp at Camp Chaffee, Arkansas. We were in Dog Company, No. 47, 5th Armored Division.

The Army didn't seem to particularly like how it worked out with us there. Every time they turned around, there was another guy from Vernor Highway acting up. We had such good times that they fixed us after the eight weeks there. Since it was only promised we'd be together through basic training, they split everybody up after that and sent us all over the country. All over the world, even.

Having all of us there was probably pretty hard on some of the other guys. They were lonely, they were by themselves, and there were the 15 of us. One guy would get in line for dinner and 14 would cut in. We brought Detroit to Arkansas.

We had three dormitories, and it worked out that five of us were in each dorm. But I can't say it was all goofing off.

We had a prisoner with us in basic training — he had gone absent without leave — and he had a guard on him with a gun every minute of the day. You couldn't even walk between him and the M.P. That influenced the heck out of us. I think they did that for a reason.

They were in your face all the time, trying to break you. In those days, they used to say, "Here's my first name. But you call me Sergeant." When we'd march by the stockade, they'd warn you, "Keep monkeying around, and you're going to be in barbed-wire city right here." And if you had to go in there, that was all bad time. In other words, if you're signed up for two years and you get 30 days in the clink, that doesn't count toward your two years.

So I never even came close to being sent in there. None of our guys ever got involved in that. As much fun as we had, we learned to respect authority. They got that across real easy in the Army.

And I always did respect authority. Even when DiBiaggio and I were battling, I never said anything bad about him and never went public. I never got into a debate with him in the media. And even when President McPherson fired me, I didn't retaliate or say anything negative about him or Michigan State. I've always watched myself closely on that kind of stuff; I figured only a loser did things that way.

When we finished basic training, we chartered a plane and all came home to Detroit and rented a hall for a big party. All of our parents came and brought a dish. It was like a wedding.

And then we all went off in different directions. Some stayed in Arkansas. Teets went to Alaska. Farrell went to Korea. We had guys all over. I went to cook school at Fort Knox, Kentucky, for two months, then to Fort Hood, Texas.

Why cook school? I had heard for a private being a cook was a good deal. And I'd say I probably beat the system a little bit.

I didn't want to do any K.P., and cooks never had to do that detail. And I definitely didn't want to do guard duty, which cooks also weren't required to do. It wasn't that I was lazy, but I was worried about falling asleep on guard duty. I was a pretty good sleeper in those days, and I didn't want to chance that happening because guard duty was a pretty serious matter — even if it was just practice.

So cook school was pretty easy. You read the book they gave you, and the Army has a master menu. If you just do what the book tells you to do with the equipment you have, you almost can't make a mistake.

And you have your own cadre room, so you don't have to be out on the floor with the rest of the troops. And they didn't inspect the cadre rooms. You would work 24 hours and then be off 24 hours, and you were off every other weekend. You'd get up in the morning and make breakfast, and then the next shift came in and served you. Sunday nights were C-rations, so there was no preparation.

When they'd go out on bivouac, you'd take the truck out there with all the K.P.s and feed them. Then you'd drive the truck back and get in the nice cozy cadre room while they're out there sleeping in the field and shaving out of their helmets.

I was like "Cookie" in Beetle Bailey. We had a lot of fun with that. "You guys have a good time out there in the field," I'd tell 'em. "I'm going back to the dorm, maybe go out tonight." They'd razz you, but you could get them back. They'd say, "Hey, Cookie, how 'bout two eggs over easy?" And I'd say, "Eggs? We're all out today. And they're only made to order on Sunday. Let's go soldier, move out."

All your buddies would come in on K.P., and you'd have a good time drinking coffee and loafing. Everybody wanted to be on your good side. At night, you'd go into the kitchen and make a little sandwich for the orderly who was working all night. The equipment guys would treat you good because you never knew when they'd want some food over there. There definitely were a lot of politics in the kitchen.

After six months in Texas, I got to go home for a month for vacation before I was sent to Hawaii for the next year. Hawaii was very nice.

It took me five days to get over there on a boat from Oakland, California. When I got there, as soon as I had checked in, I found out they had seen my records as a football player and decided to throw me in with the special troops: Now I was playing football for the 89th Tank Battalion.

I was still a cook, but they sent orders down after I was cooking for about a month that I was to go out for football. No more cook duties. So now I really had it made. We had our own dormitory and no duties. We had nothing to do but play football.

We played the 24th Infantry, we played the Marines, we played them all over there. It was great competition — big leagues, really — and we won the Hawaiian championship.

And this, believe it or not, is how I finally ended up a Spartan. Duffy was over there putting on a clinic for the troops and he saw me. Then he talked to some of the coaches and looked at film of me.

I'm not sure if he remembered me from high school, but he found out I was from Detroit and he told me he'd like me to come to Michigan State after I was discharged.

"Like you should have done in the first place," he said.

It's funny, though. At that point I already knew I was going to go to Michigan State when I got back — whether I had to recruit Michigan State, or whether Michigan State recruited me. I was lucky that Duffy wanted me, too, after I turned them down before.

And, really, if he hadn't been there, I probably would have ended up coming back and working for Ford or Tastee Bread. Would have been a little different life.

Joe Selasky and Paulie Teets are hookers at Ford Motor. They work with steel. Jimmie Teets puts up fence. Richie Teets is a retired fence man. Jerry Woods is on the production line at Ford.

I've got some friends who have very good positions, and some who are hard-working people. Some are wealthier than others. Never mattered to me. Besides, like I always say, "You can have all the money in the world, but if you ain't got your friends, you ain't got nothing."

Looking back, I'm still not really sure why I didn't go to Michigan State right away. I guess I had thought I was some kind of big shot coming out of Western. Couple of years All-State and all that. Plus, at the time I thought I wanted to get away from home. And Tennessee was one of the biggest football names in the country then and had gone for my offer about Selasky and Carruthers.

I wouldn't say I regret not going to Michigan State immediately — I don't really have any regrets — but I sometimes wonder how it would have gone if I had.

Meanwhile, after Duffy left, I still had some time left in the Army. By then I was getting pretty used to the special treatment. So it came as kind of a jolt when after football season they sent me back to the company to be a cook. Only the cooking job was filled, so they made me a ball gunner with a tank.

Ball gunner? I didn't know anything about that. That's the guy who sits next to the driver and shoots a machine gun. And those tanks, now, you've got to come in at night and shine those babies up.

I did that for two days, then I said, "This is a loser," and I went out for boxing. I could get away with things like that, because the Colonel loved us for winning the championship in football. I boxed for about a month until track started, and then I threw the shot put until I got discharged a few months later.

When I came back to Detroit in April, before I went off to school in August, I got a permit as an iron worker. I used that to work for Richie Teets for three dollars and 52 and a half cents an hour.

In April 1956, it was more than my father was making and he asked me why I was going to go to school. If I was making more than him already, he thought I ought to stay there and work. I told him I wanted to go and play football, and he didn't like that answer. He was really against it.

So my mother actually had to sneak out his suitcase to be able to take me to school while he was at work. I knew right there that I had better do well at everything or not come home, because I had really upset him by quitting a good job.

And that was all he wanted me to do: Have a good job. That was the way he was. He had been through the depression, so a job was everything. And he was worried that I was just going to school to play football and would never get an education.

But once I was in school, he was very, very supportive. Once the issue was decided, he was for me 100 percent. And probably his original feeling about it was the best thing that ever happened to me, because that really made me sure I was serious about earning my degree.

By the time I was done at Michigan State, my dad thought I invented school. He loved to come to the games. I could be on the field warming up, and I would see his face in the stands. His glare, and his pride. It was beautiful.

4

"The Right Spartan Spirit"

As it turned out, if I had gone to Michigan State just to play football, I wouldn't have gotten very far. I wasn't even eligible until my junior year, and then my career ended abruptly with a knee injury.

I had those 11 credits from Tennessee, but I was still a freshman in East Lansing. In those days, freshmen weren't eligible. There wasn't even a freshman schedule. And the transfer rule had been changed to make you ineligible for two years after you left. Pretty harsh.

Not that I didn't get some action during those two years. We scrimmaged like crazy. Our freshman coach was Doug Weaver; seems like I bumped into him all my life. He was really on me, boy, but he liked me.

I swear there were 200 guys on our freshman team; it was like a factory. In those days there were no limits on how many players you could have. There were so many of us that Bob Devaney, who was an assistant at Michigan State before he went on to Wyoming and Nebraska, would come through every spring and take the ones who weren't playing here back to Wyoming with him.

On Tuesdays as freshmen, you'd scrimmage the varsity guys who hadn't played on Saturday. A lot of them were guys I had gone to high school with, like Joe Carruthers, or played against in high school. I was ready for anything with them. Doug Weaver would tell Joe, "I don't know how tough George will be." He'd say things that he wanted to get back to me to motivate me, and they worked.

One of our freshman quarterbacks was Larry Bielat, who would become a good friend and later work with me at St. Ambrose and, of course, Michigan State.

Roger Donnahoo, a great halfback, and Dean Look, a future All-American, were on that team. So were the McNeeley brothers. The McNeeleys both left school, but Tom ended up being a boxer. He fought Floyd Patterson for the World Heavyweight Championship in Toronto. His son, Peter, fought Mike Tyson in August of 1995 after Tyson was released from prison.

As a sophomore, I was dying to play, but I spent my time on the scout team for the varsity. Just banging heads.

Finally, in my third year I was eligible. That was a thrill in itself. I started the fall practices on the third team, and it took about three games before I was on second team. Then all of a sudden I was starting against Illinois. Duffy got fed up after a loss to Purdue and changed most of the lineup.

The next game was against Wisconsin, at home and on national television. That was a big deal because in those days you could only play on national TV once a year. I knew that my relatives in New Jersey and friends would be watching and I really wanted to do well.

Instead, I got my knee torn up and I was done. For good. Waited all those years to play college football, then at 24 I finally got to start a few games . . . and it was over like that. First time in my life I was even hurt.

In those days there was no substituting. You had to play both ways, offense and defense, and on special teams, too. I was covering on a punt, and I had a burning desire to make the play. I could see the guy catching the ball and me making a strong tackle and knocking the ball loose.

Well, that didn't happen. I got blocked — fairly — when one of their linemen peeled back and hit me while my leg was planted pretty well in the ground. My ligaments were ripped. Our team physician, Dr. James Feurig, ran on the field and immediately gave me a shot of some kind of pain reliever right through my jersey. Within seconds, I felt the pain leave.

On Monday morning I had an operation. What they did in those days was drill a hole in the bone, bring the ligament through the hole and tie it up with wire. And it was a good operation. I've never had any problems with it. It was such a good operation that I always kind of thought I could have played again.

But the danger was if you ever had it injured again, you'd already used up all the elasticity in the ligament by bringing it through the bone. You'd have a stiff knee the rest of your life.

I guess it would sound silly to say this actually was a break for me, but I think that's when Duffy really noticed me and began to look after me. When he recruited me, he said, "If you put your career in my hands, I'll watch over you." And he was true to his word.

He seemed pretty sentimental when he did interviews with reporters the week after my injury.

"You know, he wasn't the greatest tackle we ever had," Duffy said. "There's a lot he doesn't know about football. But he had one thing, something every coach admires in a player. George didn't know any other way to play but all-out. He was fighting all the time, knocking somebody down. . . .

"I'll never forget when they carried him off the field on a stretcher. That knee was hurting him terribly. But he ignored his knee. . . . He sat up on the stretcher, cheering the team as the next play started."

I just remember sitting up when the pain left, and I guess I made a motion with my fist, punching the air. Dr. Feurig told a reporter the same thing that Duffy had said: "He tried to get up so he could make every one of them hear him."

Mostly what I remember about it was realizing that I would probably never play again. Today, I guess the medicine is sophisticated enough that I would at least have had a chance to get back out there. But I tried to keep my mouth shut and not bellyache.

"But did the youngster have a squawk?" Duffy said. "This I'll always remember. . . . He said to me, 'Coach, did you see the beautiful block the Wisconsin guy put on me? That's the kind of block I always wanted to make.'

"Perles has the right Spartan spirit."

Duffy, boy, he was amazing with the press. But that was really him, too. What a personality. And he was brilliant. Very, very intelligent. He made every interview a real happening.

He'd say stuff like, "We're small, but we make up for it by being slow." When writers asked who he was happiest to see returning from the previous season, he'd say, "Me." One time he was explaining the game to a group and he said, "A tight end is not necessarily intoxicated, a split end often lacks a dual personality and an ineligible receiver may be entirely eligible . . . for marriage."

His humor was second to none. And you definitely didn't want to recruit against Duffy. He would even sing to the recruits. He was an entertainer.

He was also a great humanitarian. He was one of the first major-college coaches to recruit black players from the South. He was way ahead of his time as far as equal opportunity goes. One of the reasons was he always believed in helping the poor, the underdog. And he loved old people.

And generous—Duffy was very generous. Even though he'd do everything he could to beat you at a game of golf for a buck or two — he'd cheat like crazy — after a round he'd spend 10 times what he'd made golfing buying drinks and dinner. When you went out with Duffy, he was going to pay for everything. He was a big spender, a happy-go-lucky guy who probably had more friends in the business than any other coach.

His best friends were the Bear Bryants, Bob Devaneys, John McKays and Joe Paternos. And he was a leader among them. He had a belief that coaches would like to get away and concentrate on football and exchange stories, and that's how he came to start the Coach Of The Year clinics in Grand Rapids. It's all over the country now, in places like Seattle, San Francisco, Pittsburgh, St. Louis, Philadelphia.

Duffy had succeeded Biggie Munn in 1954, when Biggie developed an ulcer and decided to become athletic director. Biggie had recommended Duffy. They were two great men . . . who didn't really get along.

Unlike Duffy, Biggie was very serious about everything. He wasn't interested in being outgoing socially, especially outside of his environment at Michigan State.

I ended up kind of in the middle of them one time in what I think was a good example of their differences.

One Friday evening we were going to have the chicken fry for the Varsity Club, after which I was going to be taking over as president of the Varsity Club. That was pretty important to me. I was going to get the gavel that night, and I needed to have a speech.

All the speeches I had ever heard from Duffy Daugherty started off with a joke, so I asked a friend if he knew a joke. He told me one that was kind of a bathroom joke, about these three mice.

I thought it was pretty funny, so when I took the gavel I proceeded to tell this joke. Kind of an involved joke. I'm cruising along, and as I'm getting to the punchline, Duffy is loving it. He's almost rolling on the ground laughing because he knows the joke.

But Duffy had a better, or at least different, sense of humor than most of the people there. Some administrators were there, and one lady dropped her chicken. It was the wrong thing to do, telling a bathroom joke in that setting.

The next day when I went by the football office, the secretary said, "Biggie wants to see you." I knew it was for the night before.

So I went down to the other end of the building, and Biggie called me into his office. Biggie was active with the Boy Scouts all his life, and he loved the Varsity Club and he liked me. But I knew this wasn't a good situation. In fact, I was scared to death. I knew he was going to rip me.

He said, "Let me tell you something. You don't have to start off every talk with a joke. We've got one funny guy around here, and that's enough." He was talking about Duffy. That's when they were really grinding each other. Different personalities.

Boy, was I glad to get out of there that day. And that was the end of jokes for me. Really. Don't forget, I was a young, impressionable student at the time. This was 1958, and all these years, still no jokes when I speak. My wife has told people many times, "George is very funny and humorous," and they ask why I don't use some of that in my talks. And I say, "I can't." Because I will never, ever forget that situation with Biggie.

But probably because of Biggie's fondness for the Varsity Club — he even built a Varsity Club room right in the stadium — I had a tremendous relationship with him after that. And Duffy, of course, was like a second father to me. And despite their differences, both had a great influence on me.

Biggie was tough. Biggie was loud and strong and would motivate you toward toughness. He was a great believer in one-on-one drills with a lot of contact. If you looked at his players, the old Spartans, you could see that in them and how it's carried over in their lives.

Even if Biggie could get hot at Duffy, I think Duffy appreciated everything Biggie had done for him. When Biggie got named to the Football Hall of Fame, Duffy joked: "You can credit me for getting Biggie to the Hall of Fame. . . . After six years of my coaching, they can appreciate what a great coach he really was."

I had a few other things going on during school, too. Some friends of mine and I tried to start our own fraternity, for example, but we never could get approval. We wanted to do our own thing. We had some of the Greek letters — I forget what we were going to call it, exactly — and we went through all the formalities, even had a picture taken for our yearbook. But it didn't work out.

And I played intramural baseball and ice hockey. We won the intramural thing in hockey a couple times.

"He was a defenseman, and he was good on the skates," Joe Farrell said. Joe Farrell played hockey with me and has been my dear friend since. Through Joe, after my football playing days were over, I later got a part-time job at a reform school in Lansing. I supervised 13- to 17-year-old kids there, mostly in a recreational environment. We'd work three hours a night, every night, and Saturday mornings.

"George got along really well with those kids," Joe said. "One reason is that he was such a self-assured guy himself that he was not easily threatened. Kids respected him, respected that he had been a varsity football player.

"But he had an easy hand with them. He didn't push them around or try to intimidate or bully them. He was just a leader — one of the great natural leaders I've ever known.

"Golf outings, softball games, picnics: You name it, he'll organize it, and it's always done well. The guy has a flair for organizing, but he also has a flair for getting people to identify with something he's doing so it gets them motivated. He's a passionate, passionate guy."

And, of course, there was the best thing that happened to me at Michigan State: During my sophomore year, I met the wonderful Sally Bradford.

My relationship with Sally actually began with a blind date that hadn't worked out. I had a blind date scheduled with her girlfriend, Joyce, but Joyce had just patched up a relationship with her ex-boyfriend and was looking for someone to take care of her blind date — me.

I guess you could say Sally was the replacement blind date.

"George for a long time tried to pull my chain about that, saying he really wanted to go out with Joyce," Sally said, laughing.

It was a successful first date, at least as far as I was concerned. We ended up at a party with a lot of my buddies. I think Sally had a good time. I didn't go too many places where we didn't have a good time. We were always laughing, and I don't think we were boring.

"There were a lot of football players there," Sally recalled, "and to be honest I was not into football too much in those days. I was not too impressed. No, I didn't exactly swoon over George right away.

"But George was really persistent, I'll say that for him. He'd call me and ask, 'How about doing something tonight?' When I'd say no, he'd say, 'How about tomorrow? How about Friday?'

"I soon found out what a terrific sense of humor he had, and what a strong sense of basic values. He's very old-fashioned in a lot of ways. One night, he just popped out and asked me to marry him. We had matching gold bands, not very elaborate, until about four years ago when George gave me this *rock*."

Sally was from Royal Oak, Michigan. Her parents were from a farm community, and all of the Bradfords raised cherries, ripe and sour. But her dad couldn't make a living just doing that, so he went to work at Chevrolet and became a machine repair man. He could make anything. Her mother was a second grade teacher, and I really looked up to her.

What I liked about Sally right away was she was easy to get along with and seemed to flow with about anything you wanted to do. She wasn't a demanding, hard-nosed person, although she likes to kid me. She'd rather kid me more than anybody; it makes her laugh.

She was easy-going, and that's a nice complement to my personality. It would have been hard if she were over-organized and over-aggressive like I am. And she was strong in all the areas I was weak in. I mean, she reads a lot of books. I'm not interested in reading a lot of books. She's interested in art, she's an artist, and I don't know much about art. She likes to go by herself to our cottage up north when she's doing her art, so she can be isolated and not have any interference.

"I'm a lot more reclusive than George," she said. "I like my space, and I like my quiet time and solitude."

Sally's very well-educated. Every place we went, she went to school. When I was coaching with the Steelers, she went to the University of Pittsburgh and got a degree in political science. Then she finished her art degree at Michigan State and got her advanced art degree here, too.

I think Sally took some of the rough edges off of me. And she still likes to keep me in my place. She's told me many times, "I'm not working for you. I'm not one of your coaches." She was always on-guard for that. I guess when you're a head coach you sometimes kind of let it carry over accidentally in some areas you shouldn't.

Sally spent a great deal of our first 20 years of marriage raising children. We had our first child in '58, our second one in '59, our third in '62 and our fourth in '63.

I probably should have worried how I would provide for us, but I didn't. I just assumed that that would work out. But we didn't have much money to work with for a long time.

My first job, as an assistant at St. Rita's in Chicago after I got my master's in secondary administration, I made $3,600. That was 1961. Oh, and I made $400 for coaching football and I used to clean the second floor of the school for $30 a week, too.

When I moved to St. Ambrose in Detroit as head coach the next year, I made $6,000, a huge increase in pay at the time. At the University of Dayton in '65, I made $8,000, and when I came back to Michigan State as an assistant in '67 I got $9,500. I started at $19,000 with the Steelers in 1972 and when I left in 1982 I was making $69,500 — a big jump, thanks to four Super Bowls.

So it was an awful, awful lot of work for Sally, raising them with a football coach just getting started and having to spend as much time in the football business as I had to spend. It's a credit to her the way the children turned out, and I'm lucky she didn't throw me out with me being gone so much. It's a hard life, being a coach's wife.

"It's not easy to carve out your life, but it wasn't really hard until we were back in East Lansing when George became head coach," Sally said. "It's a small town, and we have an unusual name that everyone recognizes. After a while, people even recognized me, and I'm not comfortable with that.

"The first thing everybody wants to talk about is football, and I just have to say, 'I don't speak for my husband.' And you hate to turn people down, but so many people ask things that if you don't watch your step you're going to be involved in everything in the city."

The way I really started in coaching, of course, was thanks to Duffy. After I got hurt, he encouraged me to be a student assistant the next year. So I did that, and I helped out with the freshmen. And then he asked me to stay on the next year as a graduate assistant.

As graduate assistants, you'd get all the gopher work. It was kind of like being back in the apartment on Pitt Street in the old neighborhood.

Henry Bullough and I worked together then, for the first of several times in our careers. I'd go get lunch for the coaches — burgers at McDonald's, 15 cents; I'd buy them by the bagful — and I'd drive the coaches where they needed to go.

We were what I call tennis-shoe coaches. We had to hustle. Since there was no room in the offices for us, we'd go over to the stadium on Sunday mornings to break down film. We'd come out around Wednesday.

When we were going into my "outstanding" season in 1994, I hired Henry away from the Detroit Lions. He was living in East Lansing, anyway, commuting to Pontiac, and I asked him if he ever thought about coming back to Michigan State since he already lived in town.

It was a big deal that I got him a five-year contract, even though I only had four years remaining myself. But Henry needed five years in a row at Michigan State to earn back pension credit he had for the 11 years he had worked here before. I thought that was important, especially to get somebody with his credentials.

He was a great player at Michigan State, and when he left he played for the Green Bay Packers. When Duffy brought him back, he was the youngest assistant Duffy ever had. I always felt that he had more respect for Henry than any assistant he had, and he had some good ones. Henry ran the Michigan State defense in the golden years of 1965 and '66, and then he went to the Baltimore Colts as an assistant and they won the Super Bowl.

That was just the start of Henry's resume: He also coached with the New England Patriots, the Cincinnati Bengals, the Packers, the Pittsburgh team in the USFL and the Buffalo Bills. When I was with the Steelers and the Bengals got Henry, I told Chuck Noll to look out for the Bengals. Getting Henry was like getting two first-round draft choices.

Anyway, after my year as a graduate assistant, I was still Duffy's man. Why? I was blessed. But you could always tell how he felt; he couldn't hide his silly grin.

He didn't have a spot for me on his staff, but he had a lot of connections. He said, "George, I want you to to go to Chicago. I want you to learn the Catholic League. It's the best high school football league in the country."

Well, I didn't have to fall off a truck to understand that he wanted me to know the Catholic League because he had plans for me.

He pulled some strings and got me the job at St. Rita's pulled some strings to get me to St. Ambrose. From there he got me a job at Dayton with John McVay, who had been his assistant. From there, he brought me back to Michigan State and when he was about to retire, he got me to the Pittsburgh Steelers and Chuck.

He took care of me from the last play I played, and when I came back to Michigan State as head coach, there was no one happier. I'm proud to say any success that I've had in this business was because of coming to Michigan State and meeting Duffy Daugherty.

5

Riddells and Rosaries

In Chicago, we lived in a flat at 47th and Sawyer on the south side. We were on the first floor, and the landlord lived upstairs but stayed in the basement most of the time. He was like a stepfather to us.

Sally and I never had much money to go out with in those days, so the few times we did he babysat for us. That was nice of him, but he also didn't want any strangers in his home. We were paying $125 a month in rent, and that was a lot of money.

Larry Bielat and I went together to St. Rita's to work for Ed Buckley. Buckley had fought at Iwo Jima and he was a Harvard man. He knew President Kennedy there. He talked about the president often. He would say the president "wasn't a strong boy, very thin. But a real nice guy."

Ed Buckley was a great coach. Brilliant offensive mind. Tough. I was lucky to work for him that one year. He took a school that hadn't had much success and went to the championship. He sent the president the game ball from the championship, but I'm not exactly sure what the president did with it.

I don't know if it was accurate, but Ed would always say he was the only football coach coaching who had graduated from Harvard. He was proud of that. I think he was implying that most of the graduates did a little better than you would as a football coach.

After that season, the real turn of events started — because of Duffy. Two assistants on Duffy's staff at the time were Danny Boisture and Bill Yeoman. Bill was a West Point graduate from Texas, and the University of Houston job had come open. Bill wanted it.

Duffy called a lot of shots around the country, and he made some phone calls to get Bill Yeoman the Houston job. Then he told Yeoman he wanted him to take care of Danny Boisture's brother, Tom, who was the head coach at the best football school in the state of Michigan: St. Ambrose.

Then he told Tom Boisture, "You recommend George Perles for the head coaching job at St. Ambrose." I got the job; a lot of strings to pull for a little Lithuanian. I mean, what the hell, Duffy had more important things to do.

So then I went to St. Ambrose for three years. We rented a home in East Detroit for $115 a month. Best high school job in Michigan. They were really ahead of the times there in terms of support from the administration and boosters. And I went in there with one thing . . . Forrest Evashevski and Davy Nelson's book on the Wing T. That was about all I had. That, and Larry Bielat and Joe Selasky to help me out.

I was real nervous about taking this job, because if I went there and laid an egg, it was all over. But I went to see my friend Al Werthmann, and his advice was, "Go for it all." So I took it. I wasn't ready, though. I mean, I knew that. I had never been a head coach, and suddenly I was the head coach at the best football school in the state?

As it turned out, we did just fine. We went undefeated our first year and outscored our opponents 274-25.

That's not a typo. I don't know how we did that, except we had dedicated kids who practiced six days a week and played once a week. They never had a day off, and they liked the challenges I gave them. I'd ask them, "Who's the toughest here?" And then I'd get the tough guys and circle them up into the ol' "bull in the ring" drill: send the whole team after one guy. We'd see who was standing at the end.

Some people didn't like how hard we were working, thought we were spending too much time at it, and there was a letter to the editor griping about that in one of the papers.

There are some people out there who want to be critical of anything. If you work too hard, they criticize you. If you don't work hard enough, they criticize that. If you start too early . . . whatever you do in athletics, it's open season for criticism. So you can't worry about those things, or you'll never get anything accomplished.

It's a good reason why, especially during the season, coaches shouldn't read the paper. I avoided reading the paper. The one who influenced me most on that was my son Patrick. How about that, a young man like him telling his father, "You have to create your own environment." You don't have to read the papers, you don't have to listen to the sports on radio and television. Create your own environment, and you won't have to listen to the negative stuff.

President Hannah at Michigan State used to tell his deans, "You know, you don't have to read the school newspaper." Because everybody's got an opinion, and one way to keep from being upset is to not read it. As long as you have confidence in yourself that you're doing the right thing. . . .

It seemed like we were doing some things right at St. Ambrose. Seven of our 12 seniors the first year earned major college scholarships. Tom Beer, our star player, went on to the University of Houston and to the NFL. And we won the Catholic school championship in the Soup Bowl, which is played for the benefit of the homeless, with 20,000 people there.

At the banquet for the game, all these poor guys from the street who eat the soup, they get on their best suit of clothes and they're the waiters. They might have on blue pants and a purple jacket, but their hair is slicked down and they shower and shave. Big thing for them, and for everybody there.

It's really a neat deal, just like the Goodfellows game for the City championship. They make an impression. When my good friend Joe Carruthers' mom passed away, they didn't want flowers. They wanted any money given to the Capuchin Guild charity, to the Soup Bowl.

I've always been pretty enthusiastic as a coach, and in those days at St. Ambrose I was almost berserk. My motivational talks, I was just yelling and screaming. But what I had to say always made a lot of sense . . . to me, at least, and maybe some of the players. Even so, after the season, the team physician put me in the hospital for observation and tests because he was worried about how hot and bothered I got. Everything was fine, but it scared him.

We didn't have our own field, and my office there was a converted coal bin. But don't let that fool you. The office was cleaned up, painted up nice, and we had everything. I mean, everything. Really, it was as good a program as any in the nation as far as support goes.

The Dad's Club did it all with year-round raffles and all kinds of fundraisers. We sold glasses, ashtrays, seat cushions, and some of the money we made I kept in my drawer and used for recruiting.

That was legal, by the way. I used to take seventh and eighth grade kids over to "Janet's Lunch" for the big hot beef sandwiches. Then we'd have them come over and check out our equipment. The finest. We'd lay out the game jerseys, by Sand-Knit, and the Rawlings pants. We had Riddell helmets, game shoes, practice shoes. We had the socks with the "A" on them.

No one could compete with us with the money we had. We had the pre-game meals at a restaurant. We had a laundry service. We had a fantastic banquet at the end of the year, and we had our own school bus. We wanted to paint it maroon and white like our helmets, but we had to keep it yellow because of the state laws.

We had about 100 boys and 100 girls in school, and about 70 of the boys were involved in football, either varsity or junior varsity. It was a storybook school, and I loved working for Father VanAntwerp, whose brother used to be mayor of Detroit, and John Tobianski, whom I named our second son after.

It was important to Father Van that St. Ambrose have a good football team. He really wasn't concerned about any other sport but football, because he saw that as an opportunity to instill discipline. So the person he hired to coach football also was hired to be the school disciplinarian. That was fine with me.

I was one of the few males in the school; all the rest of the faculty were nuns. So if someone was acting up in class, the nuns would send them down to the football office. When they got there, they'd better be ready to grab their ankles. They were going to get it. I didn't even ask what they had done. If the nuns sent them there, it was for a reason. The nuns loved it; Father loved it.

Game days were special at St. Ambrose. We'd go to the restaurant for our meal. Dry toast and steak for the players. The coaches would have banana splits, too. Then we'd take the kids back to the school, but we'd drop them off two blocks away and they'd walk together.

After they'd get taped, they'd go into the hallway and say their rosary. Then we'd all walk over to the church together, take our shoes off and go to the altar.

We'd come out to get on the bus, and the nuns were all there to wish us luck — and they had their rosaries. Then we'd go and play the game, come back to St. Ambrose and kneel on the parish steps and say a thank you prayer. Our team always went together to 9 o'clock mass on Sundays. The first six rows were saved for us.

After my first year, I was offered an assistant's job at Southern Illinois University, but I turned it down. The second year, we lost two games, which wasn't too nice, but the third year we won them all again —even if we did give up more than 25 points this time.

We ran the Wing T well, but I think we won with defense most of the time. We never threw the ball. I think we passed 18 times my first season. The last play of warmups before we went in the locker room, I'd tell the quarterback to drop back and throw it as far as he could. I didn't care if he completed it. It was just to let everybody in the press box and on the other sideline know we could throw it.

It was a great time for me, and probably my best break in coaching. I'll always be grateful to the people at St. Ambrose. But I knew all along I wanted to coach in college.

I was watching TV one Saturday night in January of 1965, and there was an announcement that John McVay had just left Michigan State and was going to be the new head coach at the University of Dayton. I got to the phone and called him as soon as I heard that, and darned if he wasn't home. I said something clever like, "Uh, hey, Coach. I'd like to apply for a job at Dayton."

Well, because of Duffy, he must have been already considering me, anyway. He said, "Are you going to the national convention?" I said, "Yeah, it's in Chicago." So we made a date that we would meet in Chicago.

We met in his hotel room, and he didn't offer me the job. But I noticed he had a map of recruiting assignments and my name was one of the ones he had on a territory. And he wanted me to bring my wife and visit the campus the following weekend, which I thought was a good sign. When I got there, it turned out I already had the job. He started to sell, and we went from being interviewed to him telling Sally what a good opportunity this would be. We thought so, too, and we accepted and went right to work.

And that's about all we did there. Work. Sally was good at managing money, so we were never worried about groceries or anything. But the only times I can remember going out in Dayton were when we went to Shakey's Pizza Parlor and we sang to the bouncing ball and ate pizza with our kids and drank some draft beer. My colleagues Tom Moore and Wayne Fontes would bring their children along, and that was our big night out.

John had gone to Michigan State from Canton Central High, where he had had some great players like Alan Page. John's a vice-president of the San Francisco 49ers now, and he doesn't get all the credit he really deserves for what they've accomplished. He did everything for them, especially in personnel and administration. He was a fine football coach —he coached the New York Giants, remember — but he really made his mark as an administrator.

During the three years John was with Duffy, I guess he saw me bringing recruits there and had a chance to observe me —with me never knowing if it would amount to a job. He took a chance on some young guys, high school coaches, on his staff, and that says a lot about him. And it panned out. Not only for Dayton, where we went 8-2 our second year after they had had a lot of bad seasons, but for the staff, too.

We had Wayne Fontes, now the coach of the Detroit Lions; Tom Moore, who became the offensive coordinator for the Lions and Jerry Hanlon, who left after our first year and joined Bo Schembechler at Miami of Ohio and later was at Michigan with Bo.

Wayne had been a couple years behind me in school at Michigan State. Excellent player. Working with him at Dayton, it was obvious to me that he had an outstanding coaching future. The kids played hard for him, and he was a complete teacher. He was always full of humor, outgoing and had a lot of friends, men and women. He was always happy and ready to have a party.

Our first year there was kind of like the pizza place: shaky. We had a record of 1-8-1, but when people asked us how we did, we'd say, "Won eight and one." But we recruited hard and worked hard, and it all turned around the next year.

"What George brought to the program was almost indescribable," John McVay said. "He was just one of those guys who had an enthusiasm that was so contagious. Very engaging. He was so much fun to be around, for the coaches and the players.

"During our spring game after the first season, we used a special point system to keep score between the offense and the defense. The whole thing was tied up as we went to the final play. We called a run on offense, and the play busted wide open.

"Our back was on his way to the end zone, but George just ran over and tackled the guy. He flipped the kid over on his back, got up and pumped both fists in the air and yelled, 'We win, we win.'"

It was just a reaction.

"Probably where we made the most strides was in our recruiting, and George was instrumental in that," John said. "He was a tremendous recruiter. He's hard to say no to.

"During that time, the University of Detroit dropped football. George spent a lot of time there. He was supposed to be going through Toledo, too, but I think he just rolled his car windows down and threw out applications as he drove by there. It didn't matter, because we took everything from the University of Detroit but their school bus. Players, uniforms, barbells, everything."

I think what helped us at Dayton, too, was the discipline. We were a demanding, aggressive young staff. We never touched the players, but we sure used our voices. Grabbing facemasks and stuff like that might have been more accepted then, but not for me with my background with Duffy. The worst language Duffy ever used was "jackass." He never tolerated cussing, and no one could ever be in a position where they could get away with touching a player.

At Michigan State in '65, Bullough put in the free safety blitz. People didn't know how to pick it up, and they had a great season. Their only loss was to UCLA in the Rose Bowl. The safety blitz was good against the pass and great against the run, too.

That year they held Ohio State to something like five yards rushing.

Over the winter, I got that defense from Henry. Everything I did I copied from somebody else. And in '66, the first eight games I think we gave up seven touchdowns. The safety blitz was beautiful.

Over the winter, I got interviewed for a job at Arizona. In fact, I got offered the job over the phone. I went out there to visit, but then I called them back and said no. It was too far from home.

The next thing I knew, I got a call from Frank Kush — another Michigan State alum — wanting to know if I'd come out there and talk. Well, of course, that was still too far from home but I listened. He told me his defensive coordinator was interviewing at Iowa, and if he left for Iowa he wanted to bring me in. I told him I wanted to bring Fontes with me as secondary coach if I got the job.

Well, his assistant went to Iowa and Frank called and said the job was mine. When I asked him about Wayne, he said, "Nah, we're all set." Well, that set me back. I didn't know what to say. Now Frank wanted an answer, I wasn't sure what to do, so I kept dodging him and dodging him.

In about a week he reached me, and he was hot. I said, "Nah, I don't think I'm coming," and he hung up on me. Boy, was he mad. I don't think he talked to me for a year. We're good friends now.

It turned out for the best. In August of 1967, Danny Boisture left Michigan State to go to Eastern Michigan. Duffy hired me as an assistant. If I'd have taken either one of those jobs in Arizona, I'd never have gotten hired here — that time, and probably not later on as head coach, either. Funny how things happen.

6

Back to the Future

Every time I went back to Michigan State, it was the happiest day of my life. I remember what I said when I went back in 1967: "I'm sure there are some people as happy as I am, but there's no one happier than I am to be back at Michigan State."

By getting an assistant's job there, and by making $9,000 like my mother-in-law the teacher, I had met the goal in life I had set when I was a student. A little different than my goal as a 10-year-old, to make $50,000 and drive a black Cadillac. But why shouldn't your dreams and goals change as you go along? I mean, I never had any ambition then to be the head coach. I never thought it would be possible.

It was a beautiful situation. We even had enough money to buy our first house, for $25,000, and when you were recruiting you had some entertaining to do so you had some free nights out.

I was an assistant freshmen coach my first two years back, working under my old high school coach, Eddie Rutherford. Then I was with the defensive backs for a year. Finally, I became defensive coordinator when Henry Bullough left for the Baltimore Colts in 1970.

I was always a defensive coach. I think it fit my personality better. Offense takes a little more patience, an understanding that there would be a slower pace of learning. Defensive coaching has a lot more to do with aggression and motivation. It suited me.

At home in the evenings, I was always sitting around with a yellow pad doodling and drawing up new and different schemes. But it almost always ends the same way when you're drawing defenses: You run out of players. You're always one man short when you add everything up. You get 11 on offense, so you need 12 on defense.

Duffy was in the twilight of his career, his last few seasons, and I'll always treasure the time I had with him then. I was always available to do anything and go any place he wanted to go. I drove him all the time. Most of the time when he was in the car, he slept — and that's how he could keep going all the time. He'd fall asleep pretty easily after we'd visited for a while.

He liked to go to the Detroit racetrack to relax, and he'd take his coaches with him. Or he'd take us with him to the Big Ten meetings in Chicago, with no responsibilities except to have a good time. He was good to his assistants. After his family, you knew his assistants were right at the top.

Duffy's wit was as sharp as ever, and as usual he kept everybody guessing. Against Notre Dame in 1968, Duffy told the media the night before the game that he was going to onside kick to start the game. They all laughed.

As assistant coaches, we didn't know anything about that . . . until game time. We were kicking off, and I was up in the coaches box hooked up with Henry on the phone downstairs. He said, "You won't believe this: Duffy is going to onside kick!" I thought, "We're nuts. The old man's nuts." And we did onside kick, on the opening kickoff, and we got the ball and went down and scored. Incredible.

For a second, I thought we were going to have an encore. Henry got on the phone again and said, "You can't believe it. He's going to do it again!" Well, Notre Dame had everybody up front so he changed his mind on that one. But we went on and won the game.

That was Duffy. He had the courage to try anything. One of the biggest games in the country, and he starts it off with an onside kick . . . and we get it. Duffy would put any play in. Did that rub off on me? Let's just say not as much as it should have. I tended to be a bit more conservative.

I had a little nickname for a while: "Ralph." That came up after our 1970 game at Michigan. One of our linemen got hurt, and Duffy yelled, "Let's get another tackle in there." I started yelling for one of our players, Ralph Wieleba. "Ralph, get in there. Hey, Ralph Wieleba."

But there was no sign of Wieleba, and I couldn't figure out what was going on. Duffy tapped me on the shoulder. He said, "George, we didn't bring Wieleba. He's back in East Lansing." Boy, did I feel like a dope.

Not everything about those days was so light, though.

In the summer of 1969, we got the kids and our Shetland sheep dog, Sundance, and took our brown Chevy station wagon to Albuquerque, New Mexico, to see Larry Bielat. It took about three days to get there. Our technique was to drive all day and get two rooms at a Holiday Inn. In those days, they were popular and pretty reasonable. We'd let the kids go swimming, get some fast food for them and put them to bed. Then Sally and I would eat.

We'd never been out West, but since Larry was coaching there, we thought it would be our chance. We went the Southern way out and planned to go home through Wyoming. When we were at Larry's house, he had a strong feeling about us going to the Grand Canyon. He thought it was not to be missed, and he called and made reservations for us at a hotel near the Grand Canyon.

When we got there, we stopped and took a little peek at it and then went to the hotel to check in. At the hotel, the fellow behind the desk said we had a message: "Before you check in, call Larry Bielat."

The family was out in the car, and I went to the pay phone and called Larry. He said, "I'm sorry to tell you, George, your dad died." He was 63, and he had a heart attack. He was at home, cleaning a lawnmower, scraping it out underneath.

I was shocked. Pretty emotional. We never checked in to the hotel. We jumped back in the car and went back to Larry's, driving almost all night. We lay down for a couple hours. He had the plane reservations, everything, taken care of, and he took us to the airport early the next morning. We arrived at the funeral home just as my mother was coming in.

We were very fortunate not to miss a minute of the service, and this is a good lesson for everybody to understand. Had we left Larry's house as we had originally planned, without anyone knowing where we were staying on the way back, we would have missed my father's funeral. And that would have been a tragedy.

Ever since then, I tell people, "You don't have the prerogative of being off by yourself for three days without anyone knowing where you are." So much can happen in three days. In three days, people can die and be buried.

At the time, I didn't care if they took our car and drove it off a bridge. But Larry later on had one of his grad assistants drive it back to Lansing, and I flew the young fellow home. But what's that saying about a friend in need is a friend indeed? Larry Bielat certainly took care of me at that time, not to mention many others.

Michigan State had had two tremendous seasons in the mid-60s, going 19-1-1 and would have gone to successive Rose Bowls if not for the no-repeat rule the Big Ten had at the time.

Duffy was only 56, but he knew he wouldn't be going much longer. Yet even at the end, he took care of me and did everything he could to recommend me to Chuck Noll and get me to Pittsburgh.

I actually interviewed with Pittsburgh twice. During spring practice of 1971, I was taking a shower in the locker room and our phone rang. It was Chuck, who had been initially pointed my way by Henry Bullough. I flew to Pittsburgh the next day to be interviewed, and I thought we really hit it off. Chuck told me he was interviewing one other candidate, though, and that was Dan Radakovich, who was at Penn State at the time. Dan got the job, but Chuck told me he was still interested and to stay the way I was. It was just a few months later when he called with an offer.

When Duffy dropped me off with Chuck, Chuck looked after me. My first 25 years, I had two guys who looked after me pretty good. When one got done, the other started.

John McVay and John Sandusky also put in good words for me in Pittsburgh, and it didn't hurt that Chuck was a graduate of Dayton. Up to then, the pros had been mostly hiring coaches who had pro experience as players. But Chuck was looking for teachers, and college position coaches were well-qualified for that.

I didn't want to leave Michigan State, but Duffy didn't think his last season would be a good time for me to stay. I didn't want to roll the dice about catching on with the new staff. And I was too young, 38, to even think about succeeding Duffy myself. I needed some more seasoning.

7

Behind the
Steel Curtain

As much as I love Michigan State, the highlight of my career wasn't there. And it wasn't coaching high school, or the one good year we had at Dayton. No, it really was with some interesting people known as the Pittsburgh Steelers.

When I joined the Steelers in February of '72, I was nervous. That was the first time in my life I was going to coach without any Michigan State people around me. I was finally on my own. It took that long to get away from the nest. And as an assistant coach, for the next 10 years I was on one-year contracts. So that kept me on my toes.

Bud Carson was the defensive coordinator, but he had all he could handle with the secondary, so I had all I could handle with the down linemen. I was nervous enough about leaving Michigan State, nervous about being in the pros, and now I had to coach someone with a big name:

Mean Joe Greene.

It was obvious to me that we had to get the most out of Joe Greene, or I might not be around too long. Luckily, Joe was the type of guy who only cared about winning. If he thought we had a good formula for winning, he didn't want to disrupt it. He was very easy for me to work with, very loyal to all the coaches.

Still, it was some time before I felt like I belonged. It took a lot of studying, and I got a lot of help from the offensive line coach, Bob Fry. He became a great friend, and I never would have made it through that first season without him.

But I knew if I could last the year, I'd be twice the coach the second year.

For our team, 1972 was a great year, and it was a lot easier for me to coach because of our success as the season went on. The town was tickled to death. Chuck was given the nickname, "The Emperor." We won the first division championship — the first championship of any kind — in the Steelers' 40-year history, and we beat the Oakland Raiders in the playoffs on the famous Immaculate Reception play where the ball got tipped to Franco Harris. I grabbed Chuck after that play and I yelled, "There is a God, there is a God!"

We lost to Miami the next week, but there was no shame in that. The Dolphins went 17-0 and won the Super Bowl.

After the season, our staff went on and coached in the Pro Bowl. What experiences I was having already in the NFL, just a few months into it. And we were finally doing OK financially, too. Sally and I made $8,000 when we sold our house in East Lansing, and I made $16,000 in bonus money in the playoffs — the first time in my life I had ever made any bonus money. That guaranteed, basically, that I was going to be able to pay for college for at least one of my four children.

The future looked bright. We had a new stadium and a good young team that was only going to get better. After all, there was still loyalty then because there was no real free agency.

And all of those things bloomed — into four Super Bowl championships. What a run. We became, I would argue, the best team ever in the National Football League. The best part? The terrific group of people I got to be associated with:

ROCKY BLEIER, running back: I remember his 1,000-yard season, standing on the sidelines during a game yelling out to him how many more yards he needed. That was a big deal for me, because I had so much compassion for him because of the injuries he got in Vietnam and the unbelievable way he worked to come back from them.

Here's the kind of guy he was: I remember him fumbling one time a few years later when I was defensive coordinator, and he ran right over to me on the sideline and said, "I'm sorry." That's unusual at any level, especially the pros.

FRANCO HARRIS, running back: Franco was quiet and bright and took care of his body. He knew he was making his living with it. He would stay late after practice to get massages and rubdowns. When he first came in, he wasn't a very good weightlifter. That embarrassed him, so he'd come in early or late by himself until he got in a position where he could compete with the other players.

As a defensive coach, you always made sure that you tried to help him in practice, not letting anything get out of hand. He was our pot of gold as far as the running game went.

TERRY BRADSHAW, quarterback: Terry probably had as much talent as anybody who's ever played the position, before or since. He had the ability to throw the ball as far as anyone, and he loved to come out to practice and throw, throw, throw. Always the last guy to leave.

Terry didn't drink, and he was very religious. The biggest vice he had was cigars. He was very close to Mr. Rooney, the owner, who loved cigars. Terry knew the people who were most complementary to him were his linemen. He knew where his bread was buttered, and he would take them out to dinner all the time. I remember once he had sketches drawn of all of them.

Someone gave him the rap early that he wasn't bright. The rap stuck, but it was false. You couldn't do the things he did, or the things he does now on TV, without a lot of gray matter. Terry, don't forget, called his own plays, and he's probably the last quarterback who did. I used to tell him all the time, "We might lose a few games with you, but we'll never win without you."

He loved to play his guitar during training camp. In his room, not bothering anybody. Lots of country. He was country and a half. He was good friends with Glen Campbell.

MIKE WEBSTER, center: Mike was the nucleus of our offensive line, and he had those arms. He probably had a great influence on weightlifting in the NFL, because he lifted so hard and his muscles bulged when he tucked his shirt sleeves in under his pads. It wasn't to show his muscles; it was so people wouldn't grab his shirt.

I remember once Mike was going out of town and wouldn't be able to lift the next day, so he lifted twice that day. When he was in the hospital, he had them bring weights over so he could lift in bed. He was as dedicated as any player I ever saw.

LYNN SWANN, wide receiver: Swann might not have been the fastest guy in the league, but he could jump as high as anybody and he could control his body in mid-air. He took ballet lessons, and he could float.

The best thing that could happen for us was Swann to drop a pass early in a game, because he would make up for it 10 times over the rest of the game. He was an acrobat, and he was super-intelligent: That's why he got out of the game early, before he got hurt. Eventually, he was going to get that big hit.

JOHN STALLWORTH, wide receiver: He had that great speed, those long strides. You couldn't double-team Stallworth, or you'd have to live with Swann. They were a problem for everybody. We were fortunate to get Stallworth. He should have been a first-round draft pick, but he went in the fourth round because someone had the wrong sprint times on him. Our scout had gone back and gotten another time on him.

JACK HAM, linebacker: I was probably as close to Jack as any player on our team. He was like a coach. He studied his game, and he was a perfectionist.

I used to have fun with him when I was writing up reports on mistakes we had made in the games. I'd always make his mistake numbers bigger than they were — and underline them — because it motivated the heck out of him. I was honest, but I just kind of wrote it bigger and accented it a bit. He knew I was doing it on purpose, but he still didn't like it. He did not like criticism at all.

He was one of the few who would come in and watch practice film on his own, and he was another guy who treated his body like a piece of gold, because he knew that was where his livelihood was coming from.

I remember he made the most remarkable play I ever saw, against Oakland. He was on his side covering a halfback, man for man, and the halfback flared around to the other side. Ham came all the way around the back of the line and intercepted the screen pass they were trying to throw to his man. Unbelievable.

When he'd come off the field, he'd come right for me to check what was going on. If the play had been on the far side of the field and I couldn't see it, I'd tell him to wait a second and

I'd call upstairs and find out what happened. He'd rip me and say, "You don't know, you don't know." He was that intense.

You know, you always think you've got to keep the player-coach relationship at a distance. But you didn't have to do that with him. He was just an unusual guy.

ANDY RUSSELL, linebacker: Andy played opposite Jack, and he played with brains. He wasn't very big, but he was as smart a player as there was. Looked like a movie star. He had a lot going for him.

Andy invented what we call the "hug-up" technique. He would fake a blitz to force the back he was supposed to pass cover to have to think about blocking him. That helped him cover more ground than his speed would let him.

Andy was the best at anticipating the play, like he somehow had been told ahead of time what was coming. A little bit of ability, but a ton of brains. After two Super Bowls, he retired. He said he had what he wanted, and he's become a very successful investor.

JACK LAMBERT, middle linebacker: Chuck drafted smart guys, and Lambert was another one of them. But he was one of those guys who really psyched himself up to play, too. Before we would go on the field, he'd have his stool turned around and his head in his locker. He'd look like he was talking to his locker to get ready. He played with all kinds of emotions. Big emotions.

If somebody on our team was screwing up, Lambert would rip him. He'd rip Joe Greene, and not too many people gave Joe Greene any noise. Joe would like it when it came from Lambert, though.

Lambert would rip anybody. One time the defense got in a huddle and a couple guys tried to hold hands in the huddle. He yelled, "There's no holding hands in the huddle." He even used to get mad at his teammates for going to religious services before the pre-game meal. "How can we tell them to turn the other cheek," he would say, "and then have them go out on the field and knock the other guys' blocks off?" It bothered him. He wanted to knock the hell out of everybody.

Ham would laugh at Lambert. I remember one time Ham didn't hold somebody up on a coverage, and Lambert was calling him every name in the book on the way back to the huddle. We had the game pretty well in hand, so Ham was cracking up. I was even laughing on the sideline at that one.

THE DEFENSIVE LINE: JOE GREENE, L.C. GREEN-WOOD, DWIGHT WHITE, ERNIE HOLMES AND STEVE FURNESS: The greatest defensive line of all time. There's not even an argument. For instance, what other front four was ever on the cover of *Time* magazine like they were on December 8, 1975? "Half A Ton Of Trouble," *Time* called them.

They weren't always a bowl of cherries to coach, but that's because they were thoroughbreds who sometimes had ideas of their own. When they'd get like that, I'd tell them, "OK, do what you want to do, I don't care. I wasn't supposed to be in this league, anyway. I'm way ahead of the game." But we didn't have many problems.

The headbutt and the uppercut were the popular techniques of the time. It's a vicious game, and we had some vicious players who could deliver some vicious headbutts. I'd always tell them if they found something that worked to stay with it. Don't try to be fancy and pretty and have all the techniques going at once. Use what you do well, like Hoyt Wilhelm. He threw 99 percent knuckleballs, because he had a good one and it worked.

I liked the swim technique for pass rushing, but that was getting tough by the end of my time in Pittsburgh because the NFL was letting offensive linemen use their hands. When you used the swim motion, you exposed your body so much that you could easily be held.

Greene was the most dominant player on defense in the NFL. He was a fantastic guy — he'd cut off his nose to help a friend. But the other teams feared him. I mean, really feared him, and with good reason.

We'd be in our end zone at Three Rivers Stadium warming up. When the other team would come out of the dugout and run by us, all their stars would go, "Hey, Joe. Uh, hi, Joe. How's it going, Joe?" They wanted to make sure they had a good relationship with Joe.

We played Cincinnati in the last game one season. Their coach, Paul Brown, was always monkeying around with silly little things — anything to get an edge. On this occasion, he had his team use the opposite bench that it normally would use and it confused our whole pre-game set-up. We were left to warm up on ice, when we were supposed to be on the other side. And, brother, did we get into it with the Bengals.

We've got both teams and the coaches in the end zone, shouting at each other, getting after each other. So I just told their quarterback, Ken Anderson, "OK, I'm going to sic Joe on you during the game." He immediately called out to his teammates, "Let's go," and they all ran down to their end. Kenny knew the last thing he wanted was Joe Greene fired up.

Not that it took much to rev Joe up. A guy on Buffalo was holding Joe all through one game, and Joe was getting sick of it. Joe had hands like big thick hams, and he pretended to use the technique of uppercutting to get past the guy but instead punched him in the gut. Joe was powerful enough to drop a guy just by unloading in his gut.

When he did the same kind of thing in Denver once, their coach, Red Miller, started getting on Joe as we were leaving the field at halftime. I went over and got Joe out of it, but got into it myself with Red. Normally that kind of thing's not a big deal— a lot of guys get hot under each other's collars— except the camera was right there shooting the teams coming off at halftime. Our little verbal scrimmage was broadcast live. I like Red, but he's a hotheaded redhead and I'm a hothead. So sometimes things like that just boil over.

Joe loved the game and wanted desperately to win. There's a story about Joe that one time in college or high school the other team drove to their one-foot line and Joe picked the ball up and threw it into the stands.

He was a violent guy sometimes, and when he was, nobody could stop him.

Against Cleveland once, their center, Bob DeMarco, snapped the ball and stood up and gave Joe a shot under the chin. Oooh, Joe was mad. He was teed off on the sideline after that. In the second half, darned if it doesn't happen again, with DeMarco running out to block for a screen after he pops Joe under the facemask.

Joe chased DeMarco about 20 yards and clotheslined DeMarco. He broke his jaw so bad that they had to carry him off on a stretcher. But Joe was not satisfied. He walked over to the Cleveland bench and said, "In case you want to know who did it, I did." Basically, he took on the whole team.

One time Dean Look, my teammate from Michigan State, was officiating one of our games against Oakland and Joe pointed out that an Oakland lineman had gone downfield. It should have been a penalty, but Dean didn't call it. Joe told him, "If I had a gun, I'd blow your head off." Dean called me at home the next day and wanted to know what was going on. What could I say? I told him, "Well, you blew a call."

We called L.C. "Hollywood Bags." He'd always have nice clothes, and he was always stylish. I remember he was angry once when another team's guard pulled and cut the back of his legs when he was in pursuit. On the next play, I'm looking out on the field and darned if Joe and L.C. haven't switched places so L.C. can get a piece of this guard. He wanted to pound on him a couple times.

We called Dwight, "Mad Dog." Dwight was mad at everybody. He was mad at officials, mad at coaches, mad at the guys on the other team. He just got after everyone and everything.

With Ernie, you were always concerned that he might not be there the next year because of his temperament, his history. One time the poor guy just snapped when he was stuck in traffic as he was driving into Pittsburgh. He ended up shooting at trucks on the highway, even shot at a police helicopter and wounded a policeman during a chase.

Ernie — "Fats" — was unbelievable. He'd wear a rubber suit under his pads in training camp, in the thick of July or August, like he wasn't human. He'd lose 15 or 17 pounds, buckets of water coming off him.

Steve might not have gotten as much attention as the other four, but he was very valuable. He was a student of the game, and he was versatile. He could play any one of the four down line positions. He could use a right-hand stance or a left-hand stance, which isn't easy. It's like being a switch-hitter, but Steve could do it. He was basically our fifth guy at the beginning of his career.

At our first Super Bowl in New Orleans, Dwight came down with pneumonia and we had to put him in the hospital the Sunday before the game. Steve was going to get to start.

Dwight kept calling me from the hospital, telling me he was going to play. I didn't put too much stock in it, but on game day he came out of the hospital and dressed. When we were warming up, I guess Dwight was trying to impress us and he took some real shots from Joe.

I didn't know what to do, but Steve Furness took me off the hook. He came up and said that he was still young and had the rest of his career to start a Super Bowl and that if Dwight could play, we should feel free to start him. That was a big thing for him to say.

So I told Chuck I was going to start Dwight, but that he'd probably only last a couple plays and we'd put Steve in after that. Well, Dwight not only played, he played very well and somehow lasted the whole game. The next day we had to take him back to the hospital.

It shows you how much emotions can play in a game. It reminds me of the concept of the person going into a burning building and throwing around furniture to save his family, and then the next day they can't even budge the same furniture.

DICK HOAK, running backs coach: Dick was my road roommate for eight years. Great friend. Every room we ever checked in, he'd throw his bags on the bed and turn on the TV. He'd always take the far bed, because if someone came to the door he wanted me to answer it.

If the TV wasn't perfect, he'd call the engineer to come up and fix it — or we'd have our room changed. He loved TV. He used to get mad at me when guests would come up and see me. He'd say, "Why do they all have to come up here? Can't you go someplace else?" As for him, he never wanted to be anyplace else: He's still with the Steelers, 24 years as an assistant and 34 years overall if you count his 10 years playing there.

CHUCK NOLL, head coach: I've always thought Chuck could have been anything he wanted. He could have been a surgeon, which in my opinion is about as high as it gets as far as gray matter goes. Totally dedicated, and totally focused. He hated distractions of any kind.

But he was very low-key. He never won coach of the year, for instance. How could you win four Super Bowls and not ever be coach of the year? Only one way: By working at it.

Chuck didn't want to be coach of the year. He didn't want to sit at speakers' tables, or go on the clinic tour. He didn't want to be noticed. I think he only did a TV show for one year, and then he said, "That's the end of that stuff." He wouldn't even do endorsements, and there was a lot of money to be had for him if he wanted it.

Chuck is very, very humble, and very well-rounded. A great family man. He never went out much except to dinner with his wife. But he would have the staff over to his house for some great parties. He would play the ukulele and the flute.

He was a religious guy, Catholic. A pilot, had his own plane. He was a diver. When we went to the Bahamas together once, he went under water and I swear he came up riding a sea turtle.

He also is very well-read. On all kinds of things. The media were afraid of him, because he didn't like dumb questions. He never enjoyed that part of the job. Just did it because he had to.

It might not sound like it, but Chuck liked being kidded. I remember one time I was walking out of a room when he was coming in, and I said, "I'm leaving because you're going to want to talk about all kinds of stuff like radial tires, or you're going to want to talk about the universe. I've got all I can handle with the defensive line. I can't cope with all that stuff."

He's a true friend. I had some great help with Duffy and John McVay and Eddie Rutherford, but Chuck was the final touch. Every time I think of Chuck I get good feelings.

ART AND DAN ROONEY, the owners: Mr. Rooney, Art Rooney, lived in walking distance from the stadium in the same house he'd lived in all his life. There will never be another Mr. Rooney. Not too many people called him anything but Mr. Rooney, but he was the most generous man I ever knew. Not only did he go to every funeral of all the people he ever knew, he paid to bury a lot of them who couldn't afford it.

He'd go home for dinner, then come back to visit us in the evenings while we were still working. He would take two members of the grounds crew — there were 16 people in the Three Rivers Stadium grounds crew — to every away game.

Mr. Rooney always operated with $50 bills. He loved the working people, so if he took a cab, for instance, he'd spend the whole $50 regardless of what the fare was. He loved Chuck. He told me one time, "You know when I knew I had a good coach? His first year, when he won one game and lost 13. He lost the games, but he never lost the team."

The Rooneys were there to support Chuck, but Chuck was running the football team — no doubt about it. Chuck always made a point of running down to Dan's office before he made any major decision, though. If he was about to finalize a trade, he'd say, "Just a minute," and he'd go down and tell Dan. Dan never heard about anything second-hand.

Dan inherited all the good features of his father. Basically, Dan was the one who turned the football team around by hiring Chuck. His father was really proud of seeing how well his son did in taking that team to the Super Bowls.

The Super Bowls never went to Mr. Rooney's head, though. I remember after our first one, the secretaries answered the phone, "Pittsburgh Steelers, home of the World Champs!" When he heard that, he instructed them that the Pittsburgh Steelers would not answer the phone any differently than they did for the first 40 years.

8

Stunted Growth

Later on, when I was back at Michigan State, we played Florida State a couple times. They beat us both times, but I'll always remember how their coach, Bobby Bowden, felt about our defensive scheme: the Stunt 4-3, a name that came about by accident.

"I didn't understand it before we played them, I didn't understand it while we were playing them and I still don't understand it," he said.

The seeds of the Stunt 4-3 were planted in Pittsburgh in 1974, our first Super Bowl season. We had been experimenting with it a little during the season, mostly just to keep the guys from getting bored. They always needed new challenges. We began to unveil it a little more after a loss to Houston late in the season. It seemed to make an immediate impact in our game against New England.

"It was the most miserable spot I've ever been in," was how the Patriots' center, Bill Lenkaitis, put it after the game. "How do you stop Greene when he's that close to you and so damn strong? There are no rules for that. Our blocking patterns were completely destroyed."

The destruction began with our tackles, Joe Greene and Ernie Holmes, usually, both lining up in a place where either or both of them could knock the center's block off. Joe eventually argued that he should line up at an angle toward the center, which had an even more intimidating effect. Joe liked that I'd let him experiment.

"George allowed me to express myself," he said on a video testimonial to me when I left Michigan State.

In the playoffs, we added another wrinkle with the middle linebacker playing games in there, too. Without getting too technical, here's what the thinking was:

When you have a man on the center in our normal 4-3, the guards aren't covered. When you have men on the guards, the center isn't covered. When your opponent knows they're not covered, they can pull out on sweeps and generally have a lot more freedom. So if you brought both tackles in on the center, you could have two guys taking care of three and they couldn't account for it all. They had to respect it. That meant there were certain plays they couldn't run against the defense.

And we had the right personnel for it. What you need is exactly what we had.

In the first round of the playoffs that year, we played Buffalo and the great O.J. Simpson. He was at the top of his game then, and we held him under 50 yards and won 32-14.

The next week, though, we played Oakland. They had a huge offensive line, and they'd beaten us 17-0 earlier in the season. That's when we added the other part we'd been tinkering with, some movement with the middle linebacker.

I didn't really talk to Chuck about any of this, because he had plenty of other things to worry about and he liked to let us do our own things. Same with Bud Carson, our coordinator. It's only when you have inferior assistant coaches that you have to coach the whole team.

Still, it was kind of a gamble. This was probably not the most ideal or logical time to be getting a brainstorm about a new defense. But I just thought it would work. Just in case, I asked Dick Hoak to help me out and watch close to see if he thought we were going to have any trouble. I was going to get out of the alignment in one play if anything went wrong. Otherwise, I knew it might mean my tail.

The first series, we held Oakland and Hoak said, "Holy Moses." He saw them on their sideline with a chalkboard trying to figure it out. They never did. They were all over the map, confused, and their blocking rules were all mixed up. We won, 24-13, and they got 29 yards rushing.

"It's time for somebody to give some credit to George Perles, our defensive line coach, and I'm going to do it," Joe told reporters after the game. "George lets us do our thing. . . . He deserves a lot of credit for the success of this team."

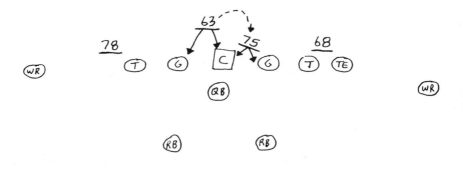

Pittsburgh Odd 4-3

As Drawn by, George J. Perles.

So we were going to the Super Bowl, against the Minnesota Vikings. On Monday after the game against the Raiders, Chuck had his press conference. The media asked him what was going on on defense, and he said, "I don't know. Go down and ask George."

The media all rushed down to my office. So I had the floor, and I had the chalk. I knew none of them really knew anything about football, as far as technique and alignment. So I decided to make up a name for the defense: the Stunt 4-3.

That just came to me. I didn't know what to call it, but they're all standing there waiting for me to give them an explanation. Since I wasn't ready for them, I was making up stuff.

When I was done, then, of course they still didn't know what I was talking about.

Ultimately, though, the Stunt 4-3 would be a big help in my career. You don't have many chances in this great game of football to invent anything, because it's all been done so many times before. But this was very close to being something different.

Two good friends of mine in the business were Jerry Burns, the Vikings coach, and Paul Roach, an assistant with the Raiders. Paul told me that Jerry called him after our game and said, "What's wrong with you guys? Twenty-nine yards rushing?" And I was worried about the Vikings, who had two weeks to devise a way to beat this whatever-it-is defense, the Stunt 4-3.

So, again, I was ready to ditch it real quick in the game if we had problems. And again, it went beautifully. We beat Minnesota 16-6, and the Vikings had 17 yards rushing. We were absolutely dominant. In a pileup during the game, their great running back, Chuck Foreman, told our guys, "C'mon, you mothers. Give us a yard."

They would have had only five yards, but late in the game they ran a draw for 12 yards when I guessed wrong and we blitzed in a passing situation. It was the last thing in the world I thought they would do in a situation where it wasn't going to help them win the game.

After the game, Paul Roach called Jerry Burns and asked him, "What's the problem? Seventeen yards rushing?"

I remember at the Super Bowl party how I wish my dad had been alive to enjoy it. That was an even stronger emotion than just wishing I had had a chance to say a last word to him.

I think our first Super Bowl bonus was $23,000, so I was pretty sure I could get at least two kids through college. And that was another great thing about Pittsburgh: the emphasis on family.

All three of my boys got to be ballboys. Since the coaches lived in the dorms with the players for the seven or eight weeks of training camp every year, it was too much burden to leave the boys at home with Sally that whole time. So I took them to training camp every year. They washed laundry, took care of the practice fields, moved the dummies around and so on. You name it.

It was their summer job, and they lived with us in the dorm. They matured very fast because of their associations with the players, and thank God most of the players were classy guys. They'd send the boys out on errands, or pay them extra to wash their cars, or ask them to carry their helmets, and the kids really felt part of the team. They had some fun at night, but they really had to work, early morning to late at night.

We were always very comfortable living in Pittsburgh. There were a lot of people who were proud of their heritage. Hard-working people. You don't find elitists there. And the Steelers fans, with things like the Terrible Towels, Gerela's Gorillas and Franco's Army, you could only tie them. There were none better.

While I was in Pittsburgh, I also had a restaurant, the Anthony House. We had tremendous business for about two years. We had live entertainment on weekends — Frank Sinatra Jr., the Platters. So we'd have 600 people in on a Friday, 600 on a Saturday and about six on a Monday.

We had a Christmas party there one year, and Ernie Holmes came late and thought everything was gone. We had a pig, so he took the head and plucked the eyes out and ate all that stuff on the head. Scared the hell out of the help.

Typical Ernie. There was a story about him that when he wanted to eat meat back in Texas he wouldn't bother going to a butcher shop. He would just go outside and personally slaughter a calf, starting with a forearm lift.

I used to go to my restaurant every weekend, but I got tired of it and I learned enough to know it wasn't the business for me. And it started to slide, so I got out.

We were having a fantastic time in Pittsburgh, but I have to admit I was always trying to keep up with things in East Lansing.

I talked about Michigan State so much that Dick Hoak used to cover his ears with his pillows. In our driveway on a hill in Upper St. Clair, I had learned that if I positioned the car just right I could tune in the Michigan State game broadcasts on Saturdays. It took a little fiddling, mostly since I didn't want the neighbors to think I was a goof out there sitting in my car in the middle of the day. So maybe I'd empty an ashtray, vacuum the carpeting, wash the wheels. Nobody ever said anything. And we'd always go to East Lansing in the summers.

Denny Stolz, who came in from Alma College and was made Duffy's defensive coordinator, took over at Michigan State in 1973. He was pretty determined to separate himself from the past, probably because of Duffy's success. That can be a hard situation. But I didn't like it when I called once and Eddie Rutherford, who still was on the staff, told me he wasn't supposed to talk to me.

In 1974, the Spartans finished a half game behind Michigan and Ohio State in the Big Ten standings. They even beat Ohio State when Ohio State was No. 1, and Denny was conference coach of the year.

But there was some monkey business going on with recruiting, and the NCAA moved in and put the school on three years' probation in January 1976. There would be no bowl games, no national TV appearances and scholarships would be reduced by 15 a year. Denny was fired.

At the time, we were just winning our second Super Bowl, and I was about to be named defensive coordinator when Bud Carson left to go to the Los Angeles Rams.

We beat Dallas 21-17 that year in Super Bowl X, thanks to a game-saving interception. We had had a punt blocked earlier in the game, and Chuck was concerned about field position late in the game. So when we had fourth down and about 3 near midfield, instead of punting, we went for it. Chuck said, "If we don't make it and we can't hold them, we don't deserve to win the game."

Well, we didn't make the first down, and all the pressure landed on the defense. Roger Staubach was throwing the ball all over the park at the end, but we managed to save the bacon. I was very relieved. I mean, "If we can't hold them, we don't deserve to win the game." Holy Moses.

When I heard about Denny being fired, I had some hope of getting a shot at the job in East Lansing. I did get an interview, but it was really just a token. The athletic director at the time, Joe Kearney, wanted Darryl Rogers from San Jose State.

I wasn't heartbroken, because I didn't know if I was ready, and everything was so good in Pittsburgh. I could have stayed there for the rest of my career.

In 1976, we probably had our best defense ever. We gave up 138 points the whole season, and 75 of those came in the first three games. We had five shutouts and gave up a total of 22 points in our last eight games. I'm not sure exactly why we were more dominant that year, but it might have been because Bradshaw got hurt and we were more close to the vest on offense.

So we took it upon ourselves to win with defense, and we did: Won our last nine games after a 1-4 start, but we lost to Oakland in the American Football Conference championship game. We lost in the first round of the playoffs in '77, and that gave us enough of a scare that we came back like demons the next year: We were back in the Super Bowl at the end of the 1978 and 1979 seasons.

In Super Bowl XIII in Miami, we beat Dallas again 35-31. Everybody remembers that game. We're beating them 35-17 in the fourth quarter, and I put in the prevent defense to keep us from giving up the quick touchdown. Staubach gets hot, and boom, boom, boom, boom, boom, they go down and score. That makes it 35-24 with about two minutes to go.

They onside kick and get the ball back. I stay in the prevent, and boom, boom, boom, boom, boom, they score again with a few seconds left. They onside kick again, Rocky recovers the ball, game's over. No sweat. We won. Chuck had taught me to play "ahead" football. You don't worry about the stats when you're ahead. Just win the game.

After the game, *Sports Illustrated* had a big party for the winner. Very fancy affair. Chuck didn't want to go, so he sent me and about half a dozen players. We had a few cocktails, and it was a good time. We were on the way to another party and one of the Pittsburgh writers, Phil Musick, grabbed me and said he'd only be a minute. He said the Dallas people were saying if the game had gone another minute, they would have beaten us.

I said, "Yeah? They couldn't beat us in a month of Sundays. I put the prevent defense in just to make sure this thing was iced. They're always shooting their mouths off. I tell you what's going to happen . . . They're coming to Pittsburgh next year, and we're going to knock their blocks off like they've never had them knocked off before."

So the next season, Dallas was coming to Pittsburgh. That week, one of the writers, Vito Stellino, said, "George, you said you're going to beat them and beat them bad." I said,

"Hey, Vito, how do you know that?" He held up his notebook and said, "That's why I keep these notes." I guess he and Musick had traded notes or something. I said, "Give me a break. I said that in January. This is October. What are you doing?" He said something like, "It's good news people want to know."

Which, by the way, is why I've kept my own notes ever since.

But, then, whew, I was uptight. This really turned the heat up on the game. No one says that kind of stuff. You've got enough problems in pro football. Luckily, Chuck didn't seem mad. He didn't say anything about it.

And darned if we didn't beat them, anyway, 14-3. In that game, Tony Dorsett's helmet came off as he was hitting the ground and our Dennis Winston was coming down on him. Dennis got him right on the face, and Dorsett was really lacerated and couldn't play any more.

I was walking off the field after the game and I said hi to their tight end, Billy Joe DuPree, a former Michigan State player. Out of the blue, Gil Brandt, one of their bigwigs, came up to me and got in my face.

He said, "I know you said all those things," and then he threw this really wacky stuff at me: "I know you're doing speaking engagements and not paying taxes and I'm going to turn you in." I had no idea what he was talking about, but I'd lost my cool and I started giving it to him. He backed away, I was walking towards him, and I ended up chasing him into their locker room.

We got back to the Super Bowl that season, against the Rams this time. It was interesting for us, because three of our assistants from our first two Super Bowls were on the Rams staff: Bud Carson, Dan Radakovich and Lionel Taylor. We won again, 31-19.

Our staff — I was assistant head coach now — had gotten very close at this time: Chuck, Dick Hoak, Woody Widenhofer, Rollie Dotsch . . . It was in those days that an aspiring young coach named Nick Saban came around to visit us in the summers. He was an assistant at Kent State at the time.

"George was just a good quality person who seemed to care about me," Nick says now, as the head coach at Michigan State. "I really appreciated what he did for me."

During the Rams' Super Bowl week in Pasadena, I had a few other things on my mind. Darryl Rogers and Joe Kearney both were leaving Michigan State for Arizona State. Joe Falls, the *Detroit News* columnist, called me up while we were in Pasadena and asked if I'd be interested in the job. I told him, "I tell you, I'd give Bo [Schembechler] something to think about."

I know I was something for Michigan State to think about. The new athletic director was my old friend Doug Weaver, and we had a terrific interview. I think I was considered the leading candidate for the job by the media, so I have to admit I was shocked when I found out from Curt Sylvester of the *Detroit Free Press* that Michigan State had named Muddy Waters the head coach.

It was the first time in my life that I lost out on something I wanted so badly. I managed to tell Curt that I would give Muddy my full support, and that turned out to be the best thing I said because I didn't burn any bridges. But I was hurting. Sally was in tears, because she knew how much it meant to me. What happened, I'm still not sure.

"President [Cecil] Mackey was told by a trustee that he had to hire someone who had head coaching experience in college," said Joel Ferguson, who was trying to get me in at the time. "This came at the 11th hour, and it left only around three candidates: Dan Devine, Rollie Dotsch and Muddy Waters. Doug wasn't going to hire Dan Devine, and President Mackey was being pushed to hire Rollie Dotsch by [another administrator] — so he wasn't going to let him be hired.

"So Doug fell on the sword and hired Muddy. Doug took all the heat, but he really had his hands tied. He would have hired George the first time if he could have, but they had this criteria that they never made public."

Here's what Doug says about it now:

"All I can say is that, given the circumstances, Muddy was the right person. I really feel badly that it didn't work out for him, and I'm sure if I were Muddy I wouldn't hold me in high esteem."

I tried to keep a brave face on, but those who knew me best knew I was in some anguish. Duffy was among the people who called to console me. He said, "George, be glad you didn't get that job. A composite of Bear Bryant and Amos Alonzo Stagg couldn't win there now, not this soon after probation."

Darryl had had a couple good years, even tied for the Big Ten championship in 1978. Of course, they couldn't play in a bowl game because of the NCAA sanctions. But the effects of those really were just starting to kick in.

"Muddy has no chance," Duffy added. "It'll come your way next time, and it'll be a better situation then."

Joe Greene had T-shirts printed up, "One For The Thumb In 1981." But we were starting to get a little old in Pittsburgh in 1980, and we didn't even get close to that fifth Super Bowl in January. We went 9-7 and missed the playoffs for the first time in eight years. You watched the playoffs on TV, and you really ate your heart out.

What hurt most was that some of our guys were really getting on their last legs. It's a young man's game, and it was a hard time. Chuck didn't want to turn his back on the guys who got us there — you hang with them, you don't throw them to the dogs. Maybe that was a weakness, but we all had it.

My wonderful parents, Julius and Nellie. He made the potato loaf; she had the cat-o'-nine-tails.

Western High: 1951 Metro League champs — and a reflection of our diverse neighborhood. Front row left to right, that's Carlton Eden, Bill Lacruenak, yours truly, Joe Selasky, Joe Carruthers, Joe Kochevar, and Harold Morris. The quarterback is Frank Nemcheck, and the running backs from left to right are Gerald Shurtz, Cliff Moon, and Sam Washington.

So what did you need a facemask for, anyway? I guess this is what they meant by "Angels with Dirty Faces."

The Buddy System at its best: Fifteen of us joined the Army at the same time, just so we could go through basic training together. Third from right, guess who? (photo by Detroit Times)

That's me in the 89th Tank Battalion.

Chef Boy-Ar-Dee, learning my trade in the Army. That's me, far left in the third row.

Hawaii Uh-Oh: Me and the boys on the beach. (left to right: Jerry Clark, me, Paul Eckelberry, and Andy O'Kulevich in front) Such was life in the Special Services.

Guess I didn't have time to get dressed up for dinner. I'm on the far right after a game in Hawaii, where Duffy recruited me.

Duffy pulled strings to get me my first team: St. Ambrose.

Not a bad start.

Finally, I'm a Spartan. (photo by MSU)

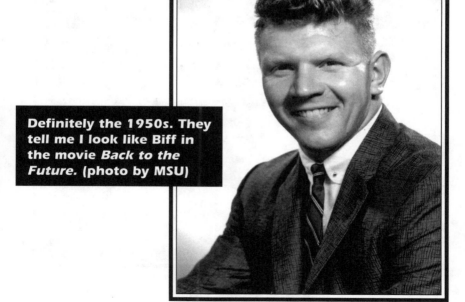

Definitely the 1950s. They tell me I look like Biff in the movie *Back to the Future.* (photo by MSU)

Does this look like a coach who would tackle a player? You betcha. (photo by University of Dayton)

Another one of my mentors, Eddie Rutherford. He was my coach at Western High, and we were reunited at Michigan State. (photo by MSU)

Proud to be a Spartan. (photo by MSU)

For some reason, Duffy always seemed to be looking over my shoulder. Here he is when he brought me back to Michigan State in 1967. (photo by MSU)

Detroit Lions coach Wayne Fontes is on the left, grinning as usual. We were teammates at Michigan State and coached together at Dayton. The Doctor of Defense, Henry Bullough, is on the right. We started together as grad assistants at Michigan State. We finished together, too.

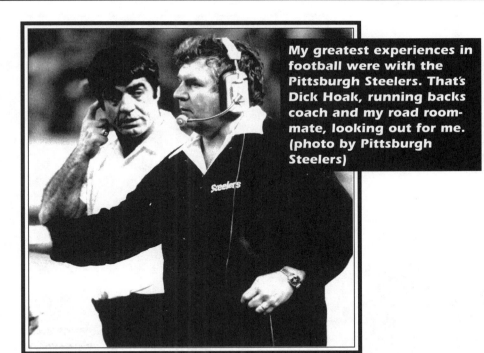

My greatest experiences in football were with the Pittsburgh Steelers. That's Dick Hoak, running backs coach and my road roommate, looking out for me. (photo by Pittsburgh Steelers)

Dan Rooney, Art Rooney, and Chuck Noll: They made the Steelers. (photo by Pittsburgh Steelers)

There was never a more generous man than Mr. Rooney—and never a more deserving man, either. (photo by Pittsburgh Steelers)

Yep, that's me. On the Scarsdale diet, and before my thyroid went on the fritz. (photo by Pittsburgh Steelers)

The greatest front four ever: Dwight White (78), Ernie Holmes (63), Joe Greene (75), and L. L. Greenwood (68). (photo by Pittsburgh Steelers)

The Perles Front Four. I'm not sure who was thrilled most when my three sons became ball boys: (left to right) John, Terry, and Pat, or me?

They said he really wasn't mean, but you never, ever wanted to cross Joe Greene. (photo by Pittsburgh Steelers)

9

A Cup of Coffee

I had learned a long time before to try not to worry about things you can't control. That's often a lot easier said than done, of course. But after Muddy got the job at Michigan State, I was wishing and hoping the program would come around and I really avoided thinking about ever getting the Michigan State job. I wanted it too bad to let myself dwell on it any more, or get my hopes up again.

In the spring of 1982, I was at a golf outing in Uniontown, Pennsylvania. I called home to say I was going to be late for dinner, and my son John answered and said there was a phone message from John Ralston, the old Stanford and Denver coach. I said, "Uh-oh, I'll be right home." I knew he was working to recruit people for the shiny new United States Football League, and I thought maybe the new Michigan Panthers team was interested in me.

John was helping the whole league out, because most of the owners didn't know coaches. They ended up with some pretty interesting names: George Allen went to the Chicago Blitz. The Denver Gold got Red Miller. The New Jersey Generals took Chuck Fairbanks. The league got a contract with ESPN right away, and with the NFL on strike during part of the 1982 season it looked like the new league might have a chance to get its foot in the door and take off.

When I called John, he said that the Philadelphia Stars and their owner, Myles Tanenbaum, wanted to talk to me. Was I interested? I said yes. A few days later, Sally called me at the Steelers offices one morning and said that Myles was flying into the Allegheny Airport on a private plane and wanted to know if I could meet with him. I went home, changed my clothes and went to meet him.

He had flown in with an alum from Notre Dame whose plane was painted in Fighting Irish colors. They had just come back from visiting Ara Parseghian, the Notre Dame coach, and checking on me with him. So we had a very basic interview. You know, "How old are you? How many children do you have?" And so on and so forth, and that was it. Myles talked about the new league, which was going to play in the spring and summer and be backed by some pretty big hitters.

A few weeks later, he called and said, "We've done all our checking, and we'd like to hire you. We'll give you $115,000 the first year, $125,000 the second year and $160,000 the third year." Four hundred thousand for three years, plus it was going to be a personal contract with him in case I was worried about the future of the USFL. I told him I wanted all the insurance benefits they had in the NFL, too, and he said, "Fine." We made a deal on the phone.

About a week later, Carl Peterson called and said he was just about sure he was going to leave the Philadelphia Eagles and come work for Myles as general manager. But he wanted to know how I thought we would get along. I thought he'd get along fine with me, I'd get along fine with him and it would be a good situation.

When I went in to tell Chuck what was happening, he was like I knew he'd be. He was all for me. Chuck and the Rooneys were very gracious. It was very hard to leave — four Super Bowls, good friends, great town, a lot of good Christmas parties — but they made it easy. Rollie left Pittsburgh for the USFL, too. He got the Birmingham job.

The Stars brought us to Philadelphia for a press conference on July 7. I remember that because it's Sally's birthday. I was 47, I'd put in 17 years as an assistant, and there I was running my first pro or college team. But Andy Russell gave me a nice endorsement in one of the Philadelphia papers.

"George is a dynamo," he said. "He's a tremendously knowledgeable coach and an excellent motivator. He had some temperamental folks on that front four [in Pittsburgh] . . . and he got them to play together in a way that was just beautiful to watch.

"When it comes to handling players, George Perles functions near a genius level. I think he'll be a dynamite head coach. I can't believe no NFL team took a shot at him before this."

Carl and I went to work pronto. Right away, I talked Steve Furness into giving up football and joining me as a coach. I hired Larry Bielat and Joe Pendry, who had been Muddy's quarterback coach at Michigan State.

In the next five months, we were scrambling. Had tryouts all over the place, and went and scouted everywhere. It was exhilarating, starting your own team. We had to go out and get the trainers, the office people, the equipment. I mean, we did everything except come up with the uniform colors, which Myles wanted to be red and gold because they had been his high school's colors.

"George was very helpful with everything," Tanenbaum said. "He even was involved in our hearings at City Council, trying to get the Veterans Stadium lease worked out with the Eagles and the Phillies."

Since we didn't have a schedule that fall — we were going to begin play in the spring of 1983 — for the first time in my life I had a chance to get around and watch from a distance how everybody else did things.

As usual, I was keeping a close eye on how the Spartans were doing. Unfortunately, it wasn't too well. They had gone 3-8 and 5-6 in the first two years under Muddy, who had played at MSU and come there from his job at Saginaw Valley State.

Muddy is a good man. A gentleman. Even though I got the job after he got fired, he went out of his way to be happy for me. He told reporters, "Isn't it great?" He said he was afraid they were going to go to Siberia for a coach and that he could kiss Doug for hiring me.

It had been tough on him as coach, though, because it hadn't been a popular decision to hire him and he didn't have an abundance of players. He also had a pretty rugged schedule: In 1982, their first five games were against Top 20 teams.

They were 2-8 when Muddy got fired on November 14, 1982. I got a strange feeling in my stomach when I heard about it happening. But I wasn't about to say anything to anyone. After all, I had just taken the job with the Stars. I hadn't even coached a game yet. And there was no way Michigan State was going to consider me . . . was there?

I was home in Pittsburgh over Thanksgiving. We hadn't sold the house yet, and I was going home on weekends. My good friend Joe Farrell was on the phone, and he asked me what was going on at Michigan State. I said I had no idea, I hadn't heard from Michigan State. I was trying to shut out the thought. But by now, I have to admit I was getting curious — and a little anxious — about what was going to happen in East Lansing. Joe suggested I call Doug Weaver.

So I called Doug, this was on a Sunday, and he wasn't home so I left a message. Monday morning as I was getting ready to leave to fly back to Philly, the phone rang. It was Doug. I told him of my interest in Michigan State, and he wanted to know where I'd be in a couple hours. I told him I was on my way back to Philly, and I gave him the number in the office. Sally woke up and wondered what I was doing. When they had hired Muddy, they offered $55,000 — was I going to take a $60,000 pay cut now that we finally had a chance to be in some comfort?

Shortly after I got into the office, Doug called and said he'd like to come to Philadelphia and see me. He was going to be in Detroit on Tuesday and Wednesday and would come to Philly on Thursday. Would I pick him up at the airport? Sure. Of course, I didn't reveal this to anybody.

I picked him up at the airport, and we went and registered at the Stadium Hilton under assumed names like "Harvey Schwartz." We took our coats off and ordered a pot of coffee, and he proceeded to explain everything about the circumstances of the Michigan State job. After explaining to me he had not talked to anybody else about the job, he asked point blank if I wanted the position.

There was no doubt: I didn't hesitate to say yes. Then he asked me if I had brought my contract. Now, there was an interesting twist here. When I was with Pittsburgh and offered the position with the USFL, I went to see the attorney that Joe Greene and Rocky Bleier used. I visited with him, and he scared the heck out of me. He thought I should have a big car in my contract, and a big car for my wife and that I should make a lot of other demands that I thought were unreasonable. I felt if I had presented those to Myles, it would have eliminated me from the position. So I didn't want to use him, and I had nowhere to go for representation.

So I made a call to a friend . . . Doug Weaver, who also was an attorney. He made suggestions and gave me the language for my contract with the Stars. When we sat down in the Hilton, then, Doug kind of gritted his teeth about the contract because now he was going to have to duplicate the language.

It was obvious to me that Michigan State already had a game plan, anyway. Doug said, "We'd like to pay you $95,000, and the president is only making $88,000." I told him I didn't want to make more than the president, but he said it was President Mackey's wish that I get a base salary of $95,000 a year for five years. The president had made a point of approving that, since he knew I was making $115,000 with the Stars. Michigan State also offered me about every perk you could imagine.

Now, we had to talk to Myles. As much as I knew going to East Lansing was what I wanted, what I had to do, I hated doing this to Myles. He was a good person, a good friend. Still, I always felt that we had an understanding that the only place I'd ever leave for would be Michigan State, so, ultimately, I didn't think there would be a problem. I didn't think he'd stand in the way.

By the time Doug and I got done, it was about 8 at night. I went back to King of Prussia, the suburb where my apartment was, and went out for a bite to eat at Charley's restaurant. I called Myles from the restaurant, and they said he was at a fundraiser for his alma mater, the University of Pennsylvania, and wouldn't be home until 10. I had time to be a little nervous.

I called him back at 10, and told him what happened. I was amazed at how understanding he was. He said he wanted the best for me and that we should meet for lunch the next day to finalize matters.

I went back to the apartment I was sharing with the other coaches, who had been wondering where I'd been all day. I told them what had happened and offered all of them spots with me. Or they could stay with the Stars and receive two-year contracts. Pendry had just left Michigan State, so he was going to stay, but Bielat and Furness said they would come with me.

If I was able to go, that is. I don't know what happened after I talked to Myles around 10, but he called me back around 1 a.m. and he was very upset. He threatened to sue me, and he wasn't going to give me his permission to leave. We were still going to meet for lunch the next day, but the complexion of our get-together had changed.

Carl came over the next morning before we met for lunch and asked what I wanted, what I needed material-wise to stay. I told him nothing. I just wanted to go home. My father-in-law lived in Lansing, my brother-in-law lived in Lansing. My mother lived in Detroit. I had a son, John, on the team there. I just wanted to go home.

So Carl and I went to meet Myles, and Myles started to explain to me how he was going to fight this. He was going to sue, and I was scared. It got kind of loud, and I don't think any of us got through any of our food.

So I excused myself, went to the phone and called Doug at the Hilton. I told him I didn't know what to do, and asked him what Michigan State's attitude was. He said his attitude was: Did I want him to come over and lock arms with me?

I said, "No, that's all I needed to hear." I had the backing, and once I had that I wasn't turning back.

"Later, I was criticized soundly for that, and probably rightly," Doug said. "It's clear there was a point where I could have walked away and saved us from the lawsuit. I never thought my job as athletic director was to take actions that would get us in a lawsuit.

"I can't say I was surprised we did get into a lawsuit, so the business decision that I made will just have to stand on its own. And as far as the economics of it, it didn't take three years to get the lawsuit money back. It took about three games. But we had a hell of a president, Cecil Mackey, who could have left me swinging and hanging slowly in the breeze after the Stars sued, but he didn't because he was a heavyweight who had vision and instinct and wisdom."

Myles also asked me to just stay through the first season, which would be over before our season would begin at Michigan State. But recruiting and organization were crucial and had to be gotten to right away.

After I talked to Doug, I explained to Myles that there was no use talking about it. "I'm going to East Lansing," I said, "if I have to walk." We went outside in the parking lot, and Myles was in tears and he hugged me even though he was going to sue.

He had to do that, really. It was his job to. He probably could have sued me for breach of contract, but he didn't want to hurt me so he sued Michigan State for tampering. I think he said the school's conduct had been "reprehensible."

"If you want to pick a guy's pocket, you've got to make [restitution]," he told *The Detroit News* at the time. "I just wish this had been handled in a more gentlemanly fashion, and [that] they wouldn't have left us in a position of responding without any confusion and backdoor manuevering."

They sued for $1 million and settled out of court for $175,000. To this day, Myles doesn't hold it against me. I don't think Carl does, either.

"The guy just had a dying desire to be coach at his alma mater," he told *The Detroit News* then. "You can't fight that. He cried like a baby when we talked this morning. And so did I."

After our meeting, I went back to the Hilton. Doug was on the phone with the board of trustees, President Mackey and Ken Thompson, the vice president for finance. They said it was OK to release the news: I was the head coach at Michigan State.

Now, this was all happening so fast that Sally didn't know any of it. We hurried to the airport, Doug went to get plane tickets and I had time for one quick call.

I said, "Yeah, honey, we're moving. But we're not going to Philadelphia. We're going back home."

The Stars went as far as the first USFL championship game, and I was only the league's big controversy for a few months. New Jersey violated the whole concept of the league in February when it signed Herschel Walker to a $16 million contract. The idea had been to keep out of bidding wars — and definitely not to raid college campuses before that year's class was supposed to graduate.

But I didn't blame New Jersey for that, because it started at the top. The commissioner, Chet Simmons, never should have let that happen, because once the owners start calling the shots there are no rules any more. The USFL folded a few years later.

10

A Can of Coke

As soon as I arrived in Lansing, I made a phone call I loved making. My son John was on the team at Michigan State — a choice I was glad to see him make, even if it did come just after I'd been turned down in 1980. But John didn't know anything yet about what was going on this time around.

"'This is your father, the coach, calling,'" I said. "'Get to the classroom, get to the weight room and get ready.'"

The press conference announcing my hiring was no different than a celebration for me. It was at Kellogg Center, and it was a beautiful scene. Right in the middle of the room, I remember, smiling from ear-to-ear, was Jack Breslin, the vice-president who was always in my corner. I know I've said it before, but it was the happiest day of my life.

"In my opinion, for my family and myself," I said that day, "this is the finest coaching position in the country. I'd rather be here . . . than any other place there is. No one can be happier than I am today.

"You know, I've been taught that you can feel what people feel toward you and what they think of you. And I know that most of the people in the state of Michigan are happy to have me here."

OK, I can get a little carried away at times. So what? I meant that, as well as the other things I said that day:

—"Our philosophy will be that we're not going to promote George Perles, or the offense, or the defense or players, coaches or statistics. We're going to promote 'Rose Bowl.' If we make all our decisions based on winning the Rose Bowl, we won't make any poor decisions."

—"I'm here, brother, and I'm going to give it all I've got."

—On recruiting: "The state of Michigan is the most important state. It's the state that will get the most attention. When we've done our work in this state, it's, I think, a natural to go to western Pennsylvania. The mothers and the fathers and the athletes in western Pennyslvania are very much into Steeler football. We're going to show some of those athletes why they should come to Michigan State. . . . I would expect the University of Pittsburgh, Penn State and Michigan to 'buckle up.' Maybe everybody in this room doesn't understand this term, but if you write it, they will."

—"I will not be the type of recruiter who works out of Mission Control. I'm going to start off by doing some leg work and dusting off the attaché case and going to the schools."

—"Three years ago, in my opinion, I think they hired the right man [Muddy]. And I think they hired the right man this time."

—I told them it would take us five years to get to the Rose Bowl.

—I said that we would run the same drills that we ran in Pittsburgh, which were a carbon copy of what I ran at St. Ambrose. "It's the same game; it's all relative."

—I gave my salary history, starting with $3600 a year I was making at St. Rita's — plus the $400 for coaching football and the $40 a week I was getting for cleaning the second floor.

When they asked why I took this job for a lesser salary, I said, "I don't know how to put a value on some of the fringes I have."

Some people thought they knew how to, though. Even though there was a lot of joy about me coming back, there was some controversy, too, because of the complications with the Stars. We think we probably would have won the case had it gone to court, but then we were worried they might file an injunction that would have kept me from coaching.

One of the trustees at the time was Peter Fletcher. He was particularly worked up about the deal, and a couple other trustees saw it the same way.

When President Mackey tried to explain his reasoning for the situation, Fletcher said, "If we are full of such ethical purity, why did we have to pay $175,000 in hush money?" He also said he didn't think there was any such thing as a "Pigskin Messiah."

I guess he was referring to me. In fact, he started referring to the whole thing as "Perles-gate." He did everything in his power to make things uneasy.

Before I even had been on the job a month, the *Kalamazoo Gazette* wrote an editorial warning me: ". . . If Perles doesn't produce a winner right away at Michigan State, the howls from critics, alumni and others will increase. . . . Better, win, George. And quickly."

Some honeymoon, huh?

Still, none of that stuff really bothered me. For one thing, I knew fans and alumni were behind me. I saw all the "Let George Do It" bumper stickers around town. For another thing, all of that only becomes a problem if you allow it to be a distraction. And I wasn't about to get sidetracked. In fact, I didn't even have time to think about anything but getting the program set up and jumping into recruiting. Oh, and returning phone calls kept me humping. I think there were 196 messages left for me my first two days on the job.

After the press conference, I went to Ed Rutherford's house — I had already hired him to be an administrative assistant — and had a sandwich. Then he took me to the Detroit airport so I could go back to Pittsburgh and collect a few things. This was going to be a familiar sight: Ed and I spent a lot of time together in the car the next few weeks on recruiting trips. Most of our meals came courtesy of McDonald's drive-through windows.

I began recruiting, in fact, before I even got on that flight to Pittsburgh. At the Detroit airport, I called Shane Bullough and Pat Shurmur — my first two recruits. Called 'em both, got 'em both.

When I got back to the airport in Detroit on Sunday, Lynn Henning from *The Detroit News* picked me up. Lynn was working with Joe Falls, the columnist, and they wanted the first exclusive interview. I agreed to it, because I know of all the people in the world, the only one Duffy went to his grave disliking was Joe Falls. And I wanted to make sure I didn't antagonize him — or leave my guard down against him — because I saw how he crucified Duffy.

So we had a good interview at my room in what was then known as the University Inn. From there, I had two coaches from Muddy's staff come over for interviews. The rest I was going to meet with on Monday. One who came over Sunday evening was

Steve Beckholt, Muddy's recruiting coordinator, and I told him to keep recruiting and that he was going to be retained. The other was Ted Guthard, a personal friend.

I told Ted that I wasn't going to retain him, but that didn't mean that I might not keep him after he'd had a chance to look at other opportunities and I had a chance to look around, too. I knew I wanted to keep Ted, but I hated and resented people keeping people to use them for one year. I wanted him, but I didn't want him to just stay on: I wanted him to leave and come back and know that I wanted him.

We had an office party on December 22, and I invited him to come over and offered him a job. I changed his office, and he moved everything out of his old office. He was part of our staff. He wasn't left over.

The next morning I went into the office and talked to every coach of Muddy's for as long as it took. I went from 9 a.m. to 6 p.m., visited with every one and retained no one. None of them had any control of the situation. I knew what I was going to do.

I explained to them that I had worked all my life for this position, and I wanted the prerogative of having the coaches I felt comfortable around. I said if I could help any of them, I would. I recommended Sherman Lewis to John McVay and the 49ers — a job Sherm landed.

It's funny how you put together a staff, though. I always looked for the best coaches available, not how they mix and stuff like that, and somehow they fall into place. But you never know where you'll find somebody. Norm Parker knew my friend Tom Moore, who was coaching in Pittsburgh, and asked Tom the best way to get in touch with me. Tom told him, "Well, he goes to breakfast every morning at the Elias Big Boy, next to the University Inn." I went in there one morning, and Norm was sitting there waiting for me. Norm had a good Big Ten background. I told him to come over to the office later that day, and I hired him.

I hired Nick Saban because I had gotten to know him when he was hanging around the Steelers camps. Bielat and Furness, of course, had come with me from the Stars. Bill Rademacher came on board from Northern Michigan, where he had some great offenses.

We rounded it out with two great Spartans: Charlie Baggett, Michigan State's co-captain in 1975, and Buck Nystrom, a former

All-American who had been my line coach at Michigan State. He had lettered in football under Biggie in 1953 and Duffy in 1954 and 1955. Charlie and Buck understood my feelings about restoring tradition.

I wanted to be a bridge back to the glory days, so we did a few cosmetic things right away. We returned to the old block "S" for our logo, on our helmets and in the middle of the stadium. I loved the block "S." It took me back to the Varsity Club. The "S" sweater. Superman. I loved it.

And I hated all those pictures of Sparty, our mascot, that had replaced it. They had different images of him in different ways — they were even using whiskers in one — and I didn't like all those silly things. But we did one thing different. We just put it on one side of the helmet — like the Steelers' logo. We also did it so people would ask why we were doing it.

I also made a point of getting rid of the multiple stripes on the home white pants. That kind of stuff is California, not Michigan State.

Like I said, though, those things were just symbols. Important, but still symbols. What really was going to make the difference, of course, was the players. Our foundation.

I'll never forget my first meeting with them. When I looked in their eyes, I saw not defeat, but hunger. They knew they were going to have a chance to win, because they knew we had the coaches and the support.

After all, we were riding in on a white horse. Galloping in. By the time we were done, I guess it was an old gray mare. But we sure came in galloping.

When I walked into our meeting room at the Duffy Daugherty Building, one of my first observations was my son John, who was sitting right out in front of me. I could see him, but I didn't want to let on or get caught looking at him. That was really good for me to have him there, good for my perspective on how to model the program. I went into it with the thought in mind of what would be best for him.

I wanted my son to have a good education. I wanted him to have good discipline. I wanted him to win, and I wanted him to stay out of trouble. And that's what I wanted for every player. And I never changed. That's why we said, "No. 1 is your family, No. 2 is your education and No. 3 is football." I wasn't going to do anything that would emphasize anything but what was best for the kids.

Those were my principles, anyway, but John's presence that day reinforced them in my mind.

I started off the meeting saying, "There's a good percentage of you guys who want to have a good winning program, and you'll have no problem with me or us. You're going to love this.There's going to be a few of you guys who are not going to conform. You're going to be a pain in the neck, and you're not going to last.

"And you've got a whole majority in here who still have to make up your mind where you're going. I recommend that you jump aboard, because it's going to help you be a better person and a better student . . . and you'll win some football games."

At this point, I looked out at the players and I saw one slumped down in his chair, like it was an effort for him to be at my meeting. He was sipping on a can of Coke and wearing a baseball cap. Gentlemen don't wear hats when they go in a building. Not a very respectful appearance — and not very smart, either, when you're trying to make an impression on the new coach. I looked at him and yelled, "Out. OUT."

No one monkeyed around after that. There were no problems with discipline. We were great disciplinarians. So I laid out my platform for the players. I didn't take any questions from them, because there was no need to. This was going to be a dictatorship — a great form of government if you can trust the dictator.

I didn't bother spending any time evaluating any past game film of our personnel. What good was it? It was done. So after recruiting, when I got Bo kind of hot at me after I said we knocked Michigan's socks off and were in control of Michigan, we got our first chance to evaluate our players and institute our philosophies. Like, "Work hard, keep your mouth shut, and good things will happen." I gave that to the players because it's a good, honest saying that they could learn lessons from on and off the field.

We wanted to establish in spring practice that we were a tough football team, and we'd already made some points about that with our winter conditioning program. I also had the word "Pride" put up all over the place.

As it turned out, the spring's harsh weather conditions were perfect for what we were looking to do. The first day was, well, a lousy April day. Cold. Wet. We couldn't practice on our regular practice field because it was too soggy, but I was determined we go outside anyway.

So we went out into Spartan Stadium, and we went through every minute of our regularly scheduled practice just to set the tone, so they knew we were going to be tough and persistent and that there weren't going to be any distractions. It was a very important spring. Nothing was going to get in our way.

We had the philosophy that in any kind of teaching you have to be as tough as you can to start with and you can always back off. The worst scenario is to start off easy and laidback and then try to get tougher on them. And we wanted to make sure we knew our players, and which ones were going to play on Saturdays and not give up. Besides that, we had to learn their personalities and how much they could take as far as motivation and corrective criticism go.

We had to take the chance on some injuries, since we had to do a lot of contact work to get to know them. So it was a lot of basics, a lot of hitting, a lot of discipline, some "meatgrinder" drills and a lot of yelling and screaming. Probably our meanest and roughest and toughest spring.

I think the players were surprised by how enthusiastic and demanding we were. We would practice until I felt that we were finished, and sometimes that was pretty late. The players seemed to take it all to heart, though. There were so many scraps after the whistle that I was ready to issue boxing gloves to anyone who kept going after the whistle. That simmered them down.

There were a few guys who dropped out of the program because of the intensity. But the great ones, like Carl Banks, said that that spring practice set the standard for the players to know what was expected.

"From the time Coach blew his whistle," he told the *Philadelphia Daily News*, "it was non-stop. You woke up dreading it, but then you remembered how bad it felt to lose and you realized this was one way to turn it around."

Some people might have thought we were too aggressive. I always tell people, "See that chair that I sit in? It doesn't matter if it's me, or Woody Hayes or Earle Bruce or Bo Schembechler or

Bobby Knight sitting there. We all have the same personalities."
Every one of us was pretty vocal, honest, straightforward, demanded a lot of the kids and sometimes let our mouths get us in
a jam.

And then someone's going to analyze you to find out why
you're like that. And the reason is . . . that's the kind of personality it takes to lead these kids. You've got to be a demanding
guy who can back up what he says. Simple. That's why if you
look at coaching personalities, they're all similar; at least the ones
who stick around for a while are.

Some coaches like to get away from the action, up into a
tower or some other observation area. Me, I was never a tower
guy. I was always on the field. I would go around from drill to
drill, offense to defense. I spent a lot of time with the defense
that particular spring, since I wanted them to run the Stunt 4-3
and I had to teach it to Norm and Nick, too. Furness, who was
coaching the defensive line, had played it but never coached it.

Over the decade before I came in, Michigan State had gone
53-54-3, been shut out of bowl games, been on NCAA probation
and been through four coaching changes. I wanted to construct
the bridge back across those 10 years, to make the program a
continuation of Biggie and Duffy. The Spartans had gone 10-23
in the most recent three seasons, and the 2-9 record in 1982 was
our worst season since 1917. So we knew we had a stiff challenge.

We felt good enough about things coming out of spring
practice, but it was obvious it was going to take some time to get
it done. You never go in some place and have all the players
you'd like to have, since your system and your needs are likely
to be different than those of the previous staff. In our situation,
we thought we had enough good players to win some games
right away.

There was one other development that spring. My son Pat
transferred from Kent State to Michigan State. So now, after never
coaching any of my kids before, I was going to be coaching two
at once. It wasn't coincidence that I hadn't done it before. Many,
many years ago I had read an article — in *Sports Illustrated*, I
think — about Jimmy Piersall and how his father had pushed
him into baseball.

His father would have him walk around with a baseball
glove tied to his belt, things like that, and just pushed him and

pushed him and pushed him. I don't think that was a good situation for Jimmy, and with all the problems he had, I went out of my way to make sure I didn't demand that my kids play football or any sport.

And I wasn't going to coach them, no matter what. I just thought it best to stay out of that, especially when I was in the coaching business. As it turned out, I felt very fortunate that I did coach them at Michigan State. I probably wouldn't have known what I missed, but it became something I'll always cherish.

It probably helped that when I got them, they were past the stage of Little League or Pop Warner. They were mature and not self-conscious about having me as their coach, just proud of it. It was great fun to have them come home at dinner and talk about everything. I always thought it was a tremendous compliment to their mother and me that the boys chose to come live at home during that time.

We never talked about it, but I always called them by their first names on the field, and they always called me "Dad." "Coach" or "Dad" would have been fine, as long as it was one of those two options. As for having to get in their faces on the field, well, they were used to that. I'd gotten in their faces all through their upbringing.

Patrick didn't get to play that much, and John did, and I'm sure that was tough on Pat. But he handled it very well and is a better man for it. I left that entirely to the position coaches. There was no way I was going to get involved. I let the position coaches have control of who plays — I give them responsibility and authority — and this was no different.

Even though I knew we had some limitations as we entered the 1983 season, I wasn't about to let the team have any excuses. We planned on coming out of the chute hard and fast and ruffling some people's feathers whose feathers needed to be ruffled.

11

"No Earrings, Dresses, or Purses"

The night before our first game with Colorado, I was nothing but nerves. What else is new, huh? It was something I'd hoped and prayed to get to do for a long time, and it was happening. I wasn't nervous because of pressure to succeed, because I knew we'd have some time and that game and season weren't going to be held against me if they didn't work out. Besides, I could always go back to Vernor and Dix and run a fruit stand, or go to Duly's and sling out some a la modes.

I was just nervous, I guess, because I was finally going to have my chance to walk in Biggie and Duffy's shoes.

I guess my nerves might have been showing a little. For our light practice the day before the game, I forgot to have the kids get their ankles taped and forgot to have water brought out. Forgot some of the details sweating out the big things.

The night before the game we always had dinner with the team at the Kellogg Center at 6:30, and the team stayed there overnight. Before that first game, I had told the team just not to wear jeans, and most of them showed up wearing coats and ties. You know you have a good group of kids when you ask them to do something and they actually go beyond it. They were trying to please me, and I appreciated it. We also made a point of putting candles and flowers on the tables. A civilized touch.

We'd have a meeting after the meal, then I'd go home and spend time with Sally and the family and some friends. My mom was over that night, and her advice to me for the next day was, "Don't cheat, don't yell and wear nice pants." She always wanted me to dress neat. I'm lucky she didn't make me wear a coat and tie. She had a belief that you were successful if you had a job where you wore a white shirt and a tie. That's because the people she knew at Ford who wore white shirts and ties usually had pretty good jobs.

In the morning, we'd have a meeting at 8:15 then have our pre-game meal at 9. Coaches love routine. We weren't dining, we were having a pre-game meal, so I'd have the players wait outside until the tables were set and then we'd zip right in, eat and get out. We'd have a set menu of four ounces of steak, well-done, baked potato with no butter, fruit salad and pancakes.

At the meal before the Colorado game, we had some newspaper people along and they noted that I had poured honey on my steak. I didn't know what was so strange about that. It was an old tradition we had when I was an athlete at Michigan State myself. Quick energy. Everybody talks about how sugar goes right to the bloodstream, and what better way to get it than from honey?

The assistants always had a lot to do after the breakfast, but I really didn't and I was usually left alone to think. Or, more accurately, to worry. That was always the worst time for me, imagining all the possible scenarios — the interceptions you'd throw, the fumbled punts, the receiver catching the ball, then fumbling it. The day of the Colorado game, even though we had coached the hell out of our players, I imagined every possible mishap. It was hard to calm down.

As we left Kellogg and walked together to the stadium, I got a real jolt of adrenalin to go with my anxiety. Hundreds of fans watched our procession across the Red Cedar River. That walk was another of my favorite traditions that went back to Biggie and Duffy. It takes exactly nine minutes to get to the tunnel at Spartan Stadium, but it stays with you a lot longer. Greatest walk in the world.

My pre-game talks at that point were still pretty passionate but a little more sensible than they had been at St. Ambrose. The best motivation at the college and pro level is just to be honest. Say what's at risk, point out that you've got 60 minutes of work ahead and a lifetime to remember it. It's a little more dramatic than that, but you don't say things like, "Bo's a louse," because at this level kids see right through that.

It's the same thing with recruiting. If you negatively recruit instead of trying to sell your school, you'll turn off more kids than you'll turn on because no one appreciates it.

I never prepared speeches for games. I know a lot of coaches who spend time with that, but I'd just let myself get filled up with the emotion of the moment and go from there. You would think I was a phony if I did it the other way, and most people who hear me speak compliment my sincerity.

So I don't remember exactly what I said to the team before the Colorado game, but I ended with saying, "Today is a beautiful day in your life. Today is September 10, 1983 — remember it." I think I was speaking to myself, too. I also led us in prayer, and I pretty much did that the same way all the time. You pray that nobody on either team gets seriously hurt. You don't pray for victory, of course, but you might make it known that you're kind of hoping to win. Just trying to get to the good Lord a little.

To this day, as a matter of fact, I get on my knees and say prayers every night before I go to bed and every morning when I wake up.

Colorado was coached by my friend Bill McCartney, who was in his second year. He was from Riverview and had been an assistant at Holy Redeemer when I was at St. Ambrose. We beat the Buffaloes 23-17, and the storyline was great:

"Favorite Son comes home." "The white horse is shining." "Strutting around." The only thing was, I graded myself a "C" for my performance. I made some errors, just basic things, that I hoped I wouldn't make again. Lucky for me that I didn't have to make the plays. The players took care of that.

After we sang the Spartan Fight Song in the locker room, my family was waiting outside for me. My mom said, "I wish your dad was here to see this." Whew. So did I. I wish he could have seen the Super Bowls, too. He would have loved them. And I got another form of congratulations after the game. A telegram from Myles Tanenbaum. What a class guy.

The next week we played Notre Dame. Second-ranked Notre Dame. Great university, great relationship with Michigan State. We've played them all but two years since 1948. They're the ones who helped put us on the map by letting us play them when Michigan was trying to keep us down. Michigan didn't want to let us get involved in the Big Ten or get promoted from a college to a university. Since 1949 we've played the Fighting Irish for the Megaphone Trophy, half of which is blue with a gold Notre Dame monogram and the other half of which is green with "MSC" on it: Michigan State College.

We have a couple other trophy games, which are kind of silly but fun:

Against Michigan, we compete for the "Paul Bunyan Governor Of Michigan Trophy." That was started in 1953 by Gov. G. Mennen Williams, and it features a four-foot wooden statue of my man, Paul Bunyan, standing over an axe that's mounted on a five-foot stand. There's an "S" flag — a block "S", naturally — on one side of the stand, and an "M" on the other.

We play Indiana for the "Old Brass Spittoon," which might sound like kind of an odd trophy to aspire to. That tradition started in 1950. The Spittoon was supposed to have come from one of Michigan's early trading posts, more than 100 years before. Students were behind the idea. The thinking had something to do with that the Spittoon supposedly had been around when both schools were founded, Indiana in 1820 and Michigan State in 1855.

The last trophy game is one we just established with Penn State in 1993, and I'm proud of that because it's something Joe Paterno and I came up with together. The concept itself came from our ticket manager, Don Loding. Our sports information director, Ken Hoffman, gave us the actual name. It's called the "Land-Grant Trophy," which represents the fact that Penn State and Michigan State were the two pioneer land-grant schools in the country. Our schools were founded 10 days apart in 1855, and the history is that we became the prototype schools for the land-grant system that came about after the Morrill Act of 1862 — that's what Ken tells me, anyway.

In 1983, Notre Dame was going to be a real bear for us. We hadn't beaten them since 1975, and that was the only time we'd beaten them since Duffy started us off with the onside kick in 1968. They were favored by something like 27 points, we had to play them in South Bend and they had just beaten Purdue 52-6.

We didn't do anything like onside kick to start the game, but we pulled off a bomb for a touchdown and probably surprised them a little with our quarterback, Dave Yarema, and his passing game. He threw three touchdown passes, and we intercepted three passes. And we really shocked them with the final score: Michigan State 28, Notre Dame 23.

It was crazy after the game. The bus ride back to campus from South Bend was beautiful. We got back to the football offices, and the band was there. It was crowded and noisy and . . . all I wanted to do was get home.

The campus police helped out by throwing me in their squad car and taking me home. Sally had been in the other bus, and there had been no way to get together with her in all the commotion when we got back. So when I got home I just sat there alone for about an hour before she got back, just taking it all in. I sat there at the kitchen table, relaxing. Meditating. I thanked the Good Lord, because to win that game we had been very lucky. When Sally got home, Sally and George had a celebration.

That week we were ranked 19th in the United Press International poll, the first time Michigan State had been ranked since 1978. Suddenly it was, "George For Governor." We were really riding the white horse.

"The difference between this year and last year is like night and day," Carl Banks told a Philly reporter that week. I was still news in Philly.

"You walk across campus now," he added, "and everybody's saying, 'Way to go . . . Let's beat Illinois.' Last year you'd mention football around here and people would say, 'Oh, do we still have a team?'"

Even so, I knew we were living on borrowed time. No one else knew, but we knew it. We just weren't good enough yet to keep going like this. We didn't have a lot of depth — only had 79 scholarship players instead of what was then a limit of 95 — and now we weren't going to be able to take anybody by surprise again. You still go out there and expect to win, but in the back of my mind I knew we were skating on thin ice.

We played Illinois the next week on regional television. Our Big Ten opener. And who knows, maybe I jinxed us by worrying about our depth and injuries. We were leading 3-0 and driving when Yarema was rolling out to pass and suffered a separated shoulder. He was done for the season.

On the very next play — the very next play! — his backup, a walk-on named Rick Kolb, had a finger broken on his throwing hand. We fumbled the ball to Illinois, and now Kolb was out, too. We were left with Clark Brown, a freshman who had never taken so much as one snap from center in a game. We lost 20-10.

The next week we tied Purdue 29-29 on a long field goal by Ralf Mojsiejenko. Then we had Michigan, and that comment of mine about knocking their socks off in recruiting came up. That didn't help our cause.

Bo and I were friends, because Bo is a good, honest, masculine, tough guy. We only had our differences one day a year, although sometimes it bubbled over all around the week of the Michigan game.

I didn't take it too well in 1989, after they beat us 10-7, and Bo said the best team had won.

"I guess the most profound statement of the weekend was, 'the best team won,'" I said the next week. "That's right. That's a good statement. That's the truth. Nice humble statement."

But I was sad when Bo retired. When you think of college football, you think of Bo Schembechler. History will remember him in the same breath as Bear Bryant, Woody Hayes, Amos Alonzo Stagg and Eddie Robinson.

The last time I had seen him before I came back to Michigan State, I almost hate to admit it, I actually was wearing a Michigan jacket with that "M" on it. I was watching one of Bo's spring practices, and it had gotten cold. So Bo loaned me his jacket.

But Bo didn't really care how I was feeling in 1983 when we met on the field for the first time. Ooh, they were big. They beat us 42-0, and it probably wasn't that close. We knew we were a long ways from having the kind of team they had.

And it stung a lot more because it was Michigan. When you have two great universities 60 miles apart, the competition is always very keen. In the state of Michigan, it doesn't matter whether you go to Michigan or Michigan State or even whether you went to school at all, everybody chooses one or the other: Maize and Blue, or Green and White. I don't know if hate's the right word, but I didn't like Michigan very much. We always wanted to beat the Wolverines more than anyone else, but you also can't put all your shoes in one basket.

After the loss to the Wolverines, reality set in. We ended up losing five of our last seven games, and we scored more than 12 points only once in those seven games. Our offense was crippled. We finished 4-6-1, but we had gotten some good things done. We had put in the foundation, and we had sparked some interest among our fans. Attendance was up nearly 8,000 a game, and our average of 71,949 was at the time the third-highest in school history — and 13th in the nation.

I didn't lay the foundation at the expense of the kids who were already in the program. A lot of coaches come in and try to separate themselves from the previous guy by dumping on the old guy's players, and I think that's a rotten thing to do.

That wouldn't be fair, to compromise a young man's career because he had the misfortune of being in that situation. This is another area where it helped me that my son John was already on the team when I got there. What was I going to do, go out of my way to keep him from playing because he had been Muddy's recruit? It's hard enough on kids to have to go through a coaching change without dealing with political nonsense.

So I promised I would always play the best people, and my coaches understood they were to carry that out. Same thing with the idea of redshirting players, keeping them out a year to develop. If they were good enough to play now, they played. Period.

Beating Notre Dame was a big boost in recruiting after our first season. That impresses the hell out of kids. But that just helps you get in the door, and you don't want to try to sell them on just things like that, because that's kind of like smoke and mirrors.

I didn't want to trick anybody into coming to Michigan State. I wasn't going into houses, high-fiving kids and giving them all a bunch of fast-talking jive. I was just myself, because what would have been the point of getting them to Michigan State if they didn't know what they were really getting with me?

They'd end up unhappy and leave, or unhappy and stay and become a cancer, and everybody would lose. Even if you get a good player that way, if he has a bad experience he's going to let it be known back home and it will kill you. Word of mouth can make or wreck your recruiting for a long time.

I'd go into homes and be interested in letting them know that ours was a tough, disciplined program. You'd have certain kids and families who want the kind of program you're offering, and you've got others who want the kind of program someone else has got. You've got to respect that and understand that. You can't waste time hounding kids who aren't the kind of citizen you want, or kids who you don't have a chance with for one reason or another. You're kidding yourself if you think you're going to go see them and wave a magic wand and whisk them away.

It can be hard to find kids who are good students and good athletes. We had some kids who hadn't been good students but had qualified, and we had tried hard to evaluate whether they had the makeup to be serious students. And once we committed to offering them a scholarship, it became our responsibility to do everything we could within the rules to help him get his degree.

It might have meant assigning him to study tables in the mornings and evenings, or threatening him with running, or calling him to wake him up, or even someone going to the classroom to make sure he was there. People will always talk about your won-lost record, too, but the people on campus know what's going on with your players as students.

You get what you emphasize: About 80 percent of my players graduated, and we had 56 Academic All-Big Ten selections in my 12 seasons. I also had three Academic All-Americans: Shane Bullough in 1986, Dean Altobelli in 1985 and '86 and Steve Wasylk in 1992 and '93.

Sometimes you do everything you can to motivate the kid, and it still doesn't work out. But you have to make sure the environment gives them the full chance. You have to let them leave practice for tests, you have to let them schedule labs even if it conflicts with practice. You can't ever put yourself in the position where those kids think you're using them and don't care about how they develop.

Being their coach, to me, also means instilling good personal traits in them. Obviously, that helps the coach run the team, but it also is important to help give them good guidance and morals. You're going to tell them, "You take your hat off when you come in a building. You sit in the seat you're assigned on the plane. You're going to be quarantined if you don't go to study hall. You're going to wear a coat and tie."

Otherwise, they're going to say, "He's hard on us, but he doesn't care about anything but winning football games." And I cared about a lot more than that. When we were traveling, we'd get many, many compliments from airline hostesses about how well-behaved our team was. I'd swell up like a big frog when I'd hear things like that. Any time somebody would say nice things about our kids, I'd just bubble over. Just like I do when someone compliments one of my own children.

Maybe some of those rules seemed kind of arbitrary, but I had reasons for all of them.

For instance, sitting in the assigned seats on the planes. College and pro teams are notorious for walking around and shooting the fat during flights and nothing can get done by the people on the airplane. So I want them sitting. There's no reason for them to be up prancing around. Other than when we went to Tokyo in 1993, we only took short trips, so it didn't need to be an issue — and it never was.

Why the big deal about the baseball caps? It's just a matter of being a gentleman. So I'm old fashioned. So what? At the training table, we had them check their hats at the desk when they came in.

We didn't allow tank tops at the training table, either. We didn't want people reaching over the salad bar and dripping with the pits of their arms not covered. And there was no music at dinner. You sit there and think and eat and talk with your friends and relax.

Oh, and one other pet cause of mine. There are — there were, anyway — no earrings on the Michigan State University football team. Never! If I was recruiting a kid who was wearing one, I made it clear he couldn't wear one at Michigan State. I don't know why, but it is something that bothers me. I didn't want that in my building, and I didn't want that on the field.

Even if the kid wasn't wearing one when we went in on recruiting visits, the assistant coaches were supposed to make a point of letting them know that they were not allowed at Michigan State. When I was in the house, or in a team meeting, I would tell them, "I don't want any earrings, dresses or purses in my building or locker room. Now, if you guys want to go downtown and wear a dress, that's your business."

They'd laugh, but they knew I meant it. Never had a problem with that. Never saw anybody wearing one. I know that kind of garbage is popular nowadays, but no players ever even approached me about it. Of course, I didn't have any committees set up to give them forums for those kinds of concerns. It was a dictatorship; I was all the committee I needed.

12

Rose Fever

In the summers, after recruiting and spring practice and camps, there was always a little bit of time to slow down and just exhale a little bit. Usually that was our only chance to get away for a personal trip, too, and after my first year at Michigan State, Sally and I took a beautiful two-week trip to the British Isles. It was organized by Duffy as a way of thanking coaches for their participation at his Coach Of The Year clinics. Some of the others who came along were Darryl Rogers, Johnny Majors, Hayden Fry, Don James, Bill Yeoman and Jim Walden.

We played golf at Turnberry and St. Andrews, and they were amazing. I was out of my league. Their greens were immaculate, and I never saw a cart my whole time there. You had to take every shot with a tee, because they didn't want any divots. That was right up my alley. Duffy would say, "I landed in a clump," and then he'd kick the ball up 20 or 30 yards.

The people were very hospitable, and I was struck by the fact that a lot of them were poor but seemed very happy. I remember that they didn't like the Russians, either, and that they weren't too big on refrigeration or tipping.

Those trips were an annual event with Duffy, bless his heart. Probably that one and the one we took to the Orient the next summer were the most memorable for me.

When we went to North Korea, we had a chance to tour the military setup — after we signed a paper that said the government wasn't responsible if anything happened to us. We soon understood why. There was still an awful lot of tension at the 38th Parallel.

Their soldiers were maybe 10 yards away from ours, each set up about five yards from the boundary. We were forbidden to make any noise or talk, because we were told that anything we did could be used as propaganda against us. I remember looking through some binoculars at some guy . . . who was looking back at me through binoculars. Kind of spooky.

We also went to Communist China, which was not a very nice place. You had the feeling all the people there wished they could get out. You should have seen how they looked at my $8,000 Super Bowl ring. We filled up a lot on rice when we were in the Orient, because we suspected they were using dog or cat in some of the meat recipes. I don't know if they were, but I'll tell you one thing: There weren't any dogs or cats on the streets!

I had another international trip that was very important to me. Three summers ago, after the Russians had moved out of Lithuania, I went over to see my heritage first-hand. My mother has a cousin over there, so I brought supplies to their family: clothes, aspirin, money, bubble gum, all kinds of things. They really had it rough. We saw people who lined up a block to buy chickens. They lined up a block to buy potatoes, which I'd say were ones you'd question eating here.

They were poor, but they were so happy because of their new freedom. Their churches were open again, and that meant an incredible amount to them. In Vilnius, the capital, they were going to church at 7 o'clock seven nights a week. They love to read about the United States and listen to American music, which also was new to them. I don't know what the political future is there, but I'll say this: I don't think they'll ever be overrun again. They'd rather die than be captured again.

I was very moved by what I saw there, all their needs. So I put together a golf outing to raise funds for medical relief to Lithuania. In our country, we have a program where a dollar will buy $86 dollars worth of medicine to benefit others. It's based on the idea that the medicine is obsolete to us, but it's still good medicine. It hasn't expired. Last year we raised $24,000, which purchased more than $2 million worth of supplies.

I always thought those trips were good for the education and the fellowship, but I was always glad to get back to the United States. There's no place like it. This would be heaven to most people.

I already felt like I was in paradise at Michigan State, anyway, as we were getting ready for our second season. Even though I turned 50 that summer — Sally got me my own Cuisinart — I felt like my energy was increasing every day.

That fall we would greet our second recruiting class, and we now had the nucleus of what would become a Rose Bowl team. And not only were we setting a bedrock foundation of our own in the early years, we also were on the same page with the administration. You can't say enough about the difference that makes.

President Mackey was on the flight with us to Colorado for our opening game. He noticed that Sally wasn't with me, and he asked if it was a family decision that she wasn't there. Actually, she was coming later with some alumni. But he said, "Well, I just want you to know that you should feel free to bring your wife on any trips at our expense. You have an unusual job, and you're away a lot." I thought that was very kind of him. He went out of his way to do everything he could for us.

Doug Weaver was the same way. This might sound like a minor thing, but any time an assistant coach's wife made a road trip we'd provide a single room for them to be together. Not every school does things like that, and that was a credit to Doug. He had played the game and been on the sidelines, and when you go through those things you know the grief that comes with the job.

To me, you really can't know the obstacles unless you've been there. It's like sometimes we Caucasians try to tell minorities we know how they feel. That's not true. I don't think you can know that unless you've lived through the same experiences, seen the same troubles.

We beat Colorado again, 24-21 this time. Notre Dame was ready for us this time, and they hung on by the skin of their teeth and beat us 24-20. Next we faced Illinois again, and I pulled a doozy before that one.

The Illini had just been hit with NCAA and internal penalties for recruiting violations, and I thought the sanctions were kind of soft. The charges involved everything from improprieties in buying airline tickets, illegal meals and tickets and even goofy stuff like giving orange and blue socks to a recruit. The NCAA put them on two years' probation and barred them from going to a bowl for one year.

Actually, my gripe had more to do with the coaching situation than the penalties. When Michigan State was put on probation, Denny Stolz was fired. I thought their coach, Mike White, should be punished, too. And I made the mistake of going public with that.

"Fire him," I said in an interview with sportscaster Ron Cameron for Channel 62's "Sports View Today" show. "You live by the rules. If you can't, get out. . . . Those kids are being groomed for what, to cheat? They're better off losing."

Ron asked me who should fire Mike White, and then I really started ranting.

"The school," I said. "I'm talking about taking care of their own park. . . . It's a mess. I don't know if anyone can straighten it out. If that happened at Michigan State, I'd be embarrassed. I don't know if I could face people. Do it right or leave. . . . It's a fantastic conference. Most people abide by the rules."

I regretted saying all that, and it hurt Mike, who I actually liked. It was none of my business, what their administration should do to a guy caught cheating. But I was upset that it was said they were cheating, and I despised cheating. I've always said there was no shame in losing, only in cheating. It's wrong, and it can cripple you. Once you cheat, how can you discipline? The players will own you.

Anyway, I guess I asked for it that Saturday.

I went out early before the game to try to talk to him and apologize. But he didn't come out when I was out there, so the first time I saw him was halftime when our teams were crossing. I tried to go toward him, and before I could say anything, he jumped on me about it. So, of course, I retaliated and we got into a healthy shouting match at halftime.

The newspapers in Champaign reported that I had started it with Mike, and they quoted him as saying all he had said to me was, "George, you really disappointed me." Mike knows differently.

But I still get a kick out of his sense of humor. The game was a disaster for us; they beat us 40-7. Then he told a Chicago reporter, "Any coach who gets beat 40-7 ought to be fired." Hooray for Mike!

The next week, we lost 13-10 to Purdue and our season probably looked a little suspect. We were 1-3, with our Michigan game coming up.

As it turned out, there was no reason to panic: We seldom did well early in the season. In my 12 seasons, only once did we win more than two of our first four games. And our record in those first four games was 18-28-2, as opposed to 52-30-2 in our other regular season games. I don't have any excuses, reasons or clues about why. We just didn't get it done.

But we did it get done against Bo and Michigan in 1984, in Ann Arbor. We beat the Wolverines for the first time since 1978 and just the third time in 16 games.

The big play was Bobby Morse's 87-yard punt return for a touchdown. Bobby was a wonderful story, and I had a picture of that play up in my office. He wasn't supposed to make plays like that; we had wanted him to come in as a walk-on, and he got the last scholarship we gave out in 1983. It probably helped us that Michigan's fine quarterback, Jim Harbaugh, had suffered a broken arm in the game.

In the locker room, we had a true celebration. Part of my good feeling was relief that the players had bailed me out for my "knock their socks off" comment from the first recruiting class. Why did I say that garbage? Maybe I liked putting pressure on myself.

After we beat Michigan, we picked up some steam. We beat Indiana, lost a close one to Ohio State, then beat Minnesota, Northwestern and Iowa to earn a Cherry Bowl trip even though we lost the season-ending game to Wisconsin. Fantastic. It was the school's first bowl in — can you believe it? — 19 years.

We were tickled. And the Cherry Bowl, that's a collector's item. I think it only lasted two years. We played Army and we should have had a little home advantage, since it was played in the Pontiac Silverdome and more than 70,000 tickets were sold. We lost the game 10-6, but we had a true freshman running back who helped make us feel like bowls were about to become a trend.

That was Lorenzo White, whom we had broken in gradually that season to let him get his feet wet. He was definitely too good to redshirt. That would have hurt him — and there was no reason to deprive ourselves of his awesome talent. His first start was against Minnesota, the eighth game of the season, and then he rushed for 170 yards against Northwestern.

What a player he was for us. His 1,908 yards the next season as a sophomore were the most ever gained by an NCAA

Division I sophomore, and I thought he should have won the Heisman Trophy. The guy from Auburn— Bo Jackson, I guess — won it. He didn't have the stats Lorenzo had coming in, but he had the hype coming into the season and it carried him. Lorenzo finished fourth in the voting, both that year and in 1987.

What made Lorenzo so good was, well, he had it all. Durability, vision, cutback ability, speed, strength, hands. Peripheral vision, you either have that or you don't. It's easy for us to sit there and watch films and say, "Geez, you should have cut here." But they have only a split second to make that decision when they're out there, and Lorenzo just had the knack for knowing when to make his move.

He was a humble, quiet kid, and he's still a great person. He's perfect. I remember one time there was a fight at a campus dance, and he did everything he could to stay out of it. He actually climbed up on a car and got himself out of the way.

He's done everything right, even since he's been a pro. He really takes care of his mother, although there was one time I got in his face about neglecting to call her. Somebody had tipped me off that he wasn't calling her, so I gave it to him.

His mother loved him more than anybody I ever saw in my life. They were very, very tight when we recruited him out of Fort Lauderdale. His mother cried when he committed to Michigan State, but she loved him and knew it was best for him to get out of that area. When Lorenzo set our record for carries in a game with 56 against Indiana in 1987, she was very concerned and upset that he was getting the ball so much.

Everyone wanted Lorenzo, and we were pretty fortunate to get him. We had a little advantage in our recruiting. His nickname was "Franco." He really idolized Franco Harris, and I had just come from being with the Steelers and Franco. We played that up a little. He also knew I had the reputation for keeping the ball on the ground, and that was helpful.

Counting the Cherry Bowl, we finished 6-6 in the 1984 season. It wasn't over .500, but it wasn't under .500, either. The cigar box is as half full as it is half empty. Now we're really starting to get our minds on the Rose Bowl. The idea started getting under our skin. It was an itch that we wanted to scratch. Immediately, if not sooner.

And our recruiting was really starting to take off in that direction, too. We were getting some real dandies: Guys like Tony

Mandarich and Andre Rison — first-round NFL draft picks, just like Carl Banks had been and Anthony Bell and Mark Ingram were going to be. By the time I left, we'd also have Lorenzo, Percy Snow, Bobby Wilson and Rob Fredrickson plucked in the first round. Easy to look like a great coach when you get talent like that around you.

We started the 1985 season in typical Perles style — slow. Nice win over Arizona State to start the season, then we lost to the Fighting Irish and slipped by Western Michigan 7-3. Teams like that are dangerous. If you or your players take them for granted and they play their hearts out, that's a deadly combination. It's a great lesson for anybody, whether it's a Ford motor executive or a football team. You can never underestimate or disrespect your opponent. You might get away with it once in a while, but only if you're lucky.

I joked with the media after that game, because they wanted me to explain what was holding us back. They knew I was going to protect the players, and I just admitted it to them:

"So I dance with the media. Saturday after the game, I did the Fox Trot. Today I'm doing the Boogie-Woogie."

I really did know the Fox Trot, by the way. That's the dance Sally and I liked to do.

If everyone was bothered by a close game with Western Michigan, well, at least it was a win. The next week we lost to Iowa, which was ranked No. 1 at the time, and then we got blown out 31-0 by Michigan. Then we lost to Illinois again.

The last two were at home, which of course bothered me a little more. I took a lot of pride in Spartan Stadium. But I tried to keep on an even keel about the concept of playing at home and away. If you emphasize having to win all the home games too much, then you could get into the mentality where you have an excuse to lose on the road.

So there we were 2-4 and 0-3 in the Big Ten — already out of the Rose Bowl picture, and the season just started! But we had a surprise for everyone waiting just around the corner: We weren't going to lose again the rest of the regular season.

Lorenzo started running wild and our offense became unstoppable. In our final five games, we score an average of 32 points a game and we beat Purdue, Minnesota, Indiana, Northwestern and Wisconsin. We were going to the All American Bowl in Birmingham, Alabama.

There were always some fun things at these bowls. In Birmingham, just going to practice and coming back were thrills because we'd receive police escorts. The motorcycles, the sirens, I loved them. I think we all still have a lot of kid in us. To have all those lights and sirens around us, flying through red lights, that was a lot of fun no matter how old we were. At the John Hancock Bowl a couple of years later, I actually got to work the siren in a police car myself. Beautiful.

My philosophy about bowls might have been different than some. I thought they were rewards that were supposed to be part of a joyous holiday season. If we win, we win. If we don't, we don't. But most of all, enjoy it. As long as the players stayed within the rules and behaved like mature gentlemen, they had a free ride. We didn't miss many local attractions on our bowl trips.

So what do I remember most about the All American Bowl? Mostly that that was where our son John met his future wife, Amy, whose father is a Michigan State graduate who had brought his family to the game, too. John met Amy, they got married, and Sally and I got another daughter and three beautiful grandchildren. I spend a lot of time chasing the little ones around. I throw them around a lot. They like that. Some kids are lap-sitters. Mine are throw-arounders.

As for the game, we lost 17-14 to Georgia Tech. We led 7-0 at halftime, but they scored a touchdown with 1:50 left to beat us. Anthony Bell had what would have been a game-saving interception called back on a roughing-the-quarterback call that I disagreed with. Didn't matter. So we finished the season 7-5. The point is, the game brought the team new experiences. And it brought us a nice daughter-in-law and three grandkids. Can't name another football game that did that.

There was another development on our campus that school year. John DiBiaggio came in from the University of Connecticut to replace Cecil Mackey as president. He gave an interview to the *Lansing State Journal* right before he took over and gave his philosophy of sports.

"One of the things that has pleased me as much as anything is that I expected sports was going to be absolutely the first thing I would hear about," DiBiaggio said. "It's not the case. People interested in it, but there isn't this overwhelming concentration. People are absolutely interested in the quality of the academic programs. If I hear anything about athletics, it's very, very often the comment that 'we really like sports, but we're really proud of the university for maintaining standards.'"

We jazzed up our offense a little after that season. We shuffled our personnel a little when Ted Guthard left to go into private business and brought in Morris Watts, who had been with Rollie Dotsch and the Birmingham Stallions, to be the offensive coordinator. He had coached at Indiana for nearly 10 years, so he knew the Big Ten, and he was excellent working with our quarterbacks. Morris deserves a lot of credit for our reaching the Rose Bowl in 1987.

Unfortunately, we had to go through a growing-pain season in 1986 before that could happen. I'm not really sure why it went that way, because we had been climbing steadily upward and we had a good team. Maybe we just weren't ready to put that hammer on the Rose Bowl.

Maybe we were depending too much on Lorenzo, who was injured most of the season. Maybe we weren't mentally tough enough, maybe it just wasn't meant to be. In some ways, though, it was the best thing that ever happened. It really alarmed and ticked off a lot of people.

We went 6-5, but it could easily have been a lot different. We lost four games by a total of 12 points, all in the last moments. We were driving for the winning scores but threw interceptions against Iowa and Indiana, fumbled at the 1-yard-line against Northwestern and had a tying field goal blocked against Arizona State in the end.

"Another 24 yards, and we would have been 10-1," Bobby Morse told reporters after the game.

"It was a crazy season; I've never seen anything like it," was what Dave Yarema told the media. Dave had had the best statistical season of any Michigan State quarterback to that point, and he was second-team All-Big Ten.

It was kind of a flat feeling even when we beat Wisconsin 23-13 to end the season. We went from talking Rose Bowl to no bowl game at all. Still, it gave us our third winning season in a row at Michigan State for the first time since our streak of five in a row ended in 1963. You could hold your head up about that.

I couldn't help but feel bad for our seniors, though. Eighteen of them who had been in our first recruiting class were moving on, and they were very special to me. I wanted them to be rewarded for all they had done to re-establish our program, and they should all know that we wouldn't have gone to the Rose Bowl the next year without the bricks and mortar they had built in our foundation.

And our foundation was strong in another way. The new president was really in my corner. He came to my office every Friday for bagels and cream cheese. His support helped keep our momentum going in the right direction.

"I like what George stands for," he told the *Pittsburgh Press.* "I like that he's a man of real good conviction and integrity. If I had to draw a composite of a coach on the collegiate level, I'd draw George Perles."

13

The Best Cry
I Ever Had

Before the 1987 season, the geniuses at *Sports Illustrated* made me one of the features in something they ran called, "Where The Noose Meets The Neck." Pretty dramatic, huh?

The piece said, "Since [Perles] arrived in 1983, the Spartans have lost five or six games every year. Too many . . . This year, he has the talent and expectations are high. Will the noose loosen?"

Sports Illustrated also assessed our Big Ten title chances: "Not this year, unless Columbus and Ann Arbor secede." Oh. OK. I'll say this for *Sports Illustrated*: They got it right when they put me in their "Firing Line" story last summer. Guess they did some detective work when they heard about the "outstanding season." Either that, or they figured if they kept taking a chance on me every year they'd get it right sooner or later.

In general, though, I seemed pretty popular with the press then. Even Joe Falls was writing things like that if he were the governor, he'd have me out speaking for him. "George Perles is a great emissary for the state of Michigan." And why shouldn't the media have liked me? I was always accessible, always returned phone calls, I tried never to dodge them and I tried to give them a little wit, too.

I have to admit, though, I'm often amazed at how the media can see things and frame things. How did *Sports Illustrated* come to that conclusion in 1987? I certainly didn't even have a toe in any hot water, or even in lukewarm water, because my five-year contract was a rollover. More important, I had the emotional support of Doug Weaver and our new president — John DiBiaggio.

At least I had DiBiaggio's allegiance for the time being.

And the program was in beautiful shape. We had the good, classy, tough kids I wanted to have. They had the right kind of attitude about playing the game.

"He likes to take our guys in practice, line them up at the 50 and let them brawl," Tony Mandarich said in *Lindy's Football* magazine. "And we usually just pound the hell out of each other."

Besides, I'm a football coach — not a doctor, or a general. Pressure? That's pressure. In football, there's no such thing as pressure if you're prepared. I can always live with the results if I've done everything I can do.

And we were definitely going to need to be prepared in 1987. Our first five games were going to be against ranked teams: Southern Cal, Notre Dame, Florida State, Iowa and Michigan. Some people rated our schedule the second-toughest in the nation. Plus — surprise — something I had once said came back at me. It was our fifth year, and I had said when I took over that it would take us five years to get to the Rose Bowl. But that wasn't really pressure, either. I just like to keep my word.

I don't think our players were at all flustered by the schedule, either. Most of them saw it as a rich opportunity. Tim Moore, our senior linebacker, figured we'd be ranked No. 1 if we won the first five games. That's the way to go, Tim.

There was a lot of hullabaloo surrounding our opening game against USC, which was playing its first game for a new coach, Larry Smith. He was one of Bo's former assistants. Larry was familiar with Spartan Stadium because of his days at Michigan, and he knew how loud it gets because our stands are so close to the field. It's 22 feet from the sideline to the first seat. I know, because I measured it myself when we were preparing our indoor facility.

We played on Labor Day night, the first night game we'd ever had at Spartan Stadium, and the school advertised it as the "Great American Football Celebration." We had fireworks, awards for the best tailgate party, the Monday Night Football window, Lee Greenwood singing, "God Bless The USA," and a sellout crowd of more than 77,000 people. Quite a spectacle.

Before the game, I received a telegram from Duffy. He was really struggling, battling heart disease in Santa Barbara. But he somehow found the energy and the time to make this gesture. It wasn't one of those, "Win one for the Gipper," type things. It was just his way of letting us know he was thinking about us, even if he couldn't be there. Duffy was that kind of man, always thinking about others no matter what was happening with him.

We did our part, too. We scored on our first possession of the season when Lorenzo ran 9 yards for a touchdown, our defense forced five turnovers and we went on to win 27-13.

At that point, we had a pretty good idea we'd have some potent weapons to complement Lorenzo. Andre Rison, of course, already had proved he was a thoroughbred. But our new quarterback, Bobby McAllister, showed he'd get Andre the ball when we gave him a chance to throw — and sometimes even when we didn't. And our other running back, Blake Ezor, was going to keep people from being able to just gang up on Lorenzo. Nice one-two punch.

How we got Blake reminds me of how wacky the recruiting scene can be. When I was with the Steelers, Mr. Rooney set us up at the Dunes hotel in Las Vegas with a friend of his who wanted the privilege of entertaining the Super Bowl champions. The man who ran the baccarat tables was Bernie Ezor, who was originally from Pittsburgh and couldn't do enough for us. He got us into shows and restaurants and really took care of us.

In our third recruiting year at Michigan State, Bernie Ezor called me up and said he had a great player for us — his son, Blake. Blake was being recruited by everyone — Notre Dame, Miami, Penn State, Oregon — but Bernie wanted him to play for me.

Now, when you're recruiting you get a lot of dads who think their sons are a little better than we might evaluate them. And it doesn't happen very often that a great player just wants to come to you. The better they are, usually the harder you have to recruit. So I sent Ted Guthard out to look at the film and check him out.

Ted called me from Las Vegas and said, "George, you can't believe it. This guy is super. Outstanding." So that's how Blake Ezor came to Michigan State. Since he was delivered by his father, this kid became for me a bona fide fourth son. Boy, was he a great back. Fast, good hands, loved to practice. Pound for pound, he was the toughest kid I ever had.

Before Blake, I'd say the toughest college kid I'd known was a teammate of mine, Henny Young. But Blake outdid him. I'd see Blake in the shower after away games, where you'd usually have to shower with the players, and he just had bruises and red marks and scratches on every inch of his body.

Blake had a couple legal mishaps, and I was criticized for being too soft on him. But nobody but Blake knows how I dealt with him, and I know Blake doesn't feel like I was too nice.

"A lot of people thought I got off easy," he told the *Lansing State Journal*. "But these people don't know Coach Perles. He was on me day and night. I hated him when I played. But now I couldn't say anything wrong about the guy. He made me a man."

I remember after the opening game wondering whether history would repeat itself. The last time we had gone to the Rose Bowl, after the 1965 season, we had opened with a game against a Pacific 10 Conference team — UCLA — and gone on to have a rematch in the Rose Bowl, where the Big Ten champion always plays the Pac 10 champ. I told the team, "Don't be surprised if we play them again."

Our next game was with Notre Dame, and we had 12 days to get ready since we had moved back our opener to that Monday night. By then, we were ranked 17th and the Irish were seventh. The hype before the game was all about Notre Dame's Tim Brown and Lorenzo, being the two top Heisman candidates.

I have to admit Brown was amazing. He reminded me of O.J. when he was in the open field, and he almost created a draft when he ran by. But I'll always feel like Lorenzo didn't have a real chance at the Heisman because of the pre-season politics.

Notre Dame was quarterbacked by Terry Andrysiak. I busted my butt trying to recruit him out of Allen Park in 1984. He lived about five blocks from my parents' old house. There was one point where I was pretty sure we had him: His mom had made a Green and White cake for Sally and me when we visited. But Terry chose Notre Dame, a tough school to compete against for recruits.

It was Lou Holtz's second year at Notre Dame, and the reporters that week made a big thing out of him being 0-4 against Michigan State, counting his time at North Carolina State, Minnesota and Notre Dame.

It was probably obvious at the beginning of the game that Lou's streak was about to end. I mean, the very beginning. Blake caught the opening kickoff at the 1-yard-line but backed into the end zone and kneeled. He thought it would be a touchback, and we'd get the ball at our 20. Instead, it was a safety and the score was 2-0 before the clock even moved. I don't think I've ever seen that happen, before or since. Blake felt awful, and it was a tough way for him to learn that rule.

We liked safeties that year, I guess. We got another one in the second quarter, when they tackled McAllister in the end zone. Then Tim Brown ran back two punts for touchdowns in the last 2:14 of the first half. Weird stuff. Brown almost had a third one, too, which was saved by a shoestring tackle.

After the game, he said they thought they might break at least one because they expected our outstanding punter, Greg Montgomery, to outkick his coverage. Greg was too good. The Detroit Lions think the same thing.

Notre Dame also sacked us eight times on the way to the win, but I thought that was a crucial time for us to let Bobby McAllister know he was our man. I talked to him on the sidelines every chance I could, and I made it clear we weren't going to hook him or make him the goat. Bobby was a great runner, very elusive, and he could put some steam on the ball. He had been watching Dave Yarema for a couple years, and it was great for him. Now he just needed to be given some rope, because he was a natural leader. He appreciated that. It made him better.

The final score was 31-8, and we tried to get some immediate consolation by talking up our next game, our next opportunity, against Florida State. We really helped ourselves a lot: This time we took a 31-3 lump.

Duffy died the day before the Florida State game, and the whole Michigan State world mourned — no one more than me. Jack Ebling, from the *Lansing State Journal*, wrote a book, *Spartan Champions*, on the 1987 season. And he did a good job getting people's reactions.

—"Duffy was Michigan State," said former roverback George Webster, a College Football Hall of Fame inductee who had played for Duffy.

—"To me, Duffy's at the top — probably running a close first to the Pope," said Walt Kowalczyk, an All-America halfback in 1957. "He knew how to handle us and how to groom us. He turned a lot of raw young men into gentlemen, that little leprechaun."

—"The word 'legend' is often overworked in our society, diluting the real meaning," DiBiaggio said. "But 'legend' is the word to use when discussing Duffy Daugherty at Michigan State. His name, his record and his personality have become an integral part of Spartan lore."

—"I'm sure Michigan State will be affected by all this," Bobby Bowden, the Seminoles coach, said. "Duffy meant so much to George Perles, and anything that affects George Perles will affect the team."

I can't say that it didn't affect me, but I think I did a good job bottling it up — for then — and I don't think I let the team see how much it hurt. Plus, as much as I talked about tradition, I don't think the players' sense of history was that keen that Duffy's death would disrupt them.

In any case, we lost bad enough that we actually were booed by our own fans. They have the right, and I'm always glad to see the stadium packed, but I think it's a lousy thing to do to college kids. Bobby got sacked seven more times, and we were 1-2. Not the way we wanted to start, but we were very aware we hadn't lost a Big Ten game yet.

As it happened, we weren't going to lose a Big Ten game all season.

We opened conference play the next weekend in Iowa City, and the Hawkeyes had been a thorn in our butts with last-second victories in three of my previous four years.

It wasn't anything intentional, but I did something that game that I probably hadn't really done since my days at St. Ambrose. I went bonkers at halftime. The score had been tied 7-7 until we fumbled at our own 27 with about a minute left in the half. Iowa went ahead 14-7 with five seconds left, and smoke was coming out my Lithuanian ears when we went into that goofy pink locker room at halftime.

That was probably the most upset and most vocal I'd ever been in any halftime in my entire career. We didn't get much done with X's and O's. I just raved and ranted and tore into them. All of them. Nothing profound. Nothing anybody would want to copy. I surprised myself, and I'm confident the players were stunned.

"He wasn't the nice Coach Perles I know," Lorenzo told reporters after the game.

Good. That's what they needed, although stuff like that can backfire if it's contrived or you try it on the wrong group of guys. In this game, it definitely succeeded. We held them, if that's the word, to minus-47 yards rushing in the second half and outscored them 12-0 to win 19-14.

I got a nice, big hug from DiBiaggio after the game. I was his huggy bear.

Next up to the plate was Michigan, and we ran over 'em. OK, we won 17-11, but Lorenzo's 185 yards were the most any back had ever gained against any team of Bo's.

Our defense also was making our offense. We had seven interceptions, including four by John Miller, and that gave us a comfortable feeling about what might be ahead. You'll never have a championship team without an exceptional defense, and ours was only hinting at how dominant it was going to be.

I brushed off a little history that week. I remembered in 1969, Bo's first year, Duffy put in the wishbone backfield the week before the game and they beat the Wolverines. Believe it or not, that was the last time Michigan State had beaten Michigan in East Lansing. We were watching film on Sunday, and I thought maybe we could try to make history repeat itself.

After Tuesday's practice, I told the assistants that we were going to have some dinner brought in. So we had some stuffed pork chops, and we spent our dinner watching film of the wishbone. They might have thought I was nuts, but that's the beauty of a dictatorship.

Actually, they knew they could always give me their input. But no one even looked at me funny. We put it in Wednesday, and it helped us on Saturday. Duff would have loved it.

We also honored history that day by giving Dr. Hannah a No. 85 jersey for his 85th birthday. He was The Chief. I had two chiefs I worked for in my career: Mr. Rooney and Dr. Hannah. They had very much the same personalities, and they made good things happen. Fair, honest, big-hearted and bigger than life.

When I came back to Michigan State in 1982, he and his wife had lunch for us out on their farm and he gave me what his blueprint had been during the 28 years he was President. How he thought he could build a big, strong university with the publicity he could get from a winning football team . . . why he picked Biggie, who in turn brought Duffy . . . why he had the school buy all the land around it. He had unlimited vision.

President Hannah was responsible for all of the good things that came to Michigan State, and he was helped quite a lot by his great vice-president, Jack Breslin.

With that win, we changed the complexion of the season. We were still only 3-2, but we were 2-0 in the Big Ten — can you believe this? — for the first time since 1967.

We beat Northwestern the next week 38-0, and the Wild-cats only got 139 yards of total offense. Served 'em right. That 24-21 loss to them the year before had crippled our bowl chances. I don't know if you would call it revenge, but let's just say we made a point of emphasizing to the players that they shouldn't forget about the year before. A lot of our guys had watched Mike Tyson batter Tyrell Biggs on TV the night before, and our great linebacker Percy Snow said the defense was hungry to set that same tone Tyson had.

Offensively, Mandarich took the game especially seriously. He got a personal foul for clobbering a guy in the back of the head. I doubt it was on purpose, but Tony was in another world when he was playing. He was one of the finest blockers in the history of college football, and the only thing he had in mind was being the best lineman in the country. He used to take pride not only in blocking people, but in punishing them and taking them 15 yards downfield. He was mean and tough and dedicated.

Our grading system for Tony was a little different than it was for everybody else. For him, we kept track of: "pancakes," the number of times he flattened an opponent; "off the film," the number of players he would drive out of our view on the film and "no mas," for those who just gave up against him.

Tony was 6 foot 6, 315 pounds and consumed with his conditioning like no one I've ever come across. He would eat seven meals a day and take in 15,000 calories a day. He got his toughness from his parents, who escaped from the Communists in Yugoslavia. I hear his mom used to wrestle him and really fling him around, even as a teenager.

Some people thought Tony was kind of cuckoo, but all great athletes are a little different to a degree. They have to be to be as great as they are. It was even suggested by some that Tony used steroids, but he never tested positive and we didn't tolerate that in our program. I mean, I put steroids in the same category as any illegal drug, and if we had so much of a whiff of something like that going around I was right on it.

The *Detroit News* later did a long story suggesting we had a widespread problem with steroid garbage, but there was nothing ever proven that even indicated we had a minor problem.

The next week we received the only blemish we'd get in the Big Ten. My old friend Mike White and his Fighting Illini tied us 14-14. You should have heard the fans hooting over that one. Duffy used to say, "They're with you, win or tie." Now it's, "They're with you, win or win. Forget the ties."

Maybe some of the grousing was because when we scored a touchdown with 4:52 left, I decided to kick to even the score instead of risking going for two. I thought we might have a chance to score again if our defense could hold them fast enough, and I didn't want to risk a loss for our kids.

There was too much at stake, and a tie at least wasn't a loss and would still leave us with a lot to say about our own fate later. Sure, it's boring. But I don't think the fans were complaining when we earned the trip to Pasadena.

As it turned out, we did get another chance against Illinois. But John Langeloh's 28-yard attempt was the best shank of his life. He was a great kicker, though. Later on, he'd win the Rose Bowl for us. And I'd rather have the Rose Bowl kicks than that one.

There was another good reason we'd win the Rose Bowl. Actually, 11 more. Our defense wound up leading the nation against the rush and second only to Oklahoma in total defense. Those guys were everything I ever wanted in a defense. I didn't want "best dressed," or "most likely to succeed," or "cutest couple" or any of that junk.

I wanted toughness, and then I wanted them to execute the most important principles of sound defense: take away the inside running game; stay at home; never get beat deep; keep the middle linebacker clear to make tackles; make receivers pay for their catches and create turnovers. Our 1987 defense almost always epitomized those traits.

The week of the Illinois game, the *Lansing State Journal* asked some players for potential nicknames for the defense. "The Green Wall," Travis Davis said. "The Spartan Steel Curtain," Mark Nichols said. The one that stuck came from the *Journal*: "Gang Green."

"I think the characteristics of the team probably reflect the head coach, and that was true on that defense," Nick said, in his new Michigan State head football office. "He believed in playing the system and staying with the system, and every year that we played the Stunt 4-3 scheme we became a little more proficient. And this bunch kind of had an attitude, not to mention speed and size and sheer talent. If I would have let them, they would have set the Big Ten record for fewest yards given up in a season.

"But we were beating Wisconsin badly at halftime in the last regular-season game, and I told them that if we scored again we were going to play the bench. They were well aware of the record, and I was, but wasn't. So we did play the other guys, which I still think was the right thing to do because the other guys deserved a chance to contribute, but we ended up a little short of the record."

You wouldn't have thought any game in Columbus, Ohio, would have brought us closer to that record, but that's just what happened. We knocked off the 15th-ranked Buckeyes 13-7 thanks to two field goals by Langeloh, who got right back in the saddle, and more smothering defense. If you can believe it, the Buckeyes only managed to get two yards rushing on 31 carries.

We got a little fright early. On their first play from scrimmage, they completed a 79-yard touchdown pass. Fifteen seconds into the game, it was 7-0. Not quite as fast as Notre Dame went up 2-0, but close enough. Good thing we only gave them a total of 68 more yards all game.

Mark Nichols, our tackle, grabbed the team before the extra point and said we wouldn't let them score again. Eddie Rutherford remembered when I did the same thing against Denby. It came true this time, too.

Percy Snow, our sophomore middle linebacker, was from Canton, Ohio. He took particular pride in that win, and he was one of the linchpins on our defense. As a senior, Percy would become the first player ever to simultaneously win the Lombardi Award as the nation's top lineman/linebacker and the Butkus Award as the top linebacker.

Percy was very strong, but he could go from Point A to Point B as fast as anybody I'd ever seen. He could accelerate, and when he got there he could throw everything into that thrust and not only tackle people but hurt them. Like Butkus: He'd put the full weight of his body into the tackle, and when you hit the ground he'd still be driving.

Next we had Purdue, and we didn't want to look past them to Indiana, which was a half game ahead of us. The Boilermakers had our attention, because historically they've tripped us up in these kinds of situations. I drove that point in all week with the players, and I made sure they didn't take to heart the fact we were 18-point favorites.

We won 45-3. Andre Rison had two touchdown receptions in the first half. Andre was spectacular and reliable. He started his first game as a freshman and he was never out of there after that. Another great recruit we got thanks to Charlie Baggett's hard work. Like Mandarich, Andre was a little different, too. That's the way it is. They're thoroughbreds. They rear up.

Finally, we got to the Indiana game on November 14. Our day of truth. We were ranked 13th, they were ranked 16th. This was the game to determine the Rose Bowl representative from the Big Ten, and ironically it was the same day we had planned a memorial for Duffy.

The best cry I ever had was at that Mass. Because of everything that was going on at once, a lot of former players came back that weekend. That included my friend Rollie Dotsch, who was dying of pancreatic cancer.

Rollie and I marched in a procession and sat together in St. John's Catholic Center, which was packed. They played, "Ave Maria," a very sentimental song. There were a lot of people doing a lot of crying. I was looking at Duffy's wife, Francie, and thinking of Rollie, who was about to pass. Already I needed a handkerchief, and I didn't have one.

At the end of the Mass they played "Oh, Danny Boy" — which was Duffy's favorite song and Rollie's favorite song. Holy Moses, I was overwhelmed. A reporter approached me as we were leaving the Mass, and it was one of the few times I remember just being at a loss for words. That was a hell of a cry. I prayed somebody would come along and scoop me away, and Frank Kelley, the Attorney General, came along and did.

In the game, Indiana actually scored first, on a field goal, but we did all the rest. We had more than twice as many yards of total offense and more than twice the time of possession they did. The final was 27-3, and there was one other statistic that stood out:

We gave the ball to Lorenzo 56 times, and he rushed for 292 yards. No, he didn't deserve the Heisman. At one point, he carried the ball 12 times in a row. I pulled him out once, and I asked if he was tired. He said no, so I told him, "I shouldn't do this, because I might be risking you out there physically, but you're carrying the ball every down." I wanted him to break every record we had. He deserved that. And I wasn't going to lose the game with turnovers or by monkeying around.

It was chaos after the game. Fans stormed the field, and it was sheer jubilation in our locker room. Even Bill Mallory, the Indiana coach, came in. While I was talking to the team, he interrupted and said he wanted the floor. He made a great speech, a pep talk I'll never match. He said, "I just wanted to tell you we wanted this game as badly as you, but we couldn't do it. You are great champions." That was a classy and sharp move on his part, a real sign of character and guts.

The five-year plan had come true. We were going to the Rose Bowl, and the Tournament of Roses people were there to give me a nice symbolic bouquet. I told everybody, "I don't know what you're doing tonight, but none of you are going to have the time I'm going to have."

I had a quiet moment or two, though. ABC was interviewing me after the game, and I could only think about Duffy and just looked up in the heavens. And there was a sequel to the emotions of that day.

The next week, I went to see Duffy's dear friend and a friend and former teacher of mine, Father Jerome MacEachin. Father Mac. He was on his death bed in the hospital. I was leaning over his bed to hear him, and he said, "Remember, George, football's only a game." I don't know why he said that. Then he said, "I'm going to go to heaven to watch the Rose Bowl with Duffy."

Father Mac died eight days later. I figure he wanted to get there in time.

An Affair
to Remember

We beat Wisconsin 30-9 the next week, a win I was proud of because it would have been easy for us to cave in emotionally after we had clinched the Rose Bowl. The big news there was we gave up a touchdown — just 186:20 since the last one we'd surrendered on the first play of the Ohio State game. What a defense.

Two other developments were important: Bobby McAllister completed 10 of 12 passes for more than 200 yards, a performance that gave us a chance to have more balance, and we still had no major injuries. That was amazing, and it's something you could never count on.

I mean, all the pre-season predictions are based on nobody getting hurt on any team, and that just doesn't happen. But it did for us that year, and I'd like to think it had something to do with our exceptional training staff — and the advanced conditioning program that I had stolen from the Steelers a few years before.

We didn't leave for California until Christmas day, and by then it was crazy the way people were feeding off of what we had accomplished. The MSU Bookstore sold more than $500,000 of Rose Bowl merchandise in just over a month.

As for me, I was getting sick of all the roses that were coming to the office. What was I going to do with them? I threw 'em out!

I'm just kidding about that. Anyway, as we were getting prepared to play a rematch against No. 16 USC, one big theme of the writers was that the Big Ten had lost 16 of the last 18 Rose

Bowls and the last six in a row. Well, so? I said, "Don't tell me. Go tell Ohio State and Michigan and those other guys. I wasn't there, what are you telling me for?" We weren't worried about how other people had done. What control did I have over that?

I'll say this, though: I am a Big Ten guy. And I wanted to do something nice for the conference and shut up all that nonsense about how the Big Ten is inferior.

"The griping about the Pac-10's dominance in the Rose Bowl was really reaching a crescendo," Doug Weaver said. "Our victory that year was much bigger from a Big Ten, national standpoint than I believe we really understood at the time. It had a magnificent impact on our institution, a lasting impact, but it also had a great Big Ten impact."

Winning was important, but we just weren't going to sweat it like everyone else wanted us to. One media guy, for instance, said, "It's supposed to be unusually cold out there this year. What are you planning to do about it?"

I said, "I'm going to put a coat on. What do you think I'm going to do? And I'll tell you another thing: When it warms up, I'm going to take the coat off. What do you think about that?"

We went out there and did our thing our way. For instance, we were the first ones to stay out at Newport Beach. Everybody usually stayed in Pasadena, but we didn't want to be locked in up there. Some teams have gone out for the game, and their approach is so serious they might as well have stayed in a monastery.

I wanted everyone to be able to get around and enjoy themselves. First class. And I wasn't worried about the players' approach. I think Bobby McAllister spoke for all of them when he said this may be the icing on the cake but everyone knows a cake isn't any good without icing.

I had a little fun with this at one of the press conferences.

"Mother will be 80 next Tuesday, and she doesn't get around like she used to," I said. "So I thought Newport Beach would be a good place to stay. There are plenty of places for her and my wife to spend their money."

We had worked hard to get there, so we deserved to enjoy it. If we didn't win the game, we were still going to have something to remember. All work and no play makes you very, very boring. So we did as much as we could. We went to Universal Studios, where we saw everything from the flying bicycles in

"E.T." to the exterior of the house from "Psycho" to one of the mechanical sharks from "Jaws." My favorite stop probably was Disneyland. I even got a hat there. I love Pluto and Donald Duck and Mickey Mouse, and they were all there waiting to hug us. Mickey, my man! Donald was even wearing a Michigan State jersey — attaway, Donald! Our band came, too, and it marched down Main Street, USA.

We had a little preliminary competition with the Trojans at Lawry's Prime Rib Beef Bowl. Mark Nichols ate four 19-ounce steaks. He was that kind of guy. He wanted to compete in everything — running, hitting, playing — and this particular time it happened to be eating beef.

One of the days I was on "The Today Show," and to get me there without dealing with all the traffic they took me in a helicopter. That was probably even better than getting to handle the siren at the Hancock Bowl.

On the Tuesday night before the game, the Big Ten club of Southern California held a banquet for us at the Hollywood Palladium. We had more than 2,000 people there. Bob Hope performed for us, but it wasn't all yucks for me that night.

The first year I was at Michigan State, Doug and I had come out to see the game. The Big Ten invites the coach and the athletic director of each school to attend, so I came out to scout it. Doug loves the Rose Bowl, and when we were at this same dinner that year, he turned to me and said, "I hope someday I'm up at that podium." It had been a goal of mine to get Doug to that podium, and when I made reference to it in front of the crowd my dry eye got a little damp. Doug and I hugged.

The next night we had a pep rally at the Century Plaza Hotel. It became one of the most unbelievable sights I'd ever seen: There were an estimated 10,000 Spartan fans shoehorned in and around that ballroom. At the game, the estimates were that 55,000 of the 103,000 there were in Green and White. Amazing.

Somebody had tossed a red plastic rose on stage when I was addressing them, and I got all emotional again. All those roses flying around made me think we were lucky we weren't playing in the fish bowl.

We had a particularly distinguished Michigan State alum show up that night. Well, more than one. Governor James Blanchard was on hand for everything. A great supporter. And

Magic Johnson. He was a real Spartan. Magic even wore a "Big Ten Champions" sweatshirt.

We were ranked eighth in the nation entering the game, had a nine-game unbeaten streak and were playing against a team we had beaten by two touchdowns to open the season. So, naturally, we were three-point underdogs. Whoever was setting the odds, Jimmy the Greek or Louie the Piano or whoever, knew what they were doing. Maybe it was just because we were from the Big Ten, or maybe because we hadn't won a Rose Bowl since the 1956 game or even been here since the 1966 game.

But you didn't mind being insulted that way. It was a blessing for us, and yet another rallying point for the team. I always like being the underdog.

As our habit was, we fell behind 3-0. But that was the only time the oddsmakers were right the whole game. We went ahead 7-3 on a five-yard run by Lorenzo, and we led 14-3 at halftime after he scored on a three-yard run. The Trojans cut it to 14-10 early in the third quarter, and that's when John Langeloh really showed his mettle.

He made a 40-yard field goal at the beginning of the fourth quarter to put us up 17-10. USC tied it with about 8 minutes left on a Rodney Peete touchdown pass. After we got the ball back, it looked like we might be in a pickle. We had third and nine, and Bobby McAllister was being forced out of bounds as he was looking to pass.

But he made like Otto Graham and managed to complete a jump pass for 36 yards to Andre Rison. That set up Langeloh again, and he banged through a 36-yarder with 4:16 left. It was nowhere near over, though. The Trojans made it to our 23 on their next series.

But they had had trouble with the center-quarterback exchange the whole game. I think our stunting had a lot to do with it. We hadn't taken real advantage of their problems, though, because they kept getting the ball back.

I've always said Duffy and Father Mac were getting upset and restless that they kept getting the ball back after those fumbles. So this last one went up about six yards and Todd Krumm, the great safety who was second in the NCAA in interceptions, went in and grabbed it. I don't think Rodney Peete ever even touched it.

Personally, I think Duffy kicked it up a little so he could make sure we recovered this one. That came with a little more than a minute left, and we still couldn't relax. We gave them the ball back, and the game wasn't certain until John Miller intercepted their Hail Mary pass at our own 13 with three seconds left.

Final: Michigan State 20, USC 17. Percy had 17 tackles and was named Most Valuable Player. Lorenzo finished with 113 yards. But there wasn't a player on our team who hadn't made it happen.

It was the greatest day of my coaching career. The four Super Bowls were fantastic, but they were an accumulation. This was a specific, special moment, one that I wanted to savor and cradle — and one that, ironically, prevented that from being possible.

Instead, everything changed almost immediately, right before my eyes. Like I was just a passenger on a runaway train. That's because two weeks later, the Green Bay Packers came calling.

15

Curious George

Looking at it now, all the squabbles and struggles in my later years at Michigan State really can be traced to right after the Rose Bowl. When Green Bay offered me the job, probably I should have taken it. When you ring the bell like we did with the Rose Bowl, ideally you do move on. But I couldn't do it just like that. This was my school. I was a son of Michigan State. And that was the difference.

Still, I had never really been put in this position before. I didn't know exactly how to handle it when all of this came up. And it came up fast.

After we won the Rose Bowl, I came home for a few days, did a little recruiting and then went back out to California to coach in the East-West Shrine Game in Palo Alto. Hundreds of NFL scouts and personnel directors and general managers and coaches were buzzing around town. One day I got out to practice early, and a Green Bay scout pulled me aside and told me Forrest Gregg was leaving Green Bay to go back to his alma mater, Southern Methodist. He asked if I would be interested in talking to the Packers.

I had two choices for answers, yes or no. What would you have said? Without really thinking much about it, I said yes. I always like to talk and listen. There isn't anybody I would never talk to; I guess I'm a curious guy. I would recommend that to anybody in any profession. There's knowledge to be gained, and maybe an opportunity to improve your place in the world. If not, maybe you're at least put in a position to help one of your colleagues move up.

And Green Bay isn't just some measly job in some Podunk town. Great tradition — Lombardi. Good family living. Great following, great facilities, great reputation. A lot of people would go to a lot of trouble to land that job. I never applied. All I know is I was asked if I wanted to talk to the judge, Robert J. Parins, who also happened to be the Packers president. And I said yes, and had a quick thought about what it might be like to win the Super Bowl as a head coach.

Maybe this is hard for people to understand. Actually, I know this is hard for people to understand because I took a lot of heat about my willingness to listen, both at this time and especially two years later.

People said I was talking out of both sides of my mouth about loyalty. Was it disloyal to learn about other jobs, to learn if I could make my family's life better? Besides, look at the results. I never left Michigan State. I always chose to stay, even when I could have made a lot more money leaving. And in the end, my love was one-sided. I didn't fire me. Michigan State was like a dream for me. It was all I ever wanted.

But I've attained the job, and we've gone to the Rose Bowl and we've even won the Rose Bowl. At that point I had done everything I had ever hoped to do in getting the program back on the map.

And in this business, you have to understand that the first time is the best time. It would have been hard to do more than we did that season, so you're set up for criticism right there. "Why can't you do that every year?" I'm not complaining. It's human nature. But it's unrealistic.

You reach your dream, then maybe that dream has to transform into another dream. When you dream, you don't get your dream job . . . and then the world just ends. If you're lucky enough to get there, you should have new dreams and goals. If you have a dream today, do you have to have that same dream five years from now? You'd better not, or you're pretty easily satisfied and you get complacent and cozy.

People were acting like, "You've had your dream. Since you dreamed it once and got it, you're done dreaming. Don't ever dream again, don't ever talk to anybody again." Heck, my biggest dream had been to be a Michigan State assistant coach. Wasn't I allowed to dream differently after I got that job?

Maybe this is complex to some people, but it's black and white to me. It's a competitive world. We're teaching that in school — I hope we're teaching it. We don't tell recruits they can only visit one school. They get to visit five, and my feeling is they should take all their visits so they're even more inclined to come here.

That first conversation took place on January 14, and that was all that had happened. But by the end of the week out there, I had constant phone messages from the media in my hotel room because it had already leaked out of Green Bay. I told whatever reporters I did talk to that I would talk to Green Bay, but that I hadn't had any conservations with their brass. And I hadn't.

I got back to Lansing, and the rumors were really starting to fly. But I still hadn't heard back from the Packers officially. Finally, on the following Sunday, I was at the office visiting with some recruits. Sally called and said that Tom Braatz, the Packers general manager, was in town and wanted to come over. So she had told him to come over and called me. I said as soon as I finished with the recruits I'd come home.

When I got there, Tom was waiting in the living room. Sally went to the store, and Tom and I talked. He showed me brochures of their facilities, showed me their roster and we chewed the fat about Green Bay. Nothing really serious. He told me he was on his way to the Senior Bowl and asked if I'd give him a ride to the airport. I said, "Sure," took him to the airport, and that was it.

Kind of a funny little meeting was how I evaluated it when I got home. No offer of a job, no reason to even think they were going to try to hire me. Now, though, the rumors were getting real thick. Reporters were calling every five minutes. I wasn't getting any direction from the Packers, and I was concerned that it was going to hurt recruiting. I was in a vague position, and I don't like vagueness. If you want me, fine, let's talk. If not, that's it. So I called every hotel I could think of in Mobile and got in touch with Tom on Monday night.

I told him this had become a problem, I couldn't get involved and I didn't want them to consider me. He said, "Wait a minute. I understand your problem. Let's just leave it at, 'you're not interested.'" OK, done.

It was still kind of funny, because he didn't explain anything. I read between the lines that he was not in the position to offer me the job but that he was very interested and was doing homework as far as talking to other people. I knew it wasn't a dead issue. He didn't seem like he was going to take no for an answer, and it wasn't like I'd said, "I wouldn't be interested for all the tea in China, and I don't want any part of it." He read between my lines, I read between his.

So a week went by, and then they called again. They wanted to get together; Tom Braatz, the judge and me. I told them I was leaving for a recruiting trip to Ohio and Chicago, and they said they would be glad to meet me at the O'Hare Airport Hilton in Chicago in two days. So I did my recruiting and then I went to the Hilton, where they had a room for me right next to theirs.

I went right over to see them. Tom was sitting on the bed, the judge was sitting in a chair on one side of a table, and I sat on the other. We talked for an hour or so, and they offered me the job — and a very lucrative deal. I had been thinking a lot about the idea of winning a Super Bowl and about a new challenge.

They set up the structure of the job and offered me $2.4 million for five years. I wanted no less than a five-year contract, because I had already spent 10 years in the league and you needed 15 to be fully vested. And they gave it to me. What the hell was I going to do? I told them I was going to take the position, but that I could not call Doug Weaver and tell him this on the phone. I wanted to go home and tell him face-to-face.

I went back to my room, got up very, very early the next morning and got on the first plane to Detroit. Eddie Rutherford picked me up at the airport, and when I got back to my home in Okemos around 11 in the morning I called Doug. I said I had to see him about an offer I had. He came over about noon, and we went down in my basement to talk.

We talked about everything. How we got this program to where it should be. How I could be the dean of the Big Ten coaches some day. How I could be here for the rest of my life. It was a beautiful, beautiful meeting, but I told him I thought I was going to go to Green Bay. He said OK, but he had one request: Don't verify it with them until tomorrow.

It was about 5 in the afternoon, and when Sally and Nancy Weaver and Sally's brother Bill went out to Gus's to get some chicken and ribs, the media was at the front door. She told them that I wasn't going to be able to visit with them, and she came

back and said, "I'm not doing that any more." So Henry Bullough
— he was living across the street and without a doubt would
have come with me to Green Bay — was kind enough to later
tell the media that I wasn't in a position yet to give them any
stories because nothing was finalized.

I called Green Bay and told them that they couldn't release
it yet because I had promised Doug I'd talk to him again. They
knew Doug was my biggest concern because I felt so indebted
to him. David Scott, the provost, called and said some nice things,
and so did Jack Breslin, our former vice-president. DiBiaggio
was out of the country, but he called and I went into a bedroom
off our basement to take it. He said whatever was best for me
and my family was fine with him, and he would be behind me
all the way if I did go. I got off the phone and I said to Doug, "He
was great. It almost sounds like he wants me to go." I was kidding — or so I thought.

I look back and I think there came a time when DiBiaggio
started getting jealous of all the attention we were getting in football. He was with us everywhere — locker room, sideline — but
there was a moment at a Rose Bowl function that stands out to
me. People of course recognized me everywhere, since it was a
Rose Bowl setting, and not many people knew who he was.

Now that's a little embarrassing for the coach when that
happens, because the president is your superior and has given
you the chance to do what you've done. But I think it bothered
DiBiaggio a lot more than it bothered me. He said something to
Sally like, "Isn't it a shame that people know who the football
coach of a university is and they don't even know who the president is?" I can understand as an administrator how that might
hurt, but I think that maybe it hurt him more than it would some
others.

I didn't think much of that incident at the time — although
I definitely would later — because we had had such a great time
in California together. And we socialized quite a bit with
DiBiaggio, even though I didn't care much for him calling me
"Buddha" all the time. Doug and I even convinced him to buy a
summer home near us up in Northern Michigan, and in the summer of '88 I took him to the old neighborhood. Just the two of us
drove in, went to a game at Tiger Stadium. The guys had a big
party for him at Gannon's bar. He was from Detroit, too, Denby
High, and he used to say, "We're home boys."

In fact, I still like the guy. But I think he probably would have been happier if I had taken the job with the Packers. And I'm sure he wishes I would have left in the next few years, before the flap about athletic director came up.

Anyway, the phone calls kept coming in as I was racking myself trying to figure out what to do about Green Bay. Governor Blanchard and Frank Kelley, who I think of more as my friend than as the attorney general, called on their way back from Detroit. They told me I ought to stay, and I put a lot of stock in their advice. Around 9, my good friend Joe Farrell called, and I asked him to come over if he had anything he wanted to say because I was sick of answering the phone.

I showed Joe the brochures of the facilities, and we were talking about Green Bay and I said, "You know, Joe, I've been down in this basement since noon. It's almost 10 o'clock now, and I've heard from the governor, the president, vice-presidents, the provost, and no one has offered anything to compete with Green Bay. That's fine, but it's surprising."

Joe called Frank Kelley at home, and when Frank got home he came right over. Joe told Frank what I'd said, and Frank said, "What do you want?" As much as my head was spinning all day, I had kind of come across some ways I could justify staying. I told Frank I only wanted two things:

I would like to be able to stay at Michigan State the rest of my career, and that meant I would need an 8 1/2-year contract to take me up to retirement at age 62. I had a five-year rollover contract, but I had heard after we didn't go to a bowl my fourth year, one of the administrators had discussed gradually reducing the rollover from five years to one. I knew then that the only protection I ever had was my contract. I never forgot that. I knew it wasn't beyond these people to put you in the street. If they were spoiled by our first two bowls, imagine how they were going to be now.

Number two, I told Frank, I think Sally deserved to have the same kind of retirement package I would get if I went to the NFL. I shouldn't penalize her. What if something happened to me? I wasn't concerned about the salary I was giving up, which was a difference in base salary of about $400,000. I didn't care about a raise; I wanted security. Frank asked what the retirement benefits would be, and I told him it was about $45,000 more a year than if I stayed here.

I told him those two things would be the difference in me going or staying. It was starting to get pretty late, but Frank called Larry Owen, the chairman of the board of trustees, and told him the situation. Larry said he'd talk to the other board members, and he'd be over at my house at 9 a.m. Larry was on the phone until 3 a.m. working this out, and the trustees voted 5-3 among themselves to get it done.

In between, Larry also talked to Jack Breslin, and Jack said, "Are you nuts, offering an 8 1/2-year contract? We'll look like idiots doing that. Give him 10." And that's how the 10-year contract came to be.

The next morning, Frank and Larry told me it had been done. I called Sally over and said, "What do you think, kid, want to stay?" She said, "Whatever you want to do, honey." Sally's not always like that, but she was relying on my judgment on this one.

I said, "Let's stay."

I felt bad about Green Bay, because the Packers had been honest and straightforward with me and I'd been very indecisive.

When DiBiaggio found out what had happened, apparently he went berserk. But the trustees thought I was good enough to keep at the time and were just reacting because he was out of the country. If he'd have been around, he would have been in the thick of the negotiating.

"What really bothered me," DiBiaggio says now, "was that I had been informed of the 10-year contract . . . but they also had unilaterally given the annuity. I knew nothing about that. Suddenly, when I got back from Indonesia, there was this annuity that was going to be paid for out of athletic department funds."

Whatever went on, this really was pretty much the end of my relationship with DiBiaggio. The funny thing was I wasn't really aware of it then. I mean, he said nice things after I got the extension.

"It is with a great deal of satisfaction, pride and ... great relief that I have received news of Coach Perles' decision to stay at Michigan State," he said in a statement that day. ". . . George Perles is not only the kind of football coach we want — he IS the football coach we want at Michigan State in the coming years."

I guess his resentment was hidden pretty well, but it was probably just because I wasn't looking. In other ways it all adds up: If our kids got in jams after that point, suddenly he wanted them thrown off the team right away. No second chances, no explanations, no working on the growing pains. He stopped coming around as often, and we seemed to be having a harder time getting some kids into school.

For whatever reason these things were happening, it made me question whether we were all on the same side any more. It was kind of ironic that Dr. Hannah called from Florida when the Packers deal was all over and said it was a good thing I didn't go or he would have boxed my ears in. And I knew he wasn't kidding.

And most of the reaction to my staying was pretty nice. I got an ovation when I walked through one of the dining halls. Walter Adams, our economics professor and our former President, brought me a cigar. Joe Falls even seemed pleased about my sentimentality. He wrote:

"Of course it's corny, but George Perles is a corny guy . . . What we have here is what we've always had here — a man who is ruled more by his heart than by his mind."

We had a press conference later that day, and there was a great deal of interest in the length of the contract. At the time, it was probably the longest in the country.

"Not only will I be able to call our recruits tonight and tell them that I'm staying here," I said, "I can assure them I'll be here for their fourth and fifth years. And I'll be here when they go to graduate school and get their Ph.D.s.

"All I can say," I added later, "is that no one should ever bother approaching me again . . . because I'm not going anywhere."

The contract gave us all incredible security, even my assistants. It's a rare case that assistants can be that comfortable, because they almost always are on one-year contracts. But at this point they might as well have had 10-year contracts, too. After all, they knew I was never going to fire them, and Michigan State had told us numerous times we would never be fired for winning and losing, only for cheating. And we didn't cheat, or even get in any gray areas.

As I look back at it, I don't know whether you'd say I had a weakness to go and didn't go, or I had a strength to go and didn't go. One thing you could definitely underline, though: I didn't go. And I was damned happy that day.

16

Jets Lag

For all the racket the Packers situation had caused, for all the trouble that eveyone had gone to to keep me around in East Lansing, a lot of people must have gotten a real kick out of the way the next season started. I said all summer that the honeymoon would end as soon as the toe hit the ball in the opener, and boy, did it.

But we had 16 starters returning, and you couldn't even count the number of expectations we had raised. There was every reason to believe we'd be a similar team to what we were the year before. I also tried to remind people no Big Ten team had won successive titles outright since Michigan State did it in 1965 and '66.

Sure enough, what did we do? We went out and laid a few eggs.

We started the season 0-4-1, and I began to wonder why we even bother playing our September games. Maybe we should just try to begin the schedule in October. If we can't get anyone to agree to that, well, we'll just pick it up there ourselves and take the extra time to practice. We could hardly do any worse.

Rutgers beat us at Spartan Stadium 17-13 to open the season, then Notre Dame beat us at home, too, by a score of 20-3. Then it was a 30-7 loss at Florida State, in the last of three games that we didn't have Mandarich because of an NCAA suspension he received for writing a letter to an agent to inquire about coming out early for the draft.

I thought that was a low blow by the NCAA, because all Tony was trying to do was investigate the situation. I wasn't mad at him for it. This is still America. Why shouldn't he have been allowed to do that?

I think the media wanted me to get all over Tony about that, just like they always wanted me to condemn our players when they were involved in some extracurricular difficulties.

Well, that was just too bad. I had a lot of good reasons for being that way. One big reason was it's illegal. The way I read the Buckley Amendment, it's supposed to refer to a coach-player privilege. Confidentiality. You don't go around telling personal things, like medical records or grades or punishment, about your players.

Besides, I didn't like the idea of doing my wash in the streets, anyway. When your son makes a mistake, or you make a mistake, or anybody's child makes a mistake, you don't just put it in the newspaper or on TV and go public. There's no reason to shame them like that. Believe me, the players had enough problems dealing with me over what they did; they didn't deserve double medicine.

The media got upset with me, because I wouldn't tell them our family punishment. They got very critical and made it seem like players could get away with anything around me. Well, we were like any other Big Ten school. We'd have some people get off track, and we'd do our best to get them back on track.

That makes me laugh that anyone thought I was a patsy for the kids. I took those matters very seriously, but you had to use some common sense. When one of our players got arrested in what the media referred to as "the Blind Pig incident" — selling beer cups for a dollar at a keg party — I just couldn't get too worked up about it. I mean, they've been doing that since I was in school. It's like spitting on the street. Technically, you can't do it, but it's never enforced.

But it was OK with me if the media wanted to rap me for my approach. It didn't matter if they were on me. I just didn't want them taking cheap shots on my sons, my players.

As for how I gave out discipline, it depended on the case. I'd take them out for games. I'd run them. I'd take them out for practices. I'd quarantine them to their rooms at bowl games. The only time they could come out was for meals. In a couple cases, I sent some home from bowl games. No one in the media knew it, and no one knows who I did it with to this day. And that's how it's supposed to be.

I understand the media's side of it, but I took the chance of irritating them to help the kids. Once a kid's in trouble, I'm going to scold him, I'm going to discipline him and then I'm going to be like a father. I'm going to help him. And the best way I could help was not to go public with his problems.

Our problems were plenty public enough in 1988. After losing our first three games, then we had a 10-10 tie with Iowa and a 17-3 loss at Michigan and — pow! — we were written off.

The hate mail was coming in as fast as the roses had just a few months earlier. I knew I deserved it, but that's just the way football is sometimes. That's one of the reasons why you can't make it — or any other sport, or any other job, really — the whole focus of your life. There are so many things you can't control, and in the end it's nowhere near as important or rewarding as family and education. It's a means to an end.

People look at me funny when I say this, but winning never was that important to me. What I cared about was doing things right and giving our kids the tools to be the best they could on and off the field and be able to go on and be good, productive citizens. If they did that, I could always be proud of them and myself. I always said football came after family and education, and I was actually looking for a way to make football fourth or fifth.

I guess one way was to get fired.

Who knows why you get certain bounces, or why you do or don't get streaks of injuries, or why players are easier to motivate some weeks — or some whole seasons — than others? If anyone knew, I guess they could patent it, bottle it and make a fortune. I'd probably be one of the rubes who'd buy it. But, probably, that would ruin the game. Those variables, which can frustrate you so much, are at the same time a big part of the thrill of competition.

When you get into a funk like we were in that season, everyone wants you to take some dramatic action. Change the whole lineup around. Fire some assistants. Heck, fire the head man. Rip the players. Or maybe tie 'em to a tree and beat them up publicly — that would appease some fans. What's that expression: "the floggings will continue until morale improves?"

Instead of pushing the panic button, though, I'd say you have to know yourself and know your team. We weren't doing anything any differently than we had been when we went to the Rose Bowl, so I reasoned that we should just keep working hard and keep our mouths shut. Good things should happen if you do. I could tell the players — and the media — got tired of hearing that one, but I think the players tried to buy into it.

They definitely had to buy into something. Those are really traumatic times for players, and people don't understand that. They are children learning to be men, and people boo when they don't win? Even if they've got their priorities right and look at school and family first, there's nothing quite as exciting for them as the day of a game — and not much worse than the day of a losing game.

They take deeply to heart whatever happens. All of that has a tremendous effect on their self-esteem. So I told them if they couldn't handle the feeling, heck, just stay out of public for a while. Lie low. Stay in your room, and remember your family — and that includes your coaches — loves you just as much as it ever has.

As coaches, all you can do in that situation is to simplify. Get more and more back to fundamentals. That was the Chuck Noll approach, and the Steelers went through a similar situation with a 1-4 start in 1976. We went on to reach the AFC championship game.

The next week we beat Northwestern 36-3, and the whole tone of the season started to pick up. Somehow, the players had found the resolve to dig in and try harder the worse things got. Somehow, a few breaks started going our way. And what happens? We ended up winning our final six games and we were a bowl team again.

Just like that. Nothing to it.

It shows you how resilient those youngsters can be, and that season is a lesson and example that could be held up by any coach. You never quit. If you have character, you have mental toughness. And if you have mental toughness, you can accomplish anything.

I've never been prouder of a group of kids than I was of that one. What a learning experience. In the Gator Bowl, Blake Ezor ran for 136 yards and Andre Rison had a Gator Bowl-record nine catches for 252 yards but we lost to Georgia 34-27.

In 1989, we were a little slow out of the blocks again — 2-4. But this felt a little different.

For one thing, we weren't coming right off the Rose Bowl season so there was not quite the same level of expectation. For another, all four of the losses had been against excellent competition and had been close. We lost by eight to Notre Dame, by six to the Miami Hurricanes, by three to Michigan and by four to Illinois.

Losing that way repeatedly can be a complicated matter for a team. On one hand, they know they're close and might be able to break through at any moment. On the other hand, they might get into a loser's mentality that no matter what, they're never going to be quite good enough to win.

Our job as coaches was to keep them — and ourselves, for that matter — from getting into that negative thinking. And the best coaching we could do was point them right back to the last season's accomplishments.

I wouldn't have wanted to make a habit of doing things the way we did them in those two seasons, but 1989 ended up almost exactly the same way. We won our next five in a row to qualify for a bowl.

One of our wins in our streak was 76-14 over Northwestern, and I took some flak for that score. But it was just one of those games, and I went out of my way to try to keep us from getting to 70 points. We had scored a touchdown to reach 69, and I made us down the extra point instead of kicking it.

Then we kicked off, and Northwestern fumbled it inside their own 20. We had all our reserves in, and we tried to run it up the middle and run out the clock. But our back kept getting yards, so I ordered a quarterback sneak. So, oops, the quarterback runs for a touchdown.

Not much you can do there. You never want to be mean-spirited and pile it on in those situations, but you also can't ever tell your players not to do their best. The guys you have in there at that point probably don't get to play that much, and they deserve to be able to cut loose on those occasions when they are in there.

We had some strange games with Northwestern. In that same game, we had some snow beforehand, and we scored first to take a 7-0 lead. Then they came down and scored, but before they kicked the extra point our students threw quite a good number of snowballs at them. At the time their coach was Francis Peay, and Francis walked out to the middle of the field and told the officials to have me come out, too.

I went to the middle of the field, and Francis said, "George, if they don't quit throwing those snowballs at us, I'm taking my team and walking in." At the time I thought to myself, "Boys, keep throwing those snowballs." I thought we might be in for a long day. Then we ended up with 76 points. Blake Ezor had 36 of them on six touchdowns. No other Michigan State player ever had more than four touchdowns in a game.

That fall, Doug Weaver, the greatest guy in the world, told me he was going to retire as of the following July 1. It took me about a week to get over it. He announced it in early December, a few days after he told me. During that time in between, Doug and I talked about the job and who might be coming in next. And I got to thinking about how much I'd enjoy running the athletic department — I had hundreds of ideas.

It seemed like that would also be a way to honor Doug by continuing his good work. And one other thing: I have to admit I also didn't like the idea of working as football coach for somebody who didn't hire me. You had no way of knowing what the new person's agenda might be, or how they might regard you. I didn't want to roll the dice. I thought I'd feel pretty secure as the coach if I were athletic director, too.

I dusted off my little attaché case and followed the chain of command. I went over to see Roger Wilkinson, our vice-president for finance. He told me, "Just put your name in like anybody else, and we'll review it." So that's what I did. He said with my background he thought I would probably be an interesting candidate.

We beat Wisconsin 31-3 in our final regular season game, and we were tremendously excited about going to a bowl. We could have gone to a lot of bowls, but we chose the Aloha Bowl because of where it was — Honolulu. It doesn't make as much money as some of the others, but it's a great trip. We had people in the locker room after the Wisconsin game wearing leis around their heads, and we were very happy.

Then I went out into the press conference, and one of *The Detroit News* reporters started off right away in his mean way with,

"When's Ezor going to jail?" Ezor had just gotten a drunk driving conviction. He said he hit a mailbox when somebody cut him off, and Blake was actually the one who called the police. He was going to have to serve a week of jail time, because he had had a driving under the influence charge the year before and was on probation.

I felt horrible enough about it, anyway, and I really lost my temper at the reporter and called him a lousy so-and-so and raised some Cain with him. All the media tape recorders were on, and it really looked bad. It was bad. I was kind of rude, and I don't like the way I handled it. I shouldn't have yelled, and I shouldn't have taken it so personally — but Blake was a personal thing for me.

I think what partly provoked me was that this reporter was rumored to have some problems of his own that already had made me question whether he should be covering our football team, and I said something to that effect when I was ripping him. Whew, I was hot.

As much as I regret that, because it embarrassed him publicly, I think I did do a proper thing when I called their publisher the next week and asked him to come to East Lansing to talk about the situation. He was sympathetic and took care of the problem. But I don't think *The Detroit News* ever forgave me, and I probably never forgave them.

So we were 7-4 when we went to the Aloha Bowl to play against the Hawaii Rainbows, and we were in Hawaii practicing when the news broke that Penn State had been admitted to the Big Ten. There was a fan on the sideline with a cellular phone, and my emotions got the best of me. I asked him if I could use the phone, and I called Joe Paterno to congratulate him from right there on the field during practice. He loved that phone call.

And it was good for Michigan State that I have a good relationship with Joe, because we now play Penn State to end every season. The last game of the season in Big Ten country is always difficult in terms of being attractive to fans. It's cold, it's hunting season and if your team is having a bad season or out of the running for a bowl, nobody is going to show up.

That's why Michigan plays Ohio State last, and Minnesota plays Iowa last and Purdue plays Indiana last. You need a built-in attraction, and a rival game does that for you. We tried it with

Wisconsin and with Illinois, but it didn't work. Obviously, it wouldn't work with Northwestern — you can't fill up a stadium with them very often even in the middle of a season.

So to have the Michigan State-Penn State game be the last game of the year forever is a tremendous development for us. Getting that done was a little complicated, but not too bad. We had to give up playing the Saturday before Thanksgiving for a few years because with 11 teams on the schedule, for some reason, the computer couldn't get that worked out. That will be corrected, though, and we'll be playing them on the Saturday before Thanksgiving in another year.

Talking to Joe Paterno wasn't the only interesting conversation I had back to the mainland when we were in Hawaii. We were having a brunch with the team, and I was sitting down with my three sons and my pals Frank Kelley and Doug Weaver. We were drinking some coffee, reading the papers and keeping an eye on the players going through the buffet.

I saw in the paper that Dick Steinberg was leaving the New England Patriots and going to the New York Jets. A few minutes after that Sally came down to the table and said, "George, can I see you for a minute?" Sally normally won't do something like that. Usually, she just says what she wants to get across, but evidently this was confidential.

I stepped away with her, and she said, "Dick Steinberg just called from the New York Jets, and he wants you to call him." Despite Sally's hush-hush approach, I assumed he called just to talk about some of our players, or maybe he wanted some information about somebody he was considering hiring.

So I went up to the room and called him back, and his secretary said he was in a very important meeting and couldn't be disturbed. I thought that was kind of strange, considering he had just called me. Now he's in a meeting and can't be disturbed? I put two and two together, and I thought he was probably firing Joe Walton even as I was calling back. Maybe he was interested in me?

I went to practice, and when I got back to the room the phone rang. It was Dick Steinberg. He said, "Hi, George. We're going to have a coaching change after the game this Sunday. Would you be interested in talking to me?"

I said, "Yes."

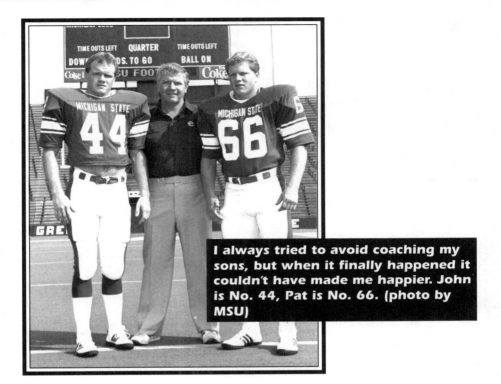

I always tried to avoid coaching my sons, but when it finally happened it couldn't have made me happier. John is No. 44, Pat is No. 66. (photo by MSU)

A handshake meant everything to Jack Breslin, our former vice-president. He was a giant of a man. (photo by MSU)

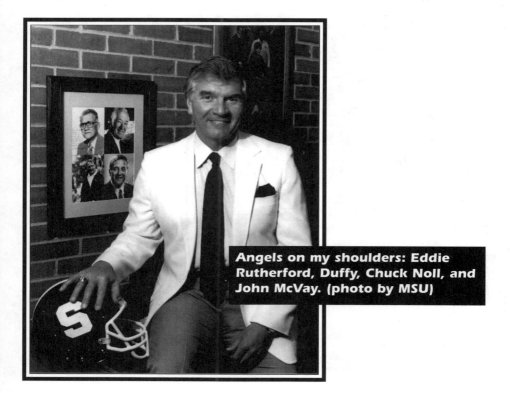

Angels on my shoulders: Eddie Rutherford, Duffy, Chuck Noll, and John McVay. (photo by MSU)

Game Day in East Lansing. The players had to hold my hand to settle me down. (photo by MSU)

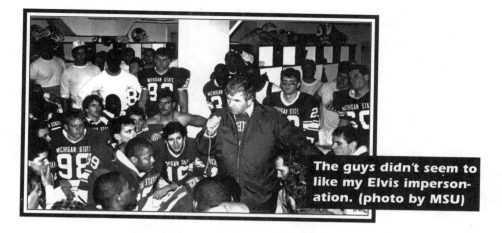

The guys didn't seem to like my Elvis impersonation. (photo by MSU)

But they did like the news we were going to the Rose Bowl. (photo by MSU)

Our facilities were second to none—and I was darned proud of it. (photo by MSU)

In Pasadena, we were determined to have a good time. Mickey, Donald, and Magic helped, and Brent Musburger showed up, too. (photo by MSU)

One of what seemed like hundreds of press conferences in my era.

At the Hancock Bowl, that's Norm Parker's beautiful son Jeffrey wearing the hat and looking up. Jeffrey's one of the reasons the Special Olympics are so important to me.

Lorenzo White (34) and "Gang Green" meant celebration for Michigan State. (photos by MSU)

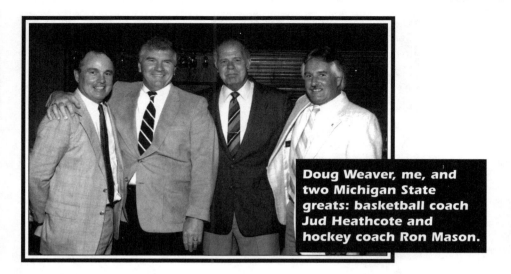

Doug Weaver, me, and two Michigan State greats: basketball coach Jud Heathcote and hockey coach Ron Mason.

Former Governor James Blanchard, former president John DiBiaggio, me, and our escorts at the All-American Bowl in Birmingham, Alabama. DiBiaggio and I were friends at the time.

I was the first to welcome Coach Paterno and Penn State into the Big Ten. (photo by Harrisburg Patriot-News)

Sally and I had an audience with the Pope in Rome, Italy 1990.

Father MacEachin and Duffy, not long before they went to heaven to watch our Rose Bowl season. (photo by MSU)

Spartie—my kind of guy. (photo by MSU)

Merrily Dean Baker and I never hit it off. (photo by MSU)

Joel Ferguson: He was with me a lot of the way but bailed out. (photo by MSU)

Perles family (left to right): my daughter-in-law Amy with grandson Michael, son John, standing behind my mother Nellie and me are my daughter-in-law Tracy and son Terry. On the right is son Pat, Sally, grandson Nick, and my daughter Kathy.

In the beginning we were all on one team. (photo by March of Dimes)

In the end I was on my own.

17

Absurd City

If I loved Michigan State so much, why did I say yes to talking to Dick Steinberg? Gut feeling.

My critics were increasing; nobody seemed happy with where we had gotten the last two seasons after the Rose Bowl. I heard DiBiaggio was calling me "a fat slob" behind my back, and more and more screws seemed to be tightening on our program from above. A new athletic director might want his or her own coach, or maybe DiBiaggio could say "make the football coach's life miserable."

Who knows what could have happened, and maybe I was being paranoid, but I had no sense of security. I'd come all the way from Vernor Highway, worked almost 40 years in the business, only to now stand still and let myself and my family become vulnerable?

Sure I had my contract, but one reason I hadn't worried too much about getting big raises was my annuity. And I still needed a few more years of service to Michigan State to guarantee my annuity, which was our assurance of being able to enjoy our retirement.

With the Jets, I had at least one very special thought: A burning desire to be the first guy to have five Super Bowl rings.

There was another reason I was considering leaving. I couldn't stand the idea of hurting Michigan State, and if there became a confrontation over my job when a new A.D. came in, I knew it would be bad for the university. When Biggie became athletic director and Duffy was coach, it became a terribly uncomfortable situation. And that happened even though Biggie had hired Duffy! I couldn't bear to be in that kind of a situation.

I never suspected what kind of a flap there could be if George the coach just had to get along with George the A.D.

I probably had been spoiled by always being protected by Duffy, Chuck Noll and Doug, and age 55 didn't seem like the time when I wanted to start gambling on pleasing a new boss. So I tried to take the pre-emptive strike, to act before I got acted on.

After I talked to Steinberg, I immediately went to find Doug in the hotel. He said, "I'll go right up and see DiBiaggio." I waited by the elevator while he went up so see DiBiaggio in his room, and then he came down and sent me up. We sat out on DiBiaggio's balcony, and I told him about the Jets situation and I asked what he thought my prospects were for succeeding Doug.

He said, "Well, George, you know I'm not going to have anything to do with this. You'll have to talk to Roger Wilkinson. He's handling all of it." I said, "If I can be athletic director, I won't pursue this at all. I won't even talk to them."

It didn't matter to him. I know I was asking them to cut through the search process. But as our trustee Joel Ferguson pointed out during that time, we had bypassed those affirmative action standards in the past when the need was great enough. And I thought keeping me at Michigan State was important, and so did a lot of people.

I think DiBiaggio considered my approaching him like this to be some kind of blackmail attempt; I considered it good negotiating. After all, he was the one who was supposed to eventually make the recommendation of an athletic director to the trustees. I wanted to be straightforward with him, and you're never going to get anything if you don't ask.

"When Doug Weaver resigned, I was taken aback because he was only going to be 60," DiBiaggio says now. "But nothing had been said to anyone about it, and George approached me at the football banquet and said he was interested in the job. That hit me like a bolt out of the blue. I should have suspected right then that it was a setup here.

"I told George I had no problem with him wanting to apply for the athletic director job but that from my vantage I couldn't see one person doing both and that we wanted an opportunity to consider a spectrum of candidates. The next time I talked to him about it was in Hawaii, and now suddenly he was being recruited by the New York Jets. When he told me about the Jets, I said, 'What the hell is this about? When the Packers offered you the job just two years ago, you said how you love the university so much — and now you're going to leave?'

"He said, 'I just want to know what's going to happen.' And I said, 'George, I just can't tell you.'"

When I walked out of DiBiaggio's room, I felt like this — pfffffft. I know when it's all over. I came down to Doug and said, "This guy doesn't want me around." Then I called Roger back in Michigan, and he gave me the runaround, too. He said, "George, we're going to have a search, and then, blah, blah, blah." So I considered that a double brush-off, and I figured the idea was dead.

Steinberg called again, and I told him that I wasn't going back to Michigan with the team. You couldn't recruit because it was a dead period, so I was going to stay for a few days and relax in Hawaii. It's a lot of work having 250 people that far away from home. Dick was going to be on the West Coast, and I was going to fly home through L.A. So we agreed I'd just get off the plane and not make the connection and meet him there. Doug liked that, too, because he was going to go to the Rose Bowl from Hawaii and wanted to talk to me after I met with Steinberg.

On December 23, CBS-TV's "NFL Today" show reported that I was a top candidate for the Jets job.

So we won the game 33-13, with Blake Ezor really teeing the media off by running for 179 yards and three touchdowns — both Aloha Bowl records. Blake had served his time in jail, and he knew the other discipline he got. But it was going to be his last college game, and I wasn't going to punish him by taking that away.

When I arrived in L.A., it was just infested with Michigan people because they were in the Rose Bowl. There was Michigan stuff all over our hotel, so Sally and I sneaked up to our room and hid out. Steinberg visited briefly, but we were pretty wiped out and agreed to meet for coffee the next morning.

We talked, a good talk about what his team is all about, but there was no offer yet. We got on the plane to go back home, and I told Doug what had happened so far. It was leaked by the time we got back, and there were little blurbs about it all over. I continued my recruiting, and Steinberg called every night for about a week, saying, "What do you think of this guy, Coach?" One time I hung up and I said, "Sally, I haven't even been offered the job, but it sounds like I'm working for the guy. I can't figure it out."

Finally, he called one day and said, "You've got to come to New York. We've got to get this thing figured out." I was supposed to go to Pittsburgh with Steve Furness and Dino Folino to recruit, so I arranged to fly from Pittsburgh to New York. While we were getting ready to fly out of Detroit, I was monkeying around at the airport and someone called an affiliate in Pittsburgh and said I was trying to ditch the press by flying through there. So when we got to Pittsburgh, the media was all over the place. Brother, these guys have unbelievable connections. So I told Dino and Furness to go on recruiting without me, because it was all over TV that I was going to the Jets.

Steinberg picked me up in New York, and we got a bite to eat. Still no offer. The next morning, he picked me up while it was still dark out and we stopped at a doughnut shop on the way to the Jets office. No one else was in when we arrived. Still no offer. Around 9, though, we met with the president of the Jets, Don Gutman. Nice guy.

Dick and I sat on one side of the desk, Don sat on the other and suddenly we were negotiating. They wanted to give me four years, I wanted five — to get vested. As for money, I told them I didn't want to be the highest-paid coach in the league, but I didn't want to play second fiddle to Bill Parcells with the Giants, either. I'd been through that enough with Bo.

We went on for a while, and we were drinking a lot of coffee. One of them got up to go to the restroom, and the other followed him in. They had a meeting. I later went to the restroom—I went by myself—and they had a meeting. I told them I was getting out-meetinged! I joked with them and said, "Hey, I'm being outclassed. You're too good for me. I'm from the Midwest. I can't compete with you guys." So that is at least one good reason why you always should have somebody else come into negotiations on your side. Good lesson.

Well, even with their home-field advantage, we got it to an agreement. They were excited, I was excited, and they called a press conference. We started talking over some of our plans for the team, and the secretary came in with a typed-up piece of Jets stationery.

"Just in case I get hit by a truck or something," Don said, "why don't you sign this to make sure we have a deal?" I wanted to call Michigan State first, and he agreed. He wanted the school's permission, because he was worried Michigan State might sue.

So I went to call Doug to fill him in, but his secretary said he was over at the hospital taking his treadmill test. I felt like I was taking a treadmill test, too. I tried to call Sally, too, but I only got the answering machine. Then I called Roger Wilkinson, and he told me that Larry Owen, the chairman of the board, was in his office. He gave me Larry.

They had had a meeting Sunday night, and I knew they hadn't gotten the votes to make me athletic director. But Larry said, "George, we need one more vote. We've got Kathy Wilbur here, and I think she's going to vote in your favor. Call me back in 45 minutes."

Now I was really fidgeting. The Jets have called the press conference, I've agreed to take the job — and now Michigan State might come through? That was one of the longest 45 minutes of my life, but Dick and I continued to work. When I called back, Larry said, "Pack your bags and come home. We got the vote."

Oh, geez. I told Larry he was going to have to talk to the Jets now. They talked to the Jets and said they wouldn't release me from my contract, but that if for some reason I didn't get the votes for athletic director at the official board meeting they would release me then.

A few months later I found out that Michigan State wouldn't have been able to enforce that. There were some loopholes in the wording of my contract that probably would have made it impossible. But I didn't know that. At the time it was written, I wasn't using an attorney or an agent to get the wording right. I was actually very naive on matters like that, and I was 55 years old at the time.

After the phone call back to campus, it was chaos. The media was right on the other side of the wall of the Jets office; I could hear them rumbling, waiting for the big announcement. The Jets snuck me out the back door, and a young equipment guy took me back to LaGuardia Airport. As I called Sally from the airport, who did I bump into but Charlie Vincent from the *Detroit Free Press*?

He had flown out just to see what was going on, and he spotted me. As long a day as this was, I didn't even look at him as a reporter. I just relaxed and talked to him, and he came along with me while I had a beer in one of the airport lounges. I told him I had to go home and talk to the administration — the *real* administration, Sally. I also told him, "George has never orchestrated anything. . . . George has never made a phone call to anybody."

Charlie wrote that I was "unashamedly corny," which I took as a compliment and I think he meant as a compliment. It was because of that he seemed to think I was going to stay, even though the choice still was mine. He also said I sometimes come across as simple, but not to be fooled by that. I liked that, too.

As I was walking toward my flight, a couple of businessmen recognized me. One said, "Did you take the Jets job?" I said, "No, not yet." He said, "Well, don't. The alumni don't want you to leave." Imagine that, in New York.

It was a little less clear how alumni stood when I got back home. There was tremendous controversy about the situation, about whether the board would try to run over DiBiaggio, so much so that the trustees moved up their meeting from February 2 to January 23.

I thought it would help loosen up some of the tension if I offered to take the A.D. job just for one year and let them evaluate me. If I wasn't doing the job, then I'd step down. And I also made a point of not asking for, or getting, any extra pay for the second job. I was trying to prove that I didn't even want a nickel. I just wanted to be able to provide the service for Michigan State, and to be able to have some more security for myself.

Even so, as much as I tried to water it down, a lot of people stayed up in arms about it. And a lot of people thought if the trustees voted me in against DiBiaggio's objections that he would leave. The *Jackson Citizen Patriot* shared a few points of view.

—"I got four phone calls from major donors asking what these people are doing to our President," said Dee Cook, who was then a university fundraiser. "They said if he leaves, they will withhold their finances."

—"I'm endorsing George for athletic director," said Jud Heathcote, our basketball coach, "because of the need for continuity, the need for understanding of the role of athletics at Michigan State University."

So it was quite a scene at the emergency trustee's meeting in the Lincoln Room at the Kellogg Center. An estimated 350 people crammed in there, probably the most people at an event like that since John Hannah was president during the Vietnam War. Some people were even sitting in windowsills.

Fourteen speakers addressed the board and President DiBiaggio, and 12 of them spoke out against me becoming A.D. while I was still football coach.

"I cannot express my outrage at what the board is about to do here tonight," one student said to them. "It's a slap in the face to affirmative action and to the integrity of this university."

"You have an obligation to the taxpayers of this state not to become an arm of the NFL," another said.

DiBiaggio made his comments, too, at the meeting and in a press release he issued. He brought up that if I were approved, they would have bypassed the affirmative action concept and said it would "jeopardize" Michigan State's credibility and integrity. He also said what he said many times before and since: the two jobs of football coach and athletic director were "separate and distinct."

"It is a matter of principle from which I cannot and will not deviate," he said after the vote. "This is not my view in the area of athletics only. I would feel exactly the same if the dean of one of our medical schools wanted to be vice provost for human health in the same school. There is an inherent need for a formal system of checks and balances in all administrative areas, a system that assures accountability. . . .

"I want it known that I do not consider this action as a personal affront, but as one that in the long run could hurt the university more than the loss of any coach [or] any recruit. . . . I am disappointed that the perceived pressures of the moment were elevated by the long-term benefits."

They also released a statement from me before the meeting — it even said, "7 p.m." on it — that assumed I would be approved. But I wasn't assuming anything. The known votes for me were 4-3 — the four were Larry Owen, Joel Ferguson, Bob Weiss and Malcolm Dade, the three against were Dean Pridgeon, Barbara Sawyer and Tom Reed — and Kathy Wilbur hadn't spoken publicly about where she stood. So everything rested on her. I was watching on TV, in Norm Parker's basement, and the crowd let out a gasp when she said, "Yes."

Kathy Wilbur had been against the idea originally, but to her credit she came to my office to see me a few weeks earlier, just to get to know me a little. I know she was still wrestling with her decision a day or so before the formal vote. She was a Republican who worked for one of our state senators, William Sederburg. The *Detroit News* printed some of the things she said were going through the rumor mill about her vote.

"Some friends called me and said they saw a guy who said he was a friend of a guy sitting next to the governor [Blanchard, a Democrat] when he called your house and said that if you or Tom [Wilbur's husband] wanted to run for the 24th Senate Seat, to go ahead and [Blanchard would] remain neutral — if you voted for Perles," Wilbur said. "Sorry. Absurd City. I mean it's just wild stuff — unless my 3-year-old son Tommy is answering the phone and making all kinds of agreements for us."

She said there was an unbelievable amount of pressure on her, both ways, in terms of phone calls and letters.

"It has totally thrown my family life out of whack," she said. "The other night I was trying to read two bedtime stories to my son and had the phone ring four times during, 'Curious George.' I kept talking to them, thinking I had the responsibility."

But she said she had been able to make a clear decision to vote her conscience by leaving the phone alone, sitting down in a room and making a list of pros and cons. It helped her, too, that the appointment was conditional for one year. She looked at that as a compromise.

Not too many people seemed to look at it as a compromise, though. Sheesh, the reaction was harsh. Like a wildfire. Some students tried to stir up a recall petition against the trustees who had voted for me, but that fizzled out since they needed 600,000 signatures. Booth Newspapers, which owns the *Lansing State Journal*, filed a lawsuit against the school, charging it with violating the Open Meetings Act by having closed-door discussions about me.

Afterwards, there were lots of opinions that weren't too nice. It made me want to add another course to the curriculum I was building. I already wanted to introduce "Common Sense" and "Supply and Demand" to the media. The new one was going to be for me: "Thick Skin 101."

The sentiment I could understand was about how DiBiaggio was being mistreated, and I had compassion for him. That put him in a bind. In a way, the vote for me was the same as a vote of no confidence in him. After that, he had to ask himself whether he was only a lame duck. Still, I don't think he had to be the bad sport about it that he was. He seemed determined not to let it work.

I mean, all of a sudden he started this "athletics are more important than education stuff." Now I'm on the side of athletics over education? That was not true at all. I value education. In my family, we have 11 degrees. Eleven bona fide degrees among six of us.

What I couldn't understand was how everybody was making me out to be an extortionist. I never lied, I never tried to deceive anyone. No question, though, that if I had known all of the repercussions I would have left.

I couldn't blame Steinberg if he thought I was a rat, but I genuinely was ready to enter into the Jets fold. I can only say that when circumstances changed, I changed my mind. From the comments I read of his, he seemed to understand me pretty well.

"You're going to say he used us to get the athletic director's job, but we don't feel that's true," he told the *New York Post*. He also described the scene when I was on the phone with Larry from his office a few days earlier. "When he heard [Owen's] answer, he would have to be one hell of an actor to have the reaction he did. He turned pale, his eyes got glassy. He acted extremely schocked and was almost speechless for several minutes. He didn't know where to go from there."

I also had some nice support from three former MSU presidents: Dr. Hannah, Walter Adams and Edgar Harden. They put together a letter to DiBiaggio and the trustees.

It said: "It is time to move forward — together. As former presidents with a life-long dedication to [Michigan State], we are troubled by the portrayal of recent events as irreconcilable differences among the top policy-makers of the university. . . . We urge the board of trustees, the president and the administration to resolve their concerns cooperatively, including the role of athletics in higher administration."

It was a noble gesture on their part, but I guess almost everybody involved in the whole confrontation probably would say it turned out to be mostly wishful thinking.

Within a few weeks after my appointment, which was to begin on July 1, DiBiaggio announced he was tightening the reins on the athletic department by having the athletic director report now to the provost, the chief academic officer, instead of to the chief financial officer. He did this at his annual "State of the University" address and said the move should "put to rest any concerns loyal Spartans anywhere might have about perceived risks to academic primacy and to accountability." He also made a point of declaring that he had "the responsibility and the authority" to run the entire university.

That was dandy with me. David Scott, the provost, seemed like someone I would enjoy working with.

But there was another development that happened right after the decision that upset me a lot. It almost seemed calculated to happen then. A booster named J.D. Anderson said I had demanded $2,500 in sponsor money from him for my TV show and that I had cut him off from team flights when he didn't pony up. There was even a ridiculous rumor — from "a Michigan State University official" — that there were tape recordings of this supposed incident taking place.

The accusations were sick, totally false and vicious. Obviously, if I were worried about money I wouldn't have turned down a multimillion dollar offer to coach in the NFL so I could do two jobs for the price of one. We bumped him for one simple reason: He was biting the hand that fed him. On our flights he was constantly complaining about our game plans, our choice of plays, about everything. He was a disruptive, negative influence, and I didn't think my assistants or I should have to put up with that garbage.

The administration conducted an internal audit of the matter and found there to be nothing amiss, and nobody ever produced those tapes, either. Another businessman pulled a copycat move a month or so later, saying I was going to cut off any business he had at the university if he didn't sponsor our show. Nasty, and not true. I think he was bitter because he had lost a bid on our championship rings. Nothing ever was proven there, either.

But that probably wasn't the point of either of those capers. It was obvious that every move I made from the time I got the athletic director job was going to be heavily scrutinized. That was fine with me, but I couldn't help but feel people were going out of their way to find trouble.

For instance, an Indiana attorney who was a Michigan State graduate came out in April and said my contract was illegal. It violated a state statute that said state officials can't hold two jobs in which one office supervises another. Now I was considered a state official? If I was a public officer, wasn't a dean who taught a class in the same position? Give me a break.

That March, The *Detroit News* came out with the results of what it said was a two-month investigation of steroids abuse in our program. This in my mind was the payback for my explosion at their reporter in December. They said they interviewed more than 100 people for the story, which didn't prove a thing. Their strongest source who spoke on the record was a former walk-on who quit the team. It quoted him and some unnamed players as saying Mandarich had been a steroids user. But even in their own story it said the walk-on had to take three polygraphs before he had a test that found him truthful in all regards, without qualification.

It also used quotes like this from one former player who had transferred and didn't want his name used: "I felt I couldn't compete. I don't know who was taking what, because I never actually saw anyone, but I assumed they did because a lot of people were really strong."

How do you like that for hard-hitting proof? We had those accusations investigated internally and independently, too, and there was no fallout. Of course, once it was in the paper people assumed it was true. I'll say what I said then. "No. Underlined. Period. N-O." We got better educated about what signs to look for.

I think our players were big and strong, but I think it reflected the emphasis we put on our weight room and a first-class training table program. We were pioneers in the college game in those areas, mostly because of the advanced ideas I had swiped and brought along from the Steelers.

That wasn't the end of the bombardment. Just before I took over as A.D., the *Lansing State Journal* did a story about the money

I was making on my TV show. It's true that Michigan State is one of the few schools in the nation that doesn't have any control over, and receives no profits of its own from the coaches' television shows.

It's true that the school probably should get something from it, since its marketability is based on the connection to the university. It's probably a source of revenue Michigan State should figure out how to tap, and most schools have some stipulations about that in the coach's basic contract.

Whether that structure was right or wrong, though, it didn't seem to be an issue during my first eight years on the job. As far as I know, it wasn't an issue during the previous coaching regimes, either.

That it came up now was just another clear message to me that Big Brother was going to be watching every move I made as athletic director.

But I was excelling in that new course: Thick Skin 101. And I welcomed the attention. I knew I was going to do a lot of good things as athletic director, no matter how little time I had to prove myself.

18

Dual—or Duel?— Citizenship

For all the shots people were taking at Michigan State and me, I thought there actually was very little made of the fact that I didn't have a known background in the job I was about to undertake. Who was I to think I could keep a budget for the entire department, or make personnel decisions on other sports? That was something I did have to prove, even though I knew I could do it. I had all kinds of ideas.

I thought the media would make more of a point about that, but I guess they had too many other fish to fry. Like questioning my integrity, and saying there would be no checks and balances. DiBiaggio kept saying I was going to be my own boss. Not true. I reported to the provost, who then reports to the president. That's not accountability?

"The fox in the hen house," some of them were calling me. That was because of DiBiaggio. "Fox in the hen house." What does that mean? What about, "the bird in the tree?" If you've got something to say, say it. "Fox in the hen house."

That bothered me, because there was no reason to suggest I was less than honest. Nobody could say I didn't work hard and lead a clean life. It was obvious we were running a clean, straight ship. And if you're honest like we had been, there shouldn't be anything to worry about in that way. If you're going to be a thief and a cheater, you would have done it as a coach.

As it turned out, no one could deny I had a knack for the athletic director job. For starters, we made $3.6 million in two years — not many schools even make a profit, and I believe no one else in the Big Ten was in the black in those years. Doug's goal was to make money to save money; my goal was to make money to spend money. And we did, on every sport.

My proudest memories of that time are of raising money so we could help so many people — and then to have at the end a surplus. Big factor, because that gives you a cushion, a chance to get some interest money and keep investing.

I trimmed a lot of fat — we didn't pay the athletic director, for instance — but found ways to build up new revenue and upgrade facilities and take care of our non-revenue sports with increased scholarship budgets. Everybody was happy, and that's how my review came out. Provost Scott, who administered it, considered it favorable to highly favorable. My grade was 77.6, with 55 to 60 considered good.

Not surprisingly under the circumstances, it was the most extensive review they've ever had around Michigan State. They interviewed in confidence 75 people, including the 36 people on the council of deans, and it took them months to get it done.

They don't even put deans through the same grinder when they give them their five-year reviews. They went over everything with a fine-tooth brush, covered compliance issues to finance to academics to external relations. Thorough.

By the time it came out, in late 1991, some of the ground rules had been changed in mid-stream under my nose because it was obvious it was going to be an excellent review. I'll say more about that later, but this is how the review came out:

—"The initiation of staff meetings and departmental meetings has served to implement his commitment to reduce barriers between revenue and non-revenue sports. . . . "

—"In the view of most, Mr. Perles is seen as an entrepreneur who seeks ways to broaden the revenue base to support a more 'all sports' orientation for the department. . . . "

—"Mr. Perles is extraordinarily accessible, even to the extent of interruptions during football practice. . . . "

—"His style is described by most as one of confronting problems, solving the problem and then going on. . . . "

—"Some interviewees expressed surprise at Mr. Perles' rapid comprehension of financial matters within the department and his ability to help design a plan for the financial health of the department. . . . "

—"His ability to listen to and recall vast amounts of new information were frequently cited strengths, while his tendency to and ability to simplify (and perhaps even oversimplify) issues . . . were regarded both as a strength and a potential weakness. . . ."

—"Interviewees commended Mr. Perles for holding high performance standards, for commitment to a team approach within the department and for a willingness to make tough decisions. . . ."

—"In addition to the significant infusion of funding for non-revenue sports, his conversations with [non-revenue coaches] have been helpful in advancing the programs. . . ."

—"Most consider Mr. Perles to be very effective with people, particularly with men and coaches of both genders. He is described as a good listener and a person who signals genuine interest and concern for others. . . ."

—"Most give Mr. Perles very high marks for his effectiveness with minorities. . . . In the view of most, [he] is very willing to take risks on the behalf of students, particularly disadvantaged students."

—"Most agreed that Mr. Perles ensured that the University's procedures were followed. . . ."

—"Most view Mr. Perles as strongly committed to Michigan State University and indicate that his commitment extends beyond the department to the University as a whole. . . ."

—"Some indicate that the controversy surrounding his appointment . . . did not reflect a commitment to the best interests of the University. Critics indicate that he bears the primary responsibility; advocates indicate that the controversy could have been defused if the representatives of the University had chosen to do so. . . ."

—"His efforts to expand academic support, substance abuse programs and training services as part of his priorities for the department were considered to reflect [a] commitment to . . . the quality of the experience of the student-athlete. . . ."

—"Student concern that football would dominate the agenda of the department has dissipated. . . . Positive attitudes of coaches because of resource infusions were cited as having a positive effect on students. Protection of media exposure of students subjected to discipline was generally considered responsible and principled. . . ."

—"Most acknowledged Mr. Perles' historical problems with the media. . . . [But] Mr. Perles apparently is excellent in press conferences with regard to 'quotable quotes' and general give-and-take. . . ."

—"Among his recognized personal strengths are self-motivation and the ability to generate new ideas. Mr. Perles appears to have almost limitless energy and to be prepared to devote extraordinary amounts of time to his work at and for Michigan State. . . ."

There were criticisms in there, too, which I took to heart and thought were useful. For instance, I knew I needed to learn more about working in a "gender-diverse environment." I never really had done it before.

I didn't mind that it said I didn't accept excuses, but I thought I could work on the part where it said when I'm under pressure I get too confrontational. I already knew that about myself, but it was different to see it in print in an objective forum.

"George has one of the top 10 tempers in intercollegiate athletics," Doug Weaver says, laughing. "But George also knows what he's doing. He would never lose his temper if he didn't want to, because he always has a plan."

One other thing about the evaluation: It was leaked early by Joel, before a vote was going to be taken by the trustees on my status. Joel did it because he said he didn't want DiBiaggio twisting things around. DiBiaggio didn't like it and said so in a statement:

"The entire process is jeopardized by the selective distribution of materials to the media, incredibly even before three-fourths of the trustees had seen these documents. Such ill-advised dissemination precludes fairness to trustees, to George Perles, to Provost Scott and to our athletic council."

That statement made me laugh. Fairness? Any chance of that started changing about four months after I started as A.D. in July 1990.

At the November election, Dee Cook and Jack Shingleton were voted in as trustees. Malcolm Dade had decided not to run again, and Larry Owen lost. Cook — remember, she was a high school classmate of DiBiaggio's — and Shingleton — a World War II pilot who really rubbed people the wrong way as an interim A.D. in the '70s — both had made a big deal in their campaigns that the trustees should not have gone against DiBiaggio.

"I felt from the beginning that that was a critical point," Shingleton told reporters after the election. "We had to speak to academics over athletics. We've got to get our priorities so that education comes first. The perception was that athletics was dominating academics on our campus. I think that was a very deciding issue for voters."

Those two coming in for Malcolm and Larry meant that five of the eight board members now would support DiBiaggio. They were swing votes. I still thought we had a deal that I would be evaluated on how I did my job over the course of a year, but something Thomas Reed said on election night should have been a good tip-off that the rug could still be pulled out even if I did get a glowing recommendation.

"If it's the proper procedure for the board to assist the president in that relationship, the board would probably take the president's recommendation. . . . ," Reed, who had voted against me getting the A.D.'s job, told *The Detroit News*. "I don't believe that the board we're about to have seated in January is going to jump into the middle of issues with the president. The president will have to bring it to us in order for us to make a change."

In other words, he was practically giving a cue to DiBiaggio to come up with some new legislation to gum up the works for me as soon as the new board formed in January. And sure enough, in June — just before my one-year anniversary — they came up with a new way to cut my legs off. This is where it became very, very naughty.

In hindsight, if I had known what could have happened, I would have asked that the resolution making me A.D. be worded differently than it was when they put it in on January 23, 1990.

"BE IT RESOLVED THAT, in addition to his head football coaching duties, George J. Perles will assume, with no additional salary, the responsibilities of the Athletic Director position effective July 1, 1990. This arrangement is subject to a one-year review based on criteria to be developed by the administration in consultation with the Athletic Council and approved by the Board of Trustees."

As we were closing in on my anniversary, DiBiaggio started making noise about how this wording meant that the review should include an evaluation of whether one person could have both jobs — not just of how well I was doing them. It doesn't seem to me that the words in the resolution say that, and that didn't come up in the 76 points of criteria they did give me. But I guess the wording didn't necessarily rule that out, either.

But just in case, DiBiaggio came to the June 7 trustees meeting with an amendment that asked the trustees to have Provost Scott judge the appropriateness of one person holding both jobs. The board approved it 6-2, so now my review also was going to include an evaluation of the very idea of having both jobs. That was a dirty gimmick.

Even though we had that resolution, I bet there were plenty of people on campus who held two positions. Some deans teach classes, for instance. How is that any different than the position I was in? Simple: They're not in the public eye.

I had an attorney, Donald Reisig, make a presentation to the board the day they approved DiBiaggio's proposal. He pointed out that these new evaluation guidelines were being brought up 18 months after I'd been named A.D., and just three weeks before my evaluation was due. He closed by making a pretty articulate appeal for fairness to them.

"I suggest that this is not the time to play out the pathos of some Greek drama or some Shakespearean tragedy," he said. "Rather, it is the time for people of integrity to put aside ego, petty past grievances and turf issues and to effectuate a permanent solution."

I don't think they heard a word he said.

So now they worked on evaluating the dual job, a task that at the time only two or three others were performing. There wasn't really a whole lot to study, in my opinion. But here was the essence of the other part of my review, which really was not of me personally but of the idea of a dual arrangement:

It may have advantages in the short term, but not for the long term.

Gee, what a surprise that they came up with that. After that, of course, the skids were greased for them to be able to get their ducks lined up to get me out.

The silly thing is, they got so caught up in the politics of it that there was no common sense involved. We had made a wheelbarrow full of money that first year, and football hadn't suffered at all. In fact, we had the best season since our Rose Bowl year.

Whew, was I glad when that season began, too. Those offseasons always seem to knock the heck out of me. I needed to be in the thick of things I could touch and feel and do, and the last few months had been really draining since there was so much sniping going on and I wasn't really in a position to act much.

That tired me out more than being busy in the fall. Once the A.D. job kicked in in July and football started in August, I was constantly on the go. I was getting up earlier and going to sleep later, but so what? That's what I signed up for, and my only hobbies are work and family.

After our 1-2-1 start — maybe those starts came from my exhibition game habits in the NFL, I don't know — we beat Michigan 28-27. They went for two on the last play of the game, and there was a lot of controversy over whether their receiver had been held in the end zone. He dropped it, anyway, and that wasn't because of any holding.

So we won, and that started us off on winning six of our last seven and got us a piece of the Big Ten championship. But we lost out on the Rose Bowl because of the tie-breaker and we went to the Hancock Bowl.

The Hancock people were tickled to death, because they knew when they got us they were going to get Southern Cal, too. Larry Smith really wanted a piece of us after we'd beaten them twice in our Rose Bowl season, but we beat them again 17-16.

The athletic director business probably was going even better, probably because I had all kinds of people there to prop me up and make me look good and since I inherited something that was already in great shape. You couldn't have had any better people than Clarence Underwood, Peggy Brown, Don Loding, Charlie Wilson and Gus Ganakas. You don't always have that chance when you take over a job in athletics.

Even so, I was still surprised at how well it was going. But there was a big factor in how I did it. Instead of sitting on my duff before I took over, I spent a couple of hours of every day of the six months before Doug left sitting in his office with him. Sometimes I read, sometimes I listened to his phone conversations, sometimes I did nothing but watch him. I'd get on another phone line and listen in when he was negotiating.

It was, to me, the most ideal way to take over a program. This way, I could be groomed for the job and not miss a stroke. No one probably ever had a chance to get tutored for a job like that like I did. Doug was very smart, had good instincts and had been there for 10 years. There was a lot to be learned from him, and I think he knew how much I admired him from the way I followed him around. One day he said to me, "You're riding this horse right into the ground, aren't you?"

I had a lot of priorities I wanted to address immediately, and one of them was making sure the people in non-revenue sports felt appreciated. They really are appreciated, but sometimes their jobs might seem thankless because football, basketball and hockey get so much attention. The thing you have to understand about them is that it really doesn't take a lot to make them happy, because they're so used to getting leftovers. When our women's basketball team played in the NCAA Tournament in 1991, I called our coach, Karen Langeland, within minutes of the game ending. She really appreciated that, and I think they all knew my attitude was sincere.

"All the coaches are real happy," our men's swim coach Richard Brader told The Associated Press in July 1991, "and I think they're happy because they see somebody who A), wants us to do well, B), is going to do whatever he can to make sure we do well and, C), he is backing up what he said he was going to do."

I wanted to let them know I cared about them and would do everything I could to increase their budgets and address their concerns. So I met one-on-one with all 22 of them before I even started the job, heard their wish lists, and I let them know I'd be allocating more funds for them as soon as we started generating the money. I meant it, too. For instance, I immediately earmarked the entire $100,000 net revenue from the Hancock Bowl to non-revenue sports.

Of course, if we didn't generate the money I would have been making promises I couldn't keep. So I went right to work on that. The first move there I actually made before I even got offered the job: no salary for me. I didn't need it, anyway, and I didn't want to destroy the budget by paying another salary. So that was a start. We also made it clear that the budgets for each sport weren't meant to be guidelines. They were rules. Everybody was going to get more than they had, but they were going to have to live within that.

Then we got to the fun part: raising money. We had to be alert and aggressive in this area, or we could get swallowed up.

The days of getting financed by a university general fund or by the legislature were long gone. We had to be creative. Football was bringing in 75 percent of the department's revenue, but we couldn't just depend on that or get complacent. The writers liked to say I had a lot more imagination in my A.D. playbook than I did in my offensive one. It kind of teed me off, but they were probably right.

The best thing we did was with the scoreboards. We needed new scoreboards for football and hockey that we normally would have had to pay for. Instead, we paid nothing for them and got a five-year, $125,000-a-year commitment from each of six sponsors who wanted their names on the boards there and in the Breslin Center. That was a $3.5 million deal.

We accepted bids on an all-sport radio contract. We took bids, had presentations. That's what you do in business. Before, we had been bringing in about $85,000 and going out on seven stations in basketball and 22 for football. The new contract was comprehensive, put us up to 44 stations in basketball and more than 50 in football. Now we could be heard all over the state. Oh, and the new contract brought in $400,000.

We took our game programs, which were losing money, and made them better and sold them for $3 instead of $2 — and had a $90,000 turnaround there in one year. We sold trading cards. We advertised an 800 number to make football and basketball games available to alumni all over the country.

We put in a Hall of Fame, put in a no-smoking policy at Spartan Stadium, renovated the outdoor track, remodeled Jenison Field House, got a new bulkhead for the pool at the Intramural Building, hired John Breslin in the new position of marketing coordinator, hired Clarence Underwood to be in charge of compliance . . . and so on.

There were plenty of other ideas, too, that we either ran out of time for or they put the kibosh on. I was going to build 48 skyboxes — two decks, 24 in a row — across from the press box and suites in Munn Arena. That would have led to a $20-30 million profit over the next 30 years, with no financial risk. It would have been a turnkey operation, with no money from us up front. The construction company was even going to spend $60,000 to do a feasibility report.

We would have realized a profit of $500,000 a year, and the rest of the money would have gone to pay off our partners over a 30-year period. Then everything would be owned by Michigan State, free and clear. The company also would have renovated our embarrassing locker rooms, which had toilets that were obsolete by 50 years, and lowered the field, giving us an extra 10 rows of quality seats.

That's the kind of deal I like, where you get facilities, make revenue and don't have to put anything up. We didn't have to borrow, we didn't have to go into hock. It was a dynamite plan. But David Scott didn't want to do it. I guess they thought it was too big of an operation and didn't want to bite it off. And now they're lowering the field and having to use their own money to do it.

We also had a plan — another Ken Hoffman idea — to build a satellite office in Detroit. Bring Michigan State to the metropolitan area. Sell season tickets there, sell shirts and other paraphernalia there, have a conference room there. It would give us a tremendous presence in Detroit, where we have a great number of advertisers, media outlets and the greatest number of MSU alumni and friends, and we'd stop being prisoners of our own campus.

Our radio station would have rented half of it, and our bookstore would have rented half, so the athletic department would have had a free office. That was the game plan. I also wanted to get a code of conduct put in for all Michigan State athletes. But we couldn't get either of those OK'd by the administration, either.

It could be frustrating to deal with those kinds of setbacks. Football coaches aren't used to dealing with waiting for answers from committees, let alone committees on top of committees on top of committees.

Even with all this going on, DiBiaggio couldn't appreciate any of it. He must have been too bitter. About the only time he spoke out during this time was after there were a few athletes and a wrestling coach arrested in a period of a few weeks. Those types of incidents were always hard for me, because about the only bases you can't completely cover are the social aspects and free time.

"Obviously there are some problems at MSU, and we have to address them," he told the *Lansing State Journal* in April 1991.

He made a point of saying he didn't blame me, but then he made that into kind of a backhanded slap: "At the same time, it's clear that the job of athletic director and head football coach are too much for one person. I've said that all along."

And he wasn't going to stop saying it, no matter what the evidence showed.

19

Separate and Distinct

Now it gets really strange and sticky. While my evaluation was going on, we started the 1991 season with a 20-3 loss to Central Michigan.

I was advised by a lot of people, Bo Schembechler one of them, that when you play someone like that you really have nothing to gain and everything to lose. But I thought we had a lot to gain, especially looking at it from my athletic director's office.

There was going to be a financial payoff, because when you play one of the smaller schools usually you give a gate guarantee that's a lot less than you would split with one of the powerhouses like Notre Dame. So already we're making more money off the game. And when you play a smaller school from nearby, they're so excited about the idea of coming in and making their season by upsetting you that they're going to bring in lots of fans and enthusiasm.

I also had great compassion for the state of Michigan, and I thought it would be neat to keep the pre-game meals, the travel, the hotels — all the money and ceremony — in our own great state. That was better for both schools than going halfway across the country to play a nonconference game. So I thought there was something in it for the state, and for both schools.

And there was another factor, and maybe I was a sap for letting myself think about this part: I thought a great school like Central Michigan should have an opportunity to come in to try to knock us off. That's the kind of thing that makes college football, or any other competition, memorable and great. The chance for the underdog to take on Goliath and win.

Having said that, though, I have to make a confession: Never in my wildest dreams did I think they would beat us, and that's where this thing backfired. Had we won the game, it would have been a good game plan. But since we went out and played without any emotion and they played at the height of their emotions, it equaled an embarrassing defeat.

I took a lot of heat for that, and I have only myself to blame. Maybe I should have listened and not played someone so close to home in the nonconference, but I swear I probably would do the same thing again. And it was even worse when they beat us again the next season 24-20. That was the absolute low point of my games at Michigan State.

As for the low point otherwise, well, I was about to get into the middle of that soup.

For one thing, we had a lousy season. When we got off to a bad start — 0-5 this time — we never could quite get it turned around. I've always found the two hardest things to handle in life are great success and great adversity.

I sat at speaker's tables and took my bows when we won, which we did in our conference second only to Michigan in Big Ten games from 1987-90, so now I was willing to take my lumps when we lost. It was just one of those cycles, and there's nothing you can say that makes it better.

When you lose, there's no justification. The worst thing a coach can do is try to rationalize it somehow. "We've got injuries. We've got this. We had that." There's no pointing the finger, and there are no excuses. You just take your medicine. Whatever is coming, you just take it and eat it.

But I ached for the players, who are too young to be able to put that in the same perspective.

"When you're winning, you have friends you've never heard of," our tailback, Tico Duckett, told reporters. "When you're losing, you find out who your friends are."

But the losing was just part of the landscape. The other part that kicked me in the gut was the final clash about my dual jobs. Did the two jobs have anything to do with our losing? No, we managed pretty well the year before. I do think the controversy and distractions had an effect, though, and those came to a loud head at the end of November.

By then, the athletic director evaluation had come out — favorable toward me, unfavorable toward one man having both jobs. David Scott made his formal recommendation — that I quit coaching to be A.D. — to DiBiaggio, who announced that I had to give up one of the jobs. Period.

Well, OK, I had been doing some thinking, and I was ready to let go of football and be athletic director. It had never been my thought to do both for an indefinite period of time; I just wanted to be A.D. to ensure stability and continuity when Doug left.

I wasn't tired of coaching, but it seemed like I'd had it all in coaching. Everything was a repeat, there was so much controversy on our campus and it seemed like it might be time. What was the difference, anyway, if I was helping kids directly on the field or if I was helping everybody else help the kids? I wanted to coach one more season, and have a search to replace myself with a new coach at the end of that season.

I thought that would make for a smooth transition, and I was already considering people like Henry Bullough, Nick Saban, Charlie Baggett and Morris Watts. It would have been a beautiful situation to be A.D. and to get that going. This is how my attorney and I wrote it in a letter to DiBiaggio on November 14, 1991:

"I believe that we would both agree that the controversy over my dual appointment has been unnecessarily divisive. I believe we would also both agree that it is time to put this issue to rest. Although I have greatly enjoyed both the achievements and challenges of serving as Michigan State University Head Football Coach, I never envisioned remaining in a dual capacity on an ongoing basis. Therefore, by way of final resolution of this issue, please be advised that I am prepared to continue my role as Michigan State University Athletic Director while resigning my duties as Head Football Coach effective December 31, 1992. This 'lead time' provides us the opportunity of ensuring an orderly succession and continuation of our football program."

But there were a few glitches with taking just the A.D. job.

I had a contract for football, and I wasn't going to give that up. The football contract had six years left, and they were only offering me 3 1/2 years as A.D. So now I would lose my outside income, which would have been fine if it were all I'd lose, and they were also going to cut into my annuity — my security. They said they would still guarantee me some kind of employment even if they didn't retain me after 3 1/2 years, but that seemed like a sketchy idea to me. I would have accepted the A.D. position if they had just crossed out "football coach" on my contract and replaced it with "A.D."

There was no way I wanted anything to do with that otherwise. To be honest, I didn't think I could trust them unless I was protected by a precise contract. I think I'd been burned by not getting some contract matters more clear in the past, and I thought they might be setting me up. If they got me from six years to 3 1/2 years, what was to keep them from trying to get rid of me in a year and a half? So I didn't want to budge on any of that.

DiBiaggio also was looking to make another power move: He was planning on asking the trustees at their December 6 meeting to be given the personal power — "total delegation," he called it — to hire not only the athletic director but the football, men's basketball and hockey coaches. He said having that clout was not a matter of opinion, but a necessity for proper management of the university.

Shoot, I wonder why he stopped there? Anyway, that obviously meant that even if I could get my contract converted, I wasn't going to be able to have anything to do with the next coach — or who knows how many other decisions an A.D. normally would make.

So then what would you need an athletic director for, exactly? You'd have one guy doing two jobs, which is exactly what DiBiaggio was objecting to with me. Oddly enough, that whole idea also reminded me a little of what DiBiaggio used to have to deal with with our board: being hired to manage something, then having others above you step in on your authority. In some ways, DiBiaggio and I went through a lot of the same problems.

Even so, I didn't exactly feel close to him or sympathetic. And I had a lot of reservations about becoming just A.D. with those terms thrown into the mix.

It seemed to me at this point that DiBiaggio had become almost obsessed with me, like getting me out was some kind of quest for him. Peter Secchia, the ambassador, is still my good friend and for a long time was close to DiBiaggio. He thinks DiBiaggio became very jealous of me, and he thought it was unfair that DiBiaggio made it sound like I was using Michigan State for leverage when DiBiaggio was known to talk to people about other jobs, too.

"When DiBiaggio looked in the mirror, he saw a cross between Mahatma Gandhi and Sylvester Stallone," Secchia says. "But he hurt this university, and . . . by the end all he wanted to do was publicly humiliate George."

Peter thinks DiBiaggio didn't like that I was making more money than him, or that I'd gotten an annuity and the board didn't get him one. I know DiBiaggio hated all the outside income opportunities coaches get, like the TV show, shoe contracts and other endorsements.

I remember Terry Denbow, DiBiaggio's spokesman, joking that DiBiaggio should talk to Gucci about a shoe contract, or that he could hold a summer fantasy camp where kids would learn how to walk around in little three-piece suits and little attaché cases.

Maybe those weren't bad ideas. His "President" camp might not have done as much business as one of our football camps, but maybe it would have done enough to tide him over.

Anyway, apparently there was a misunderstanding in our discussions in November. Because the next thing I knew, I stopped in at the House of Ing for some take-out Chinese food on my way home from work and I heard on WJR radio that I was giving up football to be A.D. for the next 3 1/2 years.

Suddenly, it was on ESPN, on the wire services, it was all over the country. Son-of-a-gun, I couldn't believe it. It was a big blunder on their part.

The university — not sports information, but the overall publicity department — had put out a news release that was worded in a vague and misleading way. It said that DiBiaggio was ready to begin a search for a football coach. The A.P. story that moved said, "Perles apparently wasn't given a choice of positions, and the only decision is whether to hold onto the A.D.'s job alone." I know DiBiaggio's quotes in the story were right:

"I have considered such a dual appointment inappropriate from the start. The jobs are separate and distinct and a mistake was made when they were joined over my objections."

I made some phone calls and got some of the confusion cleared up that night, but we addressed the matter more the next day. DiBiaggio stuck with the terms he had given, and that left me with no real choice. But I didn't want to get into a lot of questions and answers about it then, because we had a game against

Illinois the next day and I had a few alternatives I wanted to think over.

There was a twist to the timing of playing Illinois, because it was another of the few schools where the coach and the A.D. were the same man. But for some reason there was never any trouble about it for John Mackovic. Hooray for John, a good man and a good coach.

I had a game to coach, not to mention a department to manage, and I didn't appreciate the distraction. I mean, couldn't it have waited until the next week, when our season would have been over? As a matter of fact, couldn't it all have waited until after the season? It wasn't my fault the evaluation came out four months late.

I normally can ignore any distraction, but this was such a constant that I'm sure it affected the team. It wears you down after a while. I'm not saying we would have been 10-1 without all this mess, but I bet we wouldn't have been 3-8. It would have been interesting, too, to see if they would have been able to get me out if we had gone 10-1.

So all I did was clear up that I hadn't been fired as coach and that I would consider what to do next. Originally, I thought I'd try to stick both out. Let them come in and move me out. I thought the law would be on my side if I took legal action for breach of contract, and I considered taking it to court. I even went as far as to have the papers drawn up for a "wrongful termination" suit. It was never released, but part of what it said was:

"Throughout his first year, Perles served as Athletic Director under the reasonable belief that his performance would be evaluated under the Original Criteria. Perles' diligent performance of his duties as Athletic Director has been to the complete satisfaction of all the Original Criteria. . . . Regardless of Perles' performance as Athletic Director, DiBiaggio . . . has never supported the concept of Perles serving [both positions]."

DiBiaggio proposed additional criteria, the suit added, on the eve of my review. "The Original Criteria measure Perles' individual performance as Athletic Director and have been fully satisfied. The Additional Criteria do not address the merits of Perles' individual performance but rather question the propriety of one individual serving as both. . . .

"Adoption of the Original Criteria and Perles' good faith performance and reliance upon the Original Criteria throughout his first year of service bars Michigan State by estoppel [the prevention of a person from making an affirmation or a denial because it is contrary to a previous affirmation or denial that person has made] from adopting material and significant amendments to the performance criteria immediately prior to Perles' review or terminating Perles as Athletic Director on the basis of such Additional Criteria."

Whew, got that? That's the way lawyers say, "My client got railroaded." But after they drew that up, I didn't feel like pursuing it. And I later brought up the idea of binding arbitration over our differences. I mean, keep in mind that one of the reasons it had all come to this was because the trustees wouldn't release me to the Jets to make me A.D. — they even made that the second part of their resolution to make me A.D. in 1990:

"BE IT FURTHER RESOLVED the Board of Trustees does not release George J. Perles from his employment contract as Head Football Coach at Michigan State University, nor does it grant George J. Perles permission to accept employment with the New York Jets . . . or grant permission to the New York Jets to hire Mr. Perles."

Then I got an excellent job review . . . and they took the job away from me? Something definitely smelled there.

But I let go of the arbitration idea, too. It all had gotten so ugly, there was so much bad blood, anyway, that even though they did some things I didn't think were legal — or respectful — it was crazy to keep hammering away.

I was going to stick up for myself like any human being, but enough was enough. It was like the rabbit that goes on and on and on — the Energizer bunny. The whole scene had damaged Michigan State, and even though I was acting on my principles I was just sick of all the fallout.

So on November 29, it was announced that I would just be the coach.

There was an interesting development when the Board met on December 6. By a 6-2 vote, they ratified DiBiaggio's decision to force me to choose between jobs. But they didn't approve his request to have final say on the hiring of coaches and the athletic director. Too bad.

I was supposed to stay on as A.D. until we appointed a new one, and just to see what would happen I put my name in for consideration to the search committee. But Roger Wilkinson told me that they didn't feel comfortable interviewing me under the circumstances. Fair enough. I like when people are straight with me like that.

Joel Ferguson and Bob Weiss, the only two remaining board members who had voted for me to be athletic director in 1990, complained publicly about the committee declining to interview me. As usual, Joel spoke out and said the committee wasn't interested in what was best for Michigan State but was just carrying out some political game. He wanted to break the committee up and start over.

During this time, I heard from and spoke with the Indianapolis Colts. It wasn't out of anger, because I always listen, but I just wondered whether I should just get the heck out of East Lansing. I met twice with the general manager, Jim Irsay, and once with the owner, Bob Irsay, Jim's father. But it never really got serious with them, and Ted Marchibroda got the job. I have no idea whether I would have taken it if I'd gotten the offer. I don't like to play "what if?"

Meanwhile, the finalists for the Michigan State A.D job were: Merrily Dean Baker, who had been the NCAA assistant executive director for administration, Debbie Yow, the athletic director at St. Louis University; Clarence Underwood, who was my associate A.D.; Eastern Michigan A.D. Gene Smith; Washington State A.D. Jim Livengood and Iowa State A.D. Max Urick. Debbie Yow withdrew from consideration near the end because she was getting too much press.

The committee was supposed to rank the candidates for our provost, David Scott, who would make his recommendation to DiBiaggio. Unless he had some reason to disagree, DiBiaggio would present that recommendation to the board for the final approval.

I would like to have seen Clarence get the job. He had a good reputation around the Big Ten, and he would have given us continuity. Everybody would have been on the same page. Instead, they hired Merrily, whose agenda was along the lines of what DiBiaggio wanted: more emphasis on gender equity, while de-emphasizing sports in general.

They named her in April and she came in in May. After deciding I was going to keep my mouth shut about everything, I kind of blew it right away with her. The day she was hired, I said something like, "I'll be watching her." She didn't like that so much and just said she'd be keeping her eye on me, too.

But I didn't have any real problem with Merrily until a couple weeks later, when she tried to get Larry Bielat fired. Not re-assigned — fired. Larry and I had been together many, many years, from our days as undergraduates to St. Ambrose to the Philadelphia Stars and back to Michigan State. Without Larry's friendship, I probably would have missed my father's funeral.

The first time I had met Merrily or the other finalists was in the interview. Jud Heathcote, our basketball coach, and Ron Mason from hockey and I were supposed to talk to each candidate. I think David Scott set that up because it was crucial for the whole department that the revenue sports continue to be able to work together like they had under the leadership of Doug Weaver and then myself.

I had a few questions for each candidate, but the one greatest concern I had was that whoever came in wouldn't hurt anyone by coming in and making moves before they had a chance to evaluate them. That was all I asked, that the people in the department would have a chance to prove their ability. So what happened? Two weeks after she was here, Merrily notified me that she was not going to renew Larry's contract.

Larry was doing a fine job in facilities, and he certainly deserved a chance to be evaluated for a year after all his service. I understood that a new athletic director has to have people working with them that they want to work with, so I asked her if she couldn't find another spot for him. I literally begged her not to do this to Larry. In my opinion, she looked at him as just an old football coach who didn't have any other ability.

Fortunately, I was visiting with one of our former presidents, Gordon Guyer, at a recruiting party, and he thought Larry could be an asset in our alumni office. And he has been.

But I never got over that with Merrily. That's the reason that at times I didn't show as much compassion for her as I could have, and I wasn't as cooperative with her as I could have been. If I could have done that all again, I'd like that whole situation eliminated: the idea of me saying I'd be watching her, eliminated;

the idea of Merrily firing Larry, eliminated; and the idea of me not being cooperative with Merrily, eliminated.

I'm sure Merrily never understood me — maybe I'm not that easy to understand. Her time at Michigan State was pretty rough in a lot of ways, especially since DiBiaggio hired her and then left her hung out to dry by resigning a day later. DiBiaggio should never have done that to her, or he should have taken her with him to Tufts. It would have been different if the situation wasn't as complex and nasty as it was, or if we weren't talking about one of the first women to become an athletic director. That had built-in problems, I'm sure.

It ended for Merrily only a few weeks after it did for me. She resigned over the winter, less than three years after she took the job.

I called her the day after she resigned, because I cared about her. Merrily is a good person, and Merrily had a tough act to follow. Even though we had our differences, my motive never was to see her forced out. It's one thing to argue and debate and not be on the same page with someone, but it's too extreme when it costs someone her livelihood.

20

The Rubik's Circle

In case anybody misunderstands, I believe Michigan State University is a wonderful institution. My entire life has been influenced by my experiences there, my entire life has revolved around the people I met there and I could never fully express my gratitude for what the school did for a kid off Vernor Highway.

But there's no doubt that it is a very political atmosphere in East Lansing, which I'm sure makes it the same as most colleges. It may be strange that there's so much bickering in these places that exist for the noble purpose of helping raw kids become educated adults, but I guess there's a lot of turf out there to be had — and a lot of people who think they have a claim to it.

You could blame a lot of people, myself included, for the way it got out of hand in the last few years at Michigan. On the other hand, maybe nobody's to blame.

Everybody involved probably thought they were right, and everybody involved probably had good principles behind their actions. Everybody involved probably took things too personally, and everybody probably could have been more sensitive to others.

How did it get the way it did? In my mind, you could point to any number of places.

How about when we changed presidents in 1985? Not because DiBiaggio was the guy who took over, but just because now my boss hadn't hired me. Maybe he didn't want me around. Maybe he wanted to bring in his own guy — that would have been his right — but didn't feel like he could. That's never a good situation, because you really don't know how the new boss feels about you until there's some kind of test.

Or how about after I got offered the Green Bay job? That's a good one. The annuity really teed DiBiaggio off. You don't have to be a rocket scientist to look at the Jets situation as the one that really busted the camel's hump. But how much of a difference did it make when two trustee seats changed? It was everything.

The point is it was all pretty tricky, how it got to be such a sticky web. And all of that was stuff that happened beyond what can usually happen anywhere:

When you get into a new job, you've got 10 percent of the people with you just because they're your colleagues, your good friends or fans — and you've got 10 percent against you because of your nationality, your name or maybe you're replacing somebody that they liked. But the majority of the people, 80 percent, are in the middle. And every year more of them move out of the middle into liking you or disliking you. You might have stepped on a toe, not invited someone to a get-together or forgotten someone's name. Maybe they don't like your play selection. Or maybe they really come to like you, because you win or they think you're a friendly, funny guy, or they think you have character.

Who knows what can make someone think about you a certain way? You have no control over that. But after a decade, one thing's for sure: There aren't many people left in the middle. They all either like you or dislike you. Frank Kelley will tell you, on the best day of his life 51 percent of the people like him.

So when you have success, you'd better make sure you don't think you're always going to be riding that horse. That rainy day isn't far away, and we all have them.

You've heard plenty of my ideas about what happened, and what happens, at Michigan State. Who's right? Who's wrong? Who's to say? But to be fair I wanted to give some of the other people on the inner circle close to the situation a chance to talk about it all, generally and specifically. I was interested in what they had to say.

DOUG WEAVER, former athletic director: "I think that part of the reason that this institution is so great and became so great also is part of the reason it's so hard to work there in athletics. I don't mind saying that, and I played here, coached here, had all my kids go here and I was athletic director here. I don't like people saying they love Michigan State more than me — that's like saying, 'Mother loves me more than you,' or 'I love you more than you love me.' It is a marvelous place.

"But it's hard to work here. It's a school of the people, it came up the hard way — and late in this state — and there is tremendous political involvement in all decisions made. That's one reason we get such neat support from the legislature, but it's the same reason we are one of the most open athletic societies — as well as one of the most used athletic departments by all sides of the political spectrum. . . .

"When people asked me what the hardest part of my job was, I'd say, 'Keeping control.' I don't think Michigan State ever would have gotten where it has if it didn't have this pot stirring all the time. But I can tell you this: It ain't easy being in the middle of the pot. . . .

"[So many people] feel that they rightfully have enough of a vested interest that they should be able to exert influence. That includes the university presidents, the trustees, legislature, businessmen, students, alumni, the press. But without the support of those elements that led to the excesses, we wouldn't have achieved what we have as an institution.

"I think it's too late to change. I don't think we're going to put Humpty Dumpty together again. But that doesn't make me cynical about it. It's always going to be a dynamic, marvelous, wonderful institution that will always have difficulty having completely consistent athletic programs, because it's too late to stop all those elements from trying to exert themselves upon it.

"At times, of course, different athletic directors will have different powers and may be able to regulate it better. But the trend right now is for college presidents to be super-athletic directors. Maybe in 10 years that will change, and we'll go back to letting the athletic directors be like department chairman, or deans. . . .

"A friend once gave me some advice on all this. He said the only thing to remember in college athletics is . . . it's madness. Once you understand that, you can handle anything. But the people who don't understand that, they'll just go nuts. If anyone would have told them in 1845, or 1857 or whenever this stuff started, that it would have ended up like this [financially] . . . That doesn't make it bad — but it's nuts. It's not like anything else."

MERRILY DEAN BAKER, former athletic director: "I see an institution that has subordinated its values to politics. There are some major institutional problems because of that, and I think that institutional values have got to be recaptured . . . in order for the place to operate the way it should and, in fact, the way it's capable of operating. . . .

"People with petulantly political agendas have been allowed to prevail. I suspect it's a pattern that will continue to prevail until or unless someone says, 'Wait a minute, this is damaging this place enough.' Until then, you'll have individuals with either real or perceived power trying to manipulate and intimidate, and if others don't stand up to that, they will be allowed to prevail. . . .

"In some cases, there's a certain urbanity or civility on college campuses. So if you have individuals come into that environment who are hyper-political and manipulative and less than genuine, there can be abuse. . . .

"I think it's beyond a turf war, because a turf war normally is someone fighting for his or her piece of the pie. These were people fighting for personal egos and self-serving agendas, not simple turf. I did not come in here naive to the realities; I knew of the chaos. What I did not know was that the president who hired me was going to leave the first day I was here. No question, I wouldn't have come if I had known that, even if I learned it as little as a week before. As the first woman coming into that position here, there is no way on God's green earth I would have done it if I had known I would be without that support.

"I had a football coach who had previously been both athletic director and coach and had wanted to remain as athletic director. He [and DiBiaggio had differences], John DiBiaggio hired me, so by default I became George's enemy. [Trustee] Joel Ferguson looked at me the same way, and they were buddies who wanted someone else to get the job.

"So they weren't about to accept my appointment with equanimity, and [Ferguson] started undermining me before we even met. All of these things were triggered by John DiBiaggio leaving. Had he remained, he would not have allowed it to happen and, secondly, there would have been no reason for them to perpetrate them.

"With him leaving, they figured the easy way to get what they wanted was to chase this woman out. Well, this woman didn't want to be chased out.

"But it was impossible for me to manage, too, because people on my staff were allowed to be openly insubordinate — and I was refused the right to get rid of them. . . .

"I don't know what you would call my relationship with George. . . . I think George Perles came into my life, and I came into his life, at a time when it was not one of his hours of strength. So the only George Perles I know is one who was fairly insufferable as a human being. I've heard there's a different guy, and there were moments where I thought I saw that different guy. I think George would say that his personal choices during this time were not what he would uphold as, 'This is who I am.' . . .

"I hope I don't come out bitter because of all this. I don't think I will, because it's not my nature. I won't hang on to it, because who suffers but the one who hangs on? I was unable to accomplish all the things I wanted to accomplish at what could be a great institution. It was due to circumstances beyond my control, so I don't feel guilty about that. Actually, whether it was other people's fault or mine is irrelevant. I wasn't able to do it, and I will always have a little bit of regret about that. But I'm going to greener pastures. Life's too short to put up with all that, quite frankly.

"When I left, I told the president [Peter McPherson] that he must keep the politics from subordinating values and, No. 2, you've got to let the athletic director do their job. If he or she screws up, fire them. But you've got to let them do their jobs. This micro-management has to end. And No. 3, you've got to let the next athletic director clean house. Because until that happens, there will be no changes.

"Michigan State has such enormous potential, and so many talented people around. I believe that it can be a shining star, but people have to stop tripping over themselves. ... The most frustrating thing for me was that the very people who proclaim the greatness of the place are the ones who are building the walls that prevent greatness from occurring. Why would you tear down what you proclaim to love? It doesn't make sense."

JOHN DIBIAGGIO, former president: "It's all behind me now. I don't really want to get back into it. But the real issue was never George Perles. He was really insignificant in the matter. The real issue is the board of trustees' imposition on the administration.

"It started earlier with a few other appointments where the board questioned me and wanted to be involved and I said no. . . . John Hannah once told me that the biggest mistake he ever made was having elected trustees. I really believed in the place, but it became a tragedy; it was the worst situation imaginable.

"As for George and the athletic director job, I didn't see then and don't see now how a person can report to himself. And he was never interviewed by anyone regarding his ability to actually perform the job of athletic director. When the trustees voted to give him the job, that, in essence, was out of their purview. They said it was on a one-year basis, but that was ransom. It was almost conspiratorial, because some of them didn't like the fact I was standing on principle. . . .

"When the board had changed to one that supported me and decided to make George's jobs separate and distinct, I tried to concede any place I could. I told him I would protect his annuity, even if he didn't fulfill his terms. . . .

"Contrary to popular opinion, I did not make the decision to hire Merrily Dean Baker. My style is to delegate authority and responsibility, and she was David Scott's recommendation. But I didn't know I was going to leave then, either. I had met with [a board member] that spring and asked if they would consider giving me a contract. I wanted them to make a public statement of confidence. And he said, 'We can't do that.' And that's when I decided I had to leave.

"During this time, 25 schools had contacted me to see if I was going to leave. Within a month, not even a month, after that meeting, Tufts came out and recruited me. So I didn't desert her. I felt badly for her, but I had no choice. . . .

"There is no greater potential for embarrassment to a university than in athletics. That's why there must be integrity and accountability, and that's why they can not be assigned a priority that exceeds the appropriate role of athletics in the university."

JOEL FERGUSON, former trustee: "I helped bring George here. I kind of engineered behind the scenes. When he got hired, he was treated like a king, and he had a plan. I'll never forget what he told me when he came in, because I think it really illustrates why we won and why we stopped winning.

"He said, 'Joel, I've got the way to win. Back when I was with the Steelers, I went around the country to different colleges and saw how they ran their weight rooms and the mistakes they were making. I'm going to come in and make my kids bigger and stronger by teaching them how to use the weight room and having a strength coach who understands nutrition and conditioning.'

"So his first five years, we were the meanest, toughest bear in the woods. But then he lost his strength coach and replaced him with someone who had no background in that. That's how George lost it, because it was more important to him to take care of the needs of one person than those of 95 players. When he got here the weight room was his edge, and he turned around and made his edge a welfare case. . . .

"We supported George Perles because we thought George could get us to the next level. We didn't support George because he was our friend. He happened to be a guy who was a coach we liked and was a friend, but that wasn't what it was all about. We weren't satisfied with the level George had us on at the end. We weren't looking to go to the Liberty Bowl every year. He should have known he was in trouble when we went to the Liberty Bowl and only two trustees came, because they pay for everything for the trustees on the trips.

"The reason George got that big, 10-year contract after the Rose Bowl was not for George. It was for us. We wanted him. We were in shock when we thought he was leaving for Green Bay, and we got him the contract and the annuity for us. We thought he had taken us to a level we wanted to be at, so he didn't stick us up for the contract. We stuck George up to give it to him. It wasn't the way the press and everybody conveyed it, that he had put the hammer to us. It was our idea to keep him.

"DiBiaggio came to me raising hell about the annuity. He said, 'You know, I'm seriously thinking about resigning over this.' I said, 'If you're dumb enough to quit over this, you're not smart enough to be president.' That ended the discussion, but he had an attitude after that. So he was not having as much fun with football as he was before.

"When Doug Weaver left . . . I felt strongly that giving George the A.D. job would elevate his stature and help in recruiting. In college, the coach is the program. The Bear Bryants, Joe Paternos, Bobby Bowdens. It's the coaches fans identify with, not the players.

"Unfortunately, DiBiaggio went kicking and screaming and misrepresented the issue completely. He was smart enough to find the right buzz words to argue his case. And we as a board made a mistake. When he started his [garbage], we should have taken him out right then. But the governor told us we couldn't, because he was up for re-election and he didn't want that to be an issue. . . .

"DiBiaggio wanted to have the university control the coaches' outside income. I said that I would support that but that now every book deal every one of our professors makes, any honorarium any administrator gets, also have to be approved. Nobody wanted to go for that. I mean, when DiBiaggio was on the Knight Commission, he was getting paid for that. I believe that what's good for one is good for the other, but I had a feeling these educators wanted to single sports out to pick their pocket while they're running to the bank teaching eight hours a week.

"I forced John's hand when he was trying to take the A.D. job away from George. I was against us just making it a one-year thing, because when you're in a fight with someone you don't just half-kick them in the ass. My position is you slam. No mercy. That's why I leaked the evaluation, because it would never have seen the light of the day otherwise. I made it public so they had to react. So John made George an offer, but it wasn't a straight, honest offer. It was an offer with a lot of 'gotchas.' If George had accepted that offer [to become A.D. for 3 1/2 years], he'd have been an absolute idiot. What we wanted was the same thing we did in basketball with Jud. That worked wonderfully. I'm not a genius; I got this idea from what Nebraska did with Bob Devaney and Tom Osborne . . . .

"Why DiBiaggio hated all of this more than anything was he had always gone around and conveyed the image that he didn't have anybody to answer to. And all of a sudden, people discover that he can't just make any kind of pronouncement or decision he wants. He said to me one time, 'I'm going to stop inviting trustees to dinner.' I told him, 'Hey, it ain't your home.'

"I've taken a lot of heat about the things I said and did with Merrily, but she was hired based upon the wrong agenda. If I'd have been quiet about it, we'd have been getting our asses beat in football and basketball for about eight years, based on the seeds that they were sowing. We would have been a gender equity champion, and we would have been getting kicked in the major sports. I wasn't opposed to her because she was a woman — my senior righthand person in my company is a woman; I supported a woman to be president of Michigan State. I was opposed to her agenda. If she could have come in here and done the job, I wouldn't have cared who she was. . . .

"I couldn't stand what Merrily did to Larry Bielat. She came in and immediately identified him as a guy she was going to get. So when she says I was mean-spirited toward her, ain't nothing more mean-spirited than to come in here and arbitrarily cut someone's [manhood] off. I'm going to tell you something: When I watch 'The Godfather' and read all these mafia books, the one thing that really cut through it all was they were only killing folks who were killing folks. So once she took the gun and decided here's how we do [Bielat] in, she basically made her own bed. . . .

"The problem with DiBiaggio and Michigan State was we never had shared vision. His vision was to make a reputation for himself around the country as a champion of presidential reform and the Knight Commission and gender equity. And this was never a vision that was discussed with the rest of the university. Because if the rest of the university had been asked, we'd have said, 'Hey, what we want is to beat the hell out of Michigan in football.'"

NICK SABAN, head football coach: "The biggest thing I wanted to do when I came here was to stay out of the political arena. When you enter that, you have to be on one side or the other. There's always an issue, and then you either have to skirt the issue or confront the issue — and then you have to choose up sides. Then you're getting your ducks in a row, I'm getting my ducks in a row and we're going to see who's going to beat who. In the end, I don't know who wins. And I think in a university community, the university certainly doesn't win. I know an athletic progam won't."

PETER SECCHIA, former Ambassador to Italy, GOP national chairman and MSU presidential candidate: "Most people know that the [system of elected trustees] has to be changed. . . . You vote for the individual, but the individual runs on a party ticket, and usually the trustees who win are the ones whose party does the best. For instance, if you were on the ticket when Governor [John] Engler won it, most Republican education posts won, too. . . .

"DiBiaggio was a good friend of ours, but he really didn't like the fact that George had gotten the 10-year contract and the annuity. Well, it was only in the last few years that George ever made any money. It wasn't something he had been doing for decades. When the opportunity for the annuity came up, I'm sure he thought to himself, 'I'm overweight, I'm not in the best of health, my family doesn't have much, I don't have any equity, I don't have an ownership in any business.' So an annuity was a very valuable issue for the son of an ethnic.

"Meanwhile, the board hadn't cleared that part with the president, so when he came home and found they had meddled on his turf, the battle began over who was running the university — you guys, or me? . . .

"So George found himself stacked up against the political page, the education page, the editorial page, the front page and the sports page, and only a few of these writers knew the quality of this person. Meanwhile, the football was deteriorating. George would never say this because it would sound like an excuse, but there's no question that recruiting suffered with all this conflict going on. If your kid was a blue-chipper and could go anywhere, why take a chance on a university where the president was against the coach?. . .

"Another reason things got so blown up here is that it's a media center in itself. With the University of Michigan being in Ann Arbor, it's part of the Detroit news. So if there's a problem in Michigan athletics, the evening news still opens with,

'Coleman Young blasted the Governor,' or 'Detroit police have admitted to . . .' In East Lansing, the news opens with, 'Player with overdue library book reprimanded.' Or, 'Player doesn't pick up girlfriend after dance. She is found walking home.' The university dominated the emotional news, because the capital dominated the substantive news. . . .

"In the end, the university lost. Not George. The university."

21

Memos and Medicine

So for the 1992 season, I was back to just coaching again. I felt like I had learned a lot in the past few years and was a better person for it. I figure I'll be learning until they plant me.

We were still trying to make up for the players we lost after 1990 — 14 starters, seven of whom made it to the NFL — and we were very young. Our punter, for instance, turned 18 five days before the opener. But so what? Everybody's young sometime.

But we lost four of our first five, including the opener to Central Michigan, and you can imagine the fallout. It hurt at the time, but I still believe in my heart that when I'm an old man watching games here — I scheduled later games with Eastern Michigan and Western Michigan, too — I'll feel very, very good about seeing these teams playing us. We'll be giving them a chance, just like Notre Dame gave us a chance by putting us on the schedule when we weren't well known.

To complain about losing to them, though, that would just be spilled milk. Besides, we thought we were going to pull ourselves out of it. You couldn't get me to concede a game, let alone a season, if you had a bazooka to my head. And we did pick up some steam, winning four of our last six. But we lost 14-10 to Illinois in our final game, and that left us 5-6 and out of the bowl scene. Grumble, grumble, grumble.

In 1993, we returned 18 starters. I felt like we were ready to make some noise again. We won three of our first four, including back-to-back games against Michigan and Central Michigan. By then, it was almost hard to say which was a bigger victory.

I walked into my office the morning before the Central Michigan game, and some joker had put a Central Michigan Chippewas T-shirt over my chair. People had been joking that we lost our game to Notre Dame because we were looking past the Irish to Central Michigan. That was actually kind of clever humor. I was relieved when we won, though. It was 48-34, then we beat the Wolverines 17-7.

We came within a few whiskers of having a really big season. Besides the 36-14 Notre Dame loss, our other defeats were to Ohio State 28-21, Indiana 10-0 and Penn State 38-37. Oooh, that one hurt. Then we went to Tokyo to play Wisconsin.

The Badgers were playing for the chance to play in the Rose Bowl for the first time in many years, and here they were having to go for it in Tokyo. Weird. The game got set up there just the year before. I had coached in the Japan Bowl, an All-Star game, and the Coca-Cola people were trying to get a game lined up.

So they interviewed me about it. I said, sure, we'd play here, but not if we had to give up a home game to do it. We would play only if they got someone else to give up a home game, and darned if Wisconsin didn't do it. Why? The coach, Barry Alvarez, told me that since the team hadn't been to a bowl in a lot of years, and since they were trying to get the foundation built, they thought this would simulate a bowl game. Little did he know that he wouldn't have to simulate it that season.

I thought playing in a neutral spot would be a benefit for us, but the whole thing backfired. Never did we think the game would come to be for the Big Ten championship, but Wisconsin came on overnight. But I guess if we had played in Madison, there would have been even more enthusiasm for them, so that may have canceled out in some ways.

The whole thing was strange, though. You try different things, and sometimes they work out and sometimes they don't. Obviously, the bottom line is if you win the game, it seems like a good decision. If you don't win, it's a bad decision. It was something I'd never done before with one of my teams, and something I probably wouldn't do again. Not because we lost, really, but because it's too far and too hard a trip.

It wouldn't be bad if they had a real bowl game there, because then both teams would have enough time to get there and get adjusted. In this case, Wisconsin had been off the week before, and we had to play Penn State and then get on a plane almost right away. That's a tough order. We flew over with them, and that was a good time. Barry and I sat across from each other.

We lost 41-20, but we were 6-5 and going to the Liberty Bowl in Memphis, Tennessee. We went to see a memorial to Martin Luther King Jr., which really made us think. And we went to see Elvis Presley — or, I should say, Elvis' place, Graceland. I was a pretty good fan of Elvis'; I thought he was great. We got to see the pink Cadillacs and all his motorcycles. We did a bit for our TV show from a room with all his gold records on the wall.

The game itself wasn't such a swell time. It was a wet, uncomfortable night, and we lost 18-7 to Louisville when the Cardinals scored 15 points in the fourth quarter.

After that, I heard Merrily wanted me fired. We weren't getting along so well, anyway, she didn't like the comments I had made at the pre-game banquet in Tokyo and I guess this was the last straw. What I didn't know until recently was that President McPherson wanted me out then, too. That's what Joel said.

"Tokyo had cooked George's goose, and in the Liberty Bowl Louisville would have scored every damned time if they wouldn't have missed field goals or fumbled," Ferguson said. "McPherson wanted to fire him right after the game, but I still believed in George then. So [trustee] Bob Weiss and I sat in the hotel lobby talking to McPherson almost all night . . . and he held off.

"Later, the board talked and found that it had five votes to get George fired. They went to McPherson and told him that and said, 'How can you not fire him just because Ferguson doesn't want to fire him?' I convinced Peter that it was too late to fire him, because it would ruin recruiting, spring ball was about to start and so forth. So that's where we came up with the compromise: 'an outstanding season.' My position, and Peter and I talked about it, was making one of the Big Ten-designated bowls would have been acceptable."

It was around this time that some monkey business with memos seemed to be going around campus. There was a memo dated February 17 that Clarence Underwood, now our senior associate athletic director, supposedly wrote to McPherson saying it was time for our great basketball coach Jud Heathcote to either retire or be fired. Then McPherson instructed Clarence not to comment to the media about the memo. Jud obviously was hurt.

"If you think I greeted this with great elation and a smile on my face, you're on 'Dial-a-clue,'" Jud said at his press conference. "I was flabbergasted, surprised, amazed, disappointed . . . choose any words you want. . . . To be honest, my wife and children are devastated. . . .

"I did get a call from Clarence, but I was down at the [Michigan Athletic Club], pounding the handball in all my anger."

The funny thing was the actual memo never surfaced. Denbow, the university publicist, said it was "not an active memo." I heard that where the original story broke was from something that had been handwritten and crumpled up in a trash can — and that even that had been tinkered with.

It was only two days later that there was "a memo" from Merrily to McPherson that recommended firing me. That's when McPherson issued the "outstanding season" order. Merrily admitted she wanted me fired, but she said there had been no memo and I believe her. So what the heck was going on? The writers started calling all of this "Memogate," and I think that was appropriate.

"Is there a safe computer, a safe office, a safe telephone, even a safe garbage can at the athletic department offices in Jenison Field House these days?" Steve Klein wrote in the *Lansing State Journal*. "One official even asked me during a phone conversation if the phone was tapped. Really. . . . We all anxiously await the next memo, the next controversy, the next embarrassment. If you think or expect otherwise, you haven't been paying much attention to the games people play at Michigan State."

It was getting confusing again, but I knew one thing: This time, it was over for me. There may have been something we could have done to pull our fat out of the fire, but the vague "outstanding" season made it pretty rough. Once I got used to the idea, it kind of loosened me up for the season. At our preseason media day, I told them to hit me with their best shot:

"Do we have a Rose Bowl team? Yeah," I said. "And if it isn't a Rose Bowl team, it's my fault. So what?"

We started 2-2, but then we lost 40-20 to Michigan. Joel, who then was chairman of the board, said that McPherson was itching to end it then.

"After the Michigan game, McPherson called me up and said, 'Hey, we didn't look too good; I want to start the process now,'" Ferguson said. "I said, 'Bull. Go make your trip to the Far East. George is going to win the next two games.'"

Joel really was still with me then. We have an interesting relationship. We enjoy each other's company, and he was very supportive through the thick and most of the thin. He wasn't a front-runner. Our relationship at times helped him and at times hurt him. And the same with me. Sometimes it helped me, sometimes it hurt me. It was held against each of us at times that we were friends.

Well, we lost to Ohio State and Iowa. I'm not ashamed of it — somebody has to lose, and there are no coaches in the Big Ten who are wet behind the ears. But that's where McPherson made his final decision.

"If he hadn't lost to Iowa, we'd have had a chance to save him," Ferguson said. "McPherson was in Seoul at the time, and we talked the morning after. George was fired. He was dead meat. On Monday, I went to George's office and told him, 'I can't save you any more.' He says, 'You've got to do what you've got to do.'

"I told the press three things: 'George is going to coach the rest of the season, this is not an outstanding season and whatever decision the president makes, I'm with him.' That's when all the stuff about stabbing George in the back and 'stabbing a corpse' starts up, but I didn't stab George in the back."

That stabbing a corpse line was pretty clever, but it was kind of a cutting remark. My mom didn't like it much. He also went public with his words about me being beyond saving. All I could say was I expected to have my contract honored. Hey, that's America. We have tenure. We have unions. We have contracts. And you would think a place of higher learning would put a premium on matters like honoring contracts.

Since then, Joel and I have met for lunch. He apologized for saying it that way, and I certainly accepted that that's the end of it. It's very easy for me to visit with Joel again now.

McPherson got back from the Orient a couple of days later, but we didn't speak. He addressed the media at halftime of our next game, a 27-21 win over Indiana, but all he said was, "I have set expectations, but I have not had the opportunity to review the expectations against his performance."

Who knows what was up by then? I just tried to tune it all out and keep my mouth shut. But I have to admit my lips were getting pretty chapped up from being bit.

In the middle of all this, a story gets leaked that the athletic department had been investigating the football program for allegations of rules violations since September. This was October 29, and that was news to me. Then President McPherson said that the charges were running "the full gamut" and had come from one former player. That player turned out to be Roosevelt Wagner, who had started 13 games for us over two seasons but left after his junior year. We had a lot of run-ins, and I ended up kicking him off the team.

Rosie said the whole program was dirty, and then went on to make about 70 charges against us: Things like boosters giving out money, monkeying around with grades, agents. But Rosie, the poor guy, told his stories a lot of different ways, depending on who was listening. And he was saying a lot of strange things.

For instance, he told the *Lansing State Journal* that he wanted to be locked in an 8-by-6 cell with me so he could charge admission to kick my butt. He also said he was carrying a weapon with him for protection:

"Someone kept ringing my doorbell last night," he said. "When I'd go to the door, there was no one there. But I saw a car parked across the street, with a guy taking pictures. I haven't been to sleep for two days. But if they try to get me, I'm not going by myself. I'm really on the edge right now."

Then again, he told *The Detroit News* that stuff about stalking me with two loaded guns and intending to kill me. He blamed me for not being drafted by the NFL:

"At that time, my whole mental frame of being was to get back at George. . . . I had the guns sitting on my seat. I had a .38 and a 9mm. I was gonna get him with one of them. Loaded, they both was loaded, and I had cases [of extra ammunition] for both of them. I had this whole scenario made up in my mind."

He said he called off his plan after deciding killing me might mess up the rest of his life. Then he calls up ESPN to deny that was him, even though it had been on tape. Then he tells the *Detroit Free Press* that he owes me an apology. Then the *Detroit Free Press* quotes his high school coach as saying Roosevelt had "a vivid imagination." And then he tells the *Free Press'* Mitch Albom that the president's office had been encouraging him to talk because, "They wanted to clean house without burning the house down."

On top of all that, Rosie had done some things when he was in our program that should have made him suspect, anyway. I don't think it's right to reveal what those were, but let's just say they led to a lot of problems between us.

It was hard to tell what Rosie really intended in all this. I don't think he had much credibility as far as his accusations, but when it came to our safety, I thought it was best to get an anti-stalking injunction just in case. The court order said Rosie could not follow or appear within my sight, could not approach me in public or private, could not contact me by telephone or mail or appear on the Michigan State campus.

That same week, out comes another wacky rumor. There was no end to this stuff by now. This one said that I've suggested I should be made athletic director again, to save the university money on my buyout and keep me employed. Maybe I wouldn't have minded going back to that, but it wasn't even a consideration — for at least one very, very good reason . . . Merrily was still the A.D.

I phoned her right away when an anonymous-source story came out saying that was the scenario. In fact, I talked to her before she even knew about the story. I would never have tried doing anything like that to someone who still had a job. It would have been a mean, no-class move, and I'm not into that cloak-and-dagger junk.

We beat Northwestern after we beat Indiana, but finally the inevitable arrived. On November 8, McPherson called me and told me the decision was made. When I told the players just before practice, there was absolute silence. The poor kids felt abandoned, betrayed. That's always the worst part of any firing, because they came to the school counting on you and your staff being there.

Really, though, I'd been having a lot of what I call anxiety. It wasn't healthy, and I didn't like it. In fact, I don't want it ever again. I was all filled up with it.

Oddly enough, people in the media were probably as kind to me that day as they were when we won the Rose Bowl. They called me "sincere" and "a good person," and they took the school to task for not giving straight answers. And even Joe Falls, who could be so sour, wrote: "If you don't have any feelings for George Perles, you don't have feelings. He went out with class."

They asked me what I thought my legacy would be. All I could think of was, "That this guy took his medicine the best he could." But I didn't think anyone should feel sorry for me. What more could I have asked for in life — who the hell am I to deserve more?

There I was, in the building named after my great mentor, after 12 years trying to build a bridge back to him. It had been an honor to have the chance, and it was perfect to leave second to Duffy in wins. I couldn't be prouder of that, and I'll always be a son of Michigan State — until the last dog is hung.

22

The Calm After the Storm

We still had two games left, against Purdue and Penn State. They could have been bad scenes, anti-climactic. But thanks to the players being so gutsy, we got something special out of them. We fell behind Purdue 21-3 at halftime, but I knew in our locker room at halftime that there was something brewing inside those kids. Just to look at them.

And so we came out gangbusters in the second half and won the game 42-30 — the greatest comeback a Michigan State team ever had. The players carried me part of the way off the field, and my son John and my grandchildren Nicholas and Michael were there waiting for me. It was beautiful, like the end of a movie.

We shared a lot of emotions after the game. It was an emotional game, I'm an emotional person and we had some emotional players — who played emotionally.

We lost 59-31 to Penn State the next week, but there still was honor in that game. What a privilege to end my career against a man like Joe Paterno, who had an undefeated team that was just as entitled to the national championship as Nebraska was. If I had to pick one active coach who has the most respect and credibility, it's Joe — plus I think he invented those black shoes.

By then, any wounds I had from being dismissed were pretty much licked. I know that sounds crazy, but that's just the way I'm made. I've always been able to enjoy what I'm doing, and not worry about what I'm not doing. Maybe I was born that way, or maybe that's what happens when you lose forever something as precious as playing football because of a knee injury your junior year of college. You go on to the next thing.

Why wallow? I wasn't hurting, I wasn't even numb about it. Did I wish it ended differently? Sure. But it didn't. So what? I'm a big boy, and I got a lot more than I had coming.

It might feel a little different when practice begins, or the games come. But if something bothers me, I'll just shut it off. I'll create my own environment. If I'm going to the games and I can't enjoy them because it hurts too much, then I won't go. I'll go to our house up north, or I'll go to Chicago. I'm not going to be a glutton for punishment.

There was one thing I thought was very important to establish right away when I lost my job: I was going to stay in East Lansing — it's my home — but I was not going to let myself be a burden to the new coach. In fact, I planned right away to be his biggest supporter.

I said when I got fired I was going to be so supportive I'd make people sick, that whoever it was wouldn't be able to do anything wrong in my eyes. And I said at our MSU Football Bust after the season that everybody should kick in to help the new coach take Michigan State as far as he can take it. I meant it both times, and I still do.

I was extremely pleased to see Nick Saban get the job. I talked to Nick about it before he accepted, and he was concerned that I would be resentful. I told him, "Nick, somebody's going to get the job, so you might as well take it. Don't worry about me. I'm on your side." I have to admit I was a little hurt at Nick's first press conference, when somebody asked about his mentors and he didn't mention me. But Nick and I have met a few times since then — he even came over for some advice on buying a house — and I can appreciate the position he was in.

"The most difficult thing for me coming in was that George has a place in the tradition of Michigan State football, and I am connected to George," Saban said. "I'm proud of that. But because things ended the way they did for him, it was delicate to handle for me. I want to be responsible to George and give him his place in the sun, but I also have to be responsible to the people who hired me."

The MSU Football Bust was a special night for me. They had a video tribute to me, with everybody from Joe Greene to Terry Bradshaw to Courtney Hawkins to Lorenzo White speaking. The video was set against the background music of, "Our

Day Will Come" — a song that was sung by Ruby And The Romantics. What was especially neat about that is that Ruby, Ruby Garnett, is the mother of our linebacker Kevin Garnett.

What really got my dry eye going, though, were the words of some of my players who were there in person. Scott Greene, who was named most valuable player and most inspirational player, said that when I left half of him was going to leave, too. Whew, that was tough. And there was Pat Shurmur, who I called from the Detroit airport to recruit on my first day on the job. He was a great center and a captain of our Rose Bowl team, and he was one of my assistants my last five years. I was glad Nick hired him, and I think it's terrific that six people on the new staff worked for me at Michigan State at one time or another.

"I wasn't one of his first recruits, I was *the* first," Pat said that night, and I remember choking up because his voice really cracked. "For that, I'll always be proud. If I was 17 again and had the choices I had, I'd be right back here. And . . . George, it would be because of you."

Oh, man, these guys were killing me. But it's not like I was going anywhere. This is home.

Shortly after I was fired, I had an offer to join Rich Brooks, who I knew from a few different All-Star games we had coached together, with the Los Angeles Rams, who have since moved to St. Louis. But because it was so soon after my firing, I decided to say no. I'm not ruling out coaching again, but I'm not going to this season. I'll always appreciate Rich Brooks' offer, though. That was big of him.

I wouldn't say I'm retired, because I have definite plans in the next year, but right now it's kind of like being retired. No one knows how they'll handle being retired until they retire, but right now I'm at peace. If you're working like I was, 12 to 14 hours a day, seven days a week, for the last 40 years, you don't have hobbies like woodworking or collecting stamps or glasses or guns. But I have plenty to do, and plenty in mind.

My program is, up at 8 to have some coffee and breakfast with Sally. Then I go in my office and work a couple of hours a day, on finances or organizing golf outings, or whatever. Then it's swimming at the Michigan Athletic Club, a fantastic facility, and then I go to the Sip'N'Snack for lunch.

The Sip is the greatest place in America. It's not fancy. There's contractors who come in there, and carpenters and sod people. There's some painters who come in, and a lot of retirees. They're all guys like me who enjoy the basics. I feel the most comfortable in there, because it's working people. It's run by a super guy named Val Korre, who's come in to open up every morning at 4:30 a.m. for 38 years.

I like to get a Val salad, with a little Feta cheese on it, and a good bowl of soup. On Monday, it's bean soup. Tuesdays, it's split pea. On Wednesday, he has chicken noodle, on Thursday he has vegetable and on Friday it's potato. After he closes up around 3, we'll go into the back room and play gin.

On Tuesdays, though, I meet with what I call our "Flag Club" at Pistachio's. I don't know why we call it that, but it's the same group that used to come to watch my press conferences on Mondays and then came to my office and sat around my big conference table for lunch. I always knew I was just using that office, renting it.

My friends were a different matter. They usually outnumbered the media at those press conferences, and they're still strong friends of mine from inside and outside Michigan State: Ron Palmer; Ron Gibson; Bobby Popp; Larry Sierra; Russ Rivit; Joe Farrell; Terry Braverman; Larry Bielat; Henry Bullough; Walt Sorg; Andy Such; Gus Ganakas; Clarence Underwood; Don Loding; Ken Hoffman; Bill Rademacher and Gary Raff.

We solve all the world's problems.

I'm only joking about that, but there is one thing this group — and many other friends of mine — are generous about helping with: the Special Olympics. I've always felt if you don't do charity work, you're useless. That's why I've done everything I can, from playing wheelchair basketball to bowling, to help raise money for pure causes. Not because I'm a great guy, but because it's the right way to live. And since I've been in such a visible position at Michigan State, it's easy for me to be able to contribute. I mean, if corporations and athletes and successful people aren't going to do things for charities, then there aren't going to be charities.

The way I got involved in Special Olympics is kind of interesting. When I first came back as head coach, there was a tradition that in the last game of the season students would tear down a goalpost — for no reason at all, win, lose or tie. Well, the year before I came, the administration tried to beat the problem because it was expensive and they were worried about some-body getting hurt. So they put up a wooden post in the end that the students always tore down, the tunnel end.

One problem: During the game the wind came and tore down the post, and after Iowa scored they had to go all the way to the other end to kick the extra point. We were a laughing-stock.

When I came in, our facilities director, Gene Kenney, asked me what I thought about handling this problem. They were think-ing about putting up "H" posts instead of the tuning fork kind. "H" posts are strong — you couldn't tear them out without a tractor — but they're old-fashioned and ugly.

I said, "No, you can leave the tuning fork up." I decided to appeal to the students in the student newspaper and tell them if they didn't tear the posts down, I would give the cost of the goalposts to charity. We played the game and no one tore them down, so I gave $2,000 to charity.

I had no particular charity in mind, but one of my coaches, Norm Parker, had a beautiful kid named Jeffrey who was in the Special Olympics. I wanted to take the money to start a golf out-ing with Michigan, but there were some complications with that idea then, so I gave the money to Jeffrey's school.

Anyway, from there I learned more about Special Olym-pics and what a tremendous program it is. So I adopted it as my charity, and I started my own golf outing eight years ago at the Lansing Country Club. We really do it right, with sponsors like Little Caesar's, Blue Cross, Cadillac, Cellular One, Health Cen-tral, Accident Insurance, Oldsmobile, Dan Henry Distributing . . . The corporations pay for everything, and we give no free-bies on the dinners — no exceptions — so every single nickel goes to those kids.

Every year we make $40-50,000, and it's a heavy, heavy day for me — the happiest day of the year. If you could see those kids come running to you at the 18th green, feel them climbing all over your back . . . it's beautiful. A lot of the golfers are teared up before they get off that green.

I'm looking forward to this football season at Michigan State. I'll enjoy the things everyone else has enjoyed for so long. I'll be at the games in my green jacket, tailgating. I've always dreamed about tailgating: Have a little something to drink, a nice bratwurst to eat, a little mustard on my jacket. I'll go visit the club section, then I'll go to the press box. Two lifetime press passes I've got, and I'm anxious to see how they operate in there.

After I enjoy the season, then it will be time for me to get serious about my next move: running for the board of trustees. I'll get right on my campaign. Once I'm on the board — if I'm elected — I'll be overseeing Michigan State and I'll be very busy being active for the state of Michigan, which is also very important to me.

Why? I've been privileged to sit on the council of deans here. I was an athlete here, an assistant here, a head coach here and an athletic director here. I think I know the university from a few different angles, more angles than most do: from the athletics side, from the academic side and the administrative side. With all these experiences, I really think I can help the university.

If that doesn't work out, or even if it does, I'd like to look into doing some television work as an analyst. Get that telestrator out. I won't look for another coaching job. I really don't know if I still want to do that. But at my age, with my experience, I don't think you go out and look. People know you're available, people know who you are. If they don't come to you, it's no use trying to jam yourself on them.

I really want to be on the board, though. I would be good at watching over the university for the taxpayers of the state of Michigan, making sure that the funds we have are channeled in the right direction.

One action I believe we need to take right away is to eliminate waste. For instance, perks for the board. The board doesn't need any perks, and there's a tendency for people on it to get too wrapped up in where they're sitting for basketball and football games, where they're parking, how they're traveling.

The board has a job to do, and it should be willing to put in the time, do that job and get the job done. That's what I would do. I could make that a full-time job.

You want to ask, "Is George looking for revenge?" There isn't any revenge. Revenge for what? I'm not mad at anybody. I call them, they call me. I don't agree with them, they don't agree with me. So? And there was no shame in being fired.

My whole motive will be to help the state, help the school and help the taxpayers. Nothing else will be involved. My slogan will be: "To watch over Michigan State University. Period." People know the love I have for the school. I don't think I would have any trouble working with anybody on the board. Not even Dee Cook, who I think wanted me out most. She should feel very comfortable with the idea of working with me, but I guess you'd have to ask her what she thinks.

I want to give her and all the other board members the benefit of the doubt and some credit for making a decision they thought was best for Michigan State when they wanted me out. If they were making a decision based on what was best for the school, that's a pure attitude and I have to respect that.

It's going to take a lot of cooperation from a lot of people to bury all these hatchets. But if you make all your decisions based on what's best for the school and the state, then you won't make any wrong decisions. We can't have trustees wanting something, then trying to undo it, or pouting because they didn't get their way. You have your say, you can have your arguments, but when the decision is made it's done. When it's over, it's over.

I'm not sure which party I'll run with. I'll have to really study the platforms and find out exactly where I fit best. I've got plenty of friends in both. Peter Secchia is a Republican and Frank Kelley is a Democrat, and they've become good friends through me. There are many people who've said, 'I can't understand that.' But I asked them to let go of their political differences on behalf of myself and Michigan State football, and they both did. It says a lot about both of them.

Perles of Wisdom

For some reason, I've always liked issues. Why? I don't know why. I just know that I like to analyze things, and when it's something I'm really interested in I get loud and enthusiastic.

I've got a lot of opinions. Some I know are wrong, or aren't popular or what everybody else thinks they should be, but they're mine. And I have what I think are good reasons for all of them.

On agents: I don't think there's any use in them, but it's a fad: "Hey, m'man. My agent." You don't need them to get what you have coming, and they shouldn't be getting rich off of you. No wonder there's so many of them. It's lucrative because kids are getting fooled. For instance, kids who get drafted are giving them a percentage — and the kids already have their money staked out because of where they got drafted.

And any of those guys who tell you they're going to help you get drafted higher are wrong. He can hurt you, but he can't help you. The pros aren't going to be influenced to draft you higher, and if the agent's a pain in the neck to get along with they might pass you over.

Any flunky out there can be an agent, because there's no mystery to it. The NFL gives you the guidelines. They tell you what the guy who got drafted in your spot last year made, you add in the cost of living increase and that's it. Period. They've got salary caps. You're not going to get more. So don't beat your head against the wall or give your money away.

And here's another problem with agents. First you get an agent, then you get a tax man and then you get an investor —

and now you've got a team. The problem with a team is it's three against one. You should get together with your father and your family attorney. That's all you need.

As for the guys who don't get drafted, my philosophy is very simple: After your eligibility is up, work out, be in shape and go to the workouts the NFL offers.

And one other point: There's no shortcut to financial success. Sure, there are some who've hit it real lucky, but the odds are bad. The only sure things are the T-bills, C.D.s, annuities and banks and interest. You start monkeying around with real estate or oil wells or restaurants and trying to get rich quick, you're going down the drain. I saw that all the time in the NFL. When you have a big pot, you don't need to try to ring the bell.

On Title IX and gender equity: Title IX is the law. If we don't like it, then we've got to work to change the law. But if we don't change it, we've got to abide by it. But we've got to be sensible. We can't cut off our nose to spite our face. We can't bite the hand that feeds us — I'm a big cliché guy.

Sometimes we can't see trees when we're right in the middle of a forest. We all understand that if G.M. or Ford or Chrysler had 25 vehicles and 22 of them were losing money and three were making money, they'd get rid of the 22. Well, that's what we have at Michigan State, but obviously we can't do that.

So how do we keep everybody happy? How do we take care of the women without hurting non-revenue men's sports? Very simple. We take football out of the equation, because there's nothing that compares to men's football — which produces 75 percent of the athletic department revenue at Michigan State — and we'd all go broke without it. Once football's out of the equation, then we can do 50-50 between men's and women's sports' participation and nobody gets hurt.

One of these days some judge is going to wake up and have enough courage to make that ruling. There's no reason to have men and women fighting over this, but we're stimulating a real good battle of the sexes that we don't need in this country. You need to look for ways to eliminate that fighting.

When I voted against a Big Ten proposal that mandated a 60-40 participation rate of males to females, there was a lot of complaining that I was against women's sports. That wasn't the case at all, and I think any of the Michigan State women's coaches who worked for me when I was A.D. would verify that. I just thought it was very inflexible, and if the Big Ten was so fired up about cutting costs I had some other suggestions: Maybe they didn't need to have their meetings in Cape Cod, for instance.

You need to look for a compromise, and leaving football out of the equation is one way to get it done. I don't see another, and I'm not talking as a football coach. I'm talking as a citizen of the U.S.A. who cares about higher education.

On reducing football scholarships: We're down from unlimited scholarships to 105 to 95 to 85 now, but if we went down to 80 or 75 — so what? As long as the whole country is doing the same, that would be fine. Who says we're supposed to be on a mission to get kids super-ready for the pros? Our mission is to help them be the best people they can be and the best football players they can be, and less scholarships would mean more attention for each kid. But I'd hate to see the numbers get much lower, because then you're denying opportunities.

And we've already legislated down some of the crazy recruiting contacts, especially by telephone, and that's good. It's silly to be calling kids five nights a week to ask them about the weather and making him make small talk — to a bunch of different schools.

On spring practice and freshman eligibility: I think spring practice is obsolete. It was meant to help when freshmen weren't eligible, so they could get their feet wet. Well, ever since freshmen could be eligible, the only ones who need spring practice are the kids you just recruited — and they're still in high school.

So you should have one or the other, but not both. It would be ideal for freshmen not to be eligible, so they could get adjusted better. So why didn't I just make my own freshmen ineligible? Because it would be a disadvantage, both on the field and in recruiting, unless everybody else had to do it. You're not on an island, and you don't live in a vacuum.

There are many reasons why spring practice should be eliminated. First of all, it's been so watered-down that you can't get enough out of it. And I'm not sure there really ever was a tremendous carryover to the fall. So then it just becomes a lot of banging around, and there are only so many hits in each of these kids. We expose our kids enough to injury, and we take way too much of their time in the fall alone.

On Prop 48 eligibility standards: Prop 48 asked for more. Ask and ye shall receive, seek and ye shall find, knock and the door shall be opened. It's working. The kids are getting better grades and better standardized test scores. But the ones who don't make it, you can't just throw them to the wolves. They've got to have opportunities to make up for it. It's OK if they don't compete their freshman year, but I've always liked the idea of giving them an opportunity to earn that year back instead of having a year of eligibility taken away like it is now. Give them a legitimate opportunity to earn it back, and you'll still get what you want.

And the standardized tests do need to be revised. I think they're set up for a basic group of people and don't take into account the whole realm of society. We need to understand that even if we're all in the same country, different areas have different interpretations of terms, so there's a built-in bias to the tests that keeps them from being fair to everybody.

On the prospect of a college football playoff: Right now, the National Collegiate Athletic Association doesn't like the bowl situation because it doesn't realize anything from it financially. What the NCAA would like to do in my opinion is get its foot in the door with a playoff, and once it does, hold on to your hat. Because now we're really going to exploit kids. We're going to play two, three or maybe four more games, bring in more revenue and then give the revenue to everyone but the kids.

The real winner would be the NCAA. They'll have another pot of gold they can spend from. But I don't think the kids need any more games. It's just not worth what it would take out of them. Even last year, when Nebraska and Penn State both went undefeated, it wouldn't have been necessary. We had a lot of good conversations about who was No. 1, didn't we? Who says there has to be one king of the mountain? What's better for education? What's better for the kids?

On paying players: When I was in school, scholarship players got $15 a month laundry money, which probably is equivalent to $100 now. We need to shape up and start giving players modest stipends. How?

It's simple, at least for football. How many tickets does the NCAA allow each player to get from the school? Four, home and away. What's four times 25? $100. How many games are there? Eleven. How much money is that? $1100. We give you four tickets, go sell them to your dad. They get hard tickets, so if they sell them for what it's worth it's legal.

If they scalp it for more, or to a booster who wants to give them more, it's illegal. How do we police it? You educate the kids, tell them the consequences of abusing it and let them be responsible for dealing with the temptations. That's part of growing up.

On Gary Moeller's resignation/firing at Michigan after the incident at the Excalibur restaurant in Detroit last spring: I've known Gary for a long time. When he was an assistant for Bo, he'd come to see me at the Steelers camps. When I was with the Stars, he was on my list of people I wanted to hire. I don't know if he knows that.

I don't know what happened that night, but he's been so honorable for so long that he deserved a second chance. And I think it was mean and wrong for the law enforcement people, or whoever it was, to release the tapes of him afterwards.

When they announced a press conference a few days later, I suspected what was going on and I was concerned — so I got in the car and drove there. I went with two things in mind: If he was going to be fired, I was going to be there to support him. If he was going to resign, I was going to try to talk him out of it. But he didn't come to the press conference, and he resigned by way of a written statement. I had tried to call him, and I wish I could have gotten to him before then. It came out later that Michigan had actually fired him the day before.

I think there was an opportunity there to make a positive out of a negative. By that, I mean that he could have told the kids for years to come about making a mistake and paying for it and recovering from it and learning from it. He could be telling them from living experience, not something he had read or seen, and he would be able to be a tremendous example.

Gary is a very good coach and an even better person, and I predict this will all be put behind him and some day he will be a head coach in the NFL. I think that's like money in the bank. Somebody's going to get a gem.

On academics vs. athletics: People tried to put me in the camp of athletics against academics, and that never fit. There's nothing further from the truth. We always preached and believe that academics were most important and that football was important. There was no reason for any squabbling, because they could co-exist very smoothly.

I've always known you can't eat the football. I raised three sons who played football, and they heard that from me from their very early years. So I have living proof of that in my boys, who all earned degrees, and my daughter Kathleen, who is a teacher. There was a time when I thought she'd be a sportswriter. I would have loved that. Really.

You have to get an education. Education is what separates us, what gives us potential and opens doors. The only thing more important than education is your family. Football was third to me, and there were times I managed to make it fourth or fifth. I'm a strong believer that we over-emphasize the game. We can't let football get out of hand.

APPENDIX

George Perles' 12 Seasons at Michigan State

1983

(4-6-1 overall, 2-6-1 Big Ten):
MICHIGAN STATE 23, Colorado 17
Michigan State 28, NOTRE DAME 23
ILLINOIS 20, Michigan State 10
Michigan State 29, PURDUE 29
Michigan 42, MICHIGAN STATE 0
INDIANA 24, Michigan State 12
OHIO STATE 21, Michigan State 11
MICHIGAN STATE 24, Minnesota 10
Michigan State 8, NORTHWESTERN 3
Iowa 12, MICHIGAN STATE 6
WISCONSIN 32, Michigan State 0

1984

(6-6, 5-4):
Michigan State 24, COLORADO 21
Notre Dame 24, MICHIGAN STATE 20
ILLINOIS 40, Michigan State 7
Purdue 13, MICHIGAN STATE 10
Michigan State 19, MICHIGAN 7
MICHIGAN STATE 13, Indiana 6
Ohio State 23, MICHIGAN STATE 20
Michigan State 20, MINNESOTA 13
MICHIGAN STATE 27, Northwestern 10
Michigan State 17, IOWA, 16
Wisconsin 20, MICHIGAN STATE 10
Army 10, Michigan State 6 (Cherry Bowl)

1985

(7-5, 5-3)
MICHIGAN STATE 12, Arizona State 3
NOTRE DAME 27, Michigan State 10
MICHIGAN STATE 7, Western Michigan 3
IOWA 35, Michigan State 31
Michigan 31, MICHIGAN STATE 0
Illinois 31, MICHIGAN STATE 17
Michigan State 31, PURDUE 24
MICHIGAN STATE 31, Minnesota 26
Michigan State 35, INDIANA, 16
MICHIGAN STATE 32, Northwestern 0
Michigan State 41, Wisconsin 7
Georgia Tech 17, Michigan State 14 (All-American
    Bowl)

1986

(6-5, 4-4)
ARIZONA STATE 20, Michigan State 17
MICHIGAN STATE 20, Notre Dame 15
MICHIGAN STATE 45, Western Michigan 10
Iowa 24, MICHIGAN STATE 21
Michigan 27, MICHIGAN STATE 6
Michigan State 29, ILLINOIS 21
MICHIGAN STATE 37, Purdue 3
Michigan State 52, MINNESOTA 23
Indiana 17, MICHIGAN STATE 14
NORTHWESTERN, 24, Michigan State 21
MICHIGAN STATE 23, Wisconsin 13

1987

(9-2-1, 7-0-1)
MICHIGAN STATE 27, Southern Cal 13
NOTRE DAME 31, Michigan State 8
Florida State 31, MICHIGAN STATE 3
Michigan State 19, IOWA 14
MICHIGAN STATE 17, Michigan 11
Michigan State 38, NORTHWESTERN 0

MICHIGAN STATE 14, Illinois 14
Michigan State 13, OHIO STATE 7
MICHIGAN STATE 45, Purdue 3
MICHIGAN STATE 27, Indiana 3
Michigan State 30, WISCONSIN 9
Michigan State 20, Southern Cal 17 (Rose Bowl)

1988

(6-5-1, 6-1-1):
Rutgers 17, MICHIGAN STATE 13
Notre Dame 20, MICHIGAN STATE 3
FLORIDA STATE 30, Michigan State 7
MICHIGAN STATE 10, Iowa 10
MICHIGAN 17, Michigan State 3
MICHIGAN STATE 36, Northwestern 3
Michigan State 28, ILLINOIS 21
MICHIGAN STATE 20, Ohio State 10
Michigan State 48, PURDUE 3
Michigan State 38, INDIANA 12
MICHIGAN STATE 36, Wisconsin 0
Georgia 34, Michigan State 27 (Gator Bowl)

1989

(8-4, 6-2):
MICHIGAN STATE 49, Miami of Ohio 0
NOTRE DAME 21, Michigan State 13
Miami (FL) 26, MICHIGAN STATE 20
Michigan State 17, IOWA 14
Michigan 10, MICHIGAN STATE 7
Illinois 14, MICHIGAN STATE 10
Michigan State 28, PURDUE 21
Michigan State 51, INDIANA 20
MICHIGAN STATE 21, Minnesota 7
MICHIGAN STATE 76 Northwestern 14
Michigan State 31, WISCONSIN 3
Michigan State 33, Hawaii 13 (Aloha Bowl)

1990

(8-3-1, 6-2)
Michigan State 23, SYRACUSE 23
Notre Dame 20, MICHIGAN STATE 19
Michigan State 34, RUTGERS 10
Iowa 12, MICHIGAN STATE 7
Michigan State 28, MICHIGAN 27
ILLINOIS 15, Michigan State 13
MICHIGAN STATE 55, Purdue 33
MICHIGAN STATE 45, Indiana 20
Michigan State 28, MINNESOTA 16
Michigan State 29, NORTHWESTERN 22
MICHIGAN STATE 14, Wisconsin 9
Michigan State 17, Southern Cal 16 (John Hancock Bowl)

1991

(3-8, 3-5)
Central Michigan 20, MICHIGAN STATE 3
NOTRE DAME 49, Michigan State 10
Rutgers 14, MICHIGAN STATE 7
INDIANA 31, Michigan State 0
Michigan 45, MICHIGAN STATE 28
MICHIGAN STATE 20, Minnesota 12
OHIO STATE 27, Michigan State 17
Northwestern 16, MICHIGAN STATE 13
Michigan State 20, WISCONSIN 7
PURDUE 27, Michigan State 17
MICHIGAN STATE 27, Illinois 24

1992

(5-6, 5-3)
Central Michigan 24, MICHIGAN STATE 20
Notre Dame 52, MICHIGAN STATE 31
BOSTON COLLEGE 14, Michigan State 0
MICHIGAN STATE 42, Indiana 31
MICHIGAN 35, Michigan State 10
Michigan State 20, MINNESOTA 15
Ohio State 27, MICHIGAN STATE 17

Michigan State 27, NORTHWESTERN 26
MICHIGAN STATE 26, Wisconsin 10
MICHIGAN STATE 35, Purdue 13
ILLINOIS 14, Michigan State 10

1993

(6-6, 4-4)
MICHIGAN STATE 31, Kansas 14
NOTRE DAME 36, Michigan State 14
MICHIGAN STATE 48, Central Michigan 34
MICHIGAN STATE 17, Michigan 7
OHIO STATE 28, Michigan State 21
MICHIGAN STATE 24, Iowa 10
INDIANA 10, Michigan State 0
Michigan State 31, NORTHWESTERN 29
Michigan State 27, PURDUE 24
Penn State 38, MICHIGAN STATE 37
Wisconsin 41, Michigan State 20 (At Tokyo, Japan)
Louisville 18, Michigan State 7 (Liberty Bowl)

1994

(5-6, 4-4)
KANSAS 17, Michigan State 10
Notre Dame 21,   MICHIGAN STATE 20
MICHIGAN STATE 45, Miami of Ohio 10
MICHIGAN STATE 29, Wisconsin 10
MICHIGAN 40, Michigan State 20
Ohio State 23, MICHIGAN STATE 7
IOWA, 19, Michigan State 14
MICHIGAN STATE 27, Indiana 21
Michigan State 35, NORTHWESTERN 17
MICHIGAN STATE 42, Purdue 30
PENN STATE 59, Michigan State 31

Academic All-Big Ten Selections
Under George Perles

Dean Altobelli (1984, 85, 86; Academic All-America, 85-86)
Steve Bogdalek (1985)
Shane Bullough (1985, 86; Academic All-America 1986)
Pat Shurmur (1986, 87)
Kevin Robbins (1987)
Tony Briningstool (1988, 89, 90)
Josh Butland (1988)
John Kiple (1988, 89)
Chris Willertz (1988, 89)
Courtney Hawkins (1989)
Toby Heaton (1989, 90, 91, 92)
Mitch Lyons (1989, 90)
Steve Black (1990)
John Dignan (1990)
Rob Fredrickson (1990, 91, 92, 93)
Todd Grabowski (1990, 91, 92)
Mark MacFarland (1990, 91, 92)
Mike Maddie (1990, 91)
Jim Miller (1990, 91, 92)
Brian Vooletich (1990, 91)
Steve Wasylk (1990, 91, 92, 93;
    Academic All-America, 92, 93)
Mill Coleman (1991, 1992, 1993, 1994)
Colin Cronin (1991)
Peter Drzal (1993)
Brian Mosallam (1993)
Chris Salani (1993)
Anthony Folino (1994)

First-Round National Football League Draft Picks who played for George Perles

1984	Carl Banks, New York Giants
1986	Anthony Bell, St. Louis Cardinals
1987	Mark Ingram, New York Giants
1988	Lorenzo White, Houston Oilers
1989	Tony Mandarich, Green Bay Packers
1989	Andre Rison, Indianapolis Colts
1990	Percy Snow, Kansas City Chiefs
1991	Bobby Wilson, Washington Redskins
1994	Rob Fredrickson, L.A. Raiders

The All-Perles Team, as selected on The George Perles Show

Offense

Pat Shurmur	OL
Bob Kula	OL
Tony Mandarich	OL
Eric Moten	OL
Brian DeMarco	OL
Duane Young	TE
Andre Rison	WR
Mark Ingram	WR
Courtney Hawkins	WR
Bobby Morse	RB
Lorenzo White	RB
Jim Miller	QB

Defense

Bobby Wilson	DL
Travis Davis	DL
Mark Nichols	DL
Bill Johnson	DL
Carl Banks	LB
Percy Snow	LB
Carlos Jenkins	LB
Dixon Edwards	LB
Harlon Barnett	DB
Lonnie Young	DB
Todd Krumm	DB
Johnny Miller	DB

Specialists

John Langeloh	PK
Greg Montgomery	P
Mill Coleman	PR
Derrick Mason	KR